THE RELATION
BETWEEN THE
PHYSICAL AND THE
MORAL IN MAN

THE RELATIONSHIP BETWEEN THE PHYSICAL AND THE MORAL IN MAN

Maine de Biran

**Edited and translated by
Darian Meacham and Joseph Spadola**

Bloomsbury Academic
An imprint of Bloomsbury Publishing Plc

B L O O M S B U R Y
LONDON • OXFORD • NEW YORK • NEW DELHI • SYDNEY

Bloomsbury Academic

An imprint of Bloomsbury Publishing Plc

50 Bedford Square	1385 Broadway
London	New York
WC1B 3DP	NY 10018
UK	USA

www.bloomsbury.com

BLOOMSBURY and the Diana logo are trademarks of Bloomsbury Publishing Plc

Originally published in French as
Rapports du physique et du moral de l'homme (Œuvres VI)

Volume edited by F.C.T. Moore

© Librairie Philosophique J. Vrin, Paris, 1984 http://www.vrin.fr

First published in English 2016

© Copyright to the English translation Bloomsbury Publishing Plc, 2016

British Library Cataloguing-in-Publication Data

A catalogue record for this book is available from the British Library.

ISBN:	HB:	9781472579676
	PB	9781350020306
	ePDF:	9781472579683
	ePub:	9781472579690

Library of Congress Cataloging-in-Publication Data

A catalog record for this book is available from the Library of Congress.

Typeset by RefineCatch Limited, Bungay, Suffolk
Printed and bound in India

CONTENTS

ACKNOWLEDGEMENTS

The editors would like to thank most of all the contributors to this volume. We would also like to thank Liza Thompson and Frankie Mace at Bloomsbury for their support and patience throughout. Joseph Spadola carried out a massive translation effort to make this volume possible. Iain Hamilton Grant, Nicolas de Warren and David Meacham generously lent their time in helping to translate Delphine Antoine-Mahut's preface. A final word of thanks goes to the participants in the graduate seminar in 'Problems in Phenomenology' at UWE, Bristol, who so enthusiastically undertook the study of a philosopher they had never heard of before and convinced us that such a volume as this was not only possible, but perhaps necessary.

1 Editor's Preface

Darian Meacham

In his inaugural lecture at the Collège de France, the French Neurobiologist Alain Prochaintz told his audience that science is very often a story of friendships.[1] In Prochaintz's case, he was talking about the lending of microscopes or microscope time from one team to another. The endeavour of science is marked by competition but also by collaboration and the spirit of advancing a task – that of truth and discovery. The story of this edition is surely more modest, but involves the same sense of intellectual collaboration; and the story of French philosopher Maine de Biran's journey through the currents of intellectual history and especially the continual reconstruction of the history of philosophy is also marked by these same themes.[2] First, a brief recounting of how this edition came to be.

In 2012, I was teaching a graduate seminar at the University of the West of England, Bristol, on 'Problems in Phenomenology'. The aim of the seminar was to explore the development of certain problems and themes in the phenomenological tradition from their pre- or proto-phenomenological origins through to their contemporary treatment. The topic that year was 'Body and Habit'. I knew that the French philosopher François-Pierre-Gonthier Maine de Biran (1766–1824), most commonly referred to as Maine de Biran or simply Biran, had exerted a very considerable influence

---

[1] Alain Prochiantz, *Géométries du vivant*, Paris: Collège de France, Fayard, 2008, p. 17.

[2] The example of Prochiantz is not arbitrary here; in his more philosophically oriented work, Prochiantz has concerned himself with investigating the neurological and also evolutionary basis of thought, precisely the kind of explanation that Biran argues against in the text translated here, *The Relationship between the Physical and Moral in Man* (*Sur les rapports du physique et du moral de l'homme*). See, for example: Alain Prochiantz, *Les anatomies de la pensée, à quoi pensent les calamars*, Paris: Éditions Odile Jacob, 1997.

on the development of these themes in French philosophy, an influence that extended and indeed to an extent pervaded the French phenomenological tradition. I also knew that, like another influential thinker of habit, Félix Ravaisson, very few English-speaking students were familiar with his name, let alone his writings.[3] But how could it be that a philosopher studied, lauded, and sometimes critiqued by such canonical names as Arthur Schopenhauer, Henri Bergson, Jean-Paul Sartre, Maurice Merleau-Ponty, Paul Ricœur, Michel Henry and Gilles Deleuze, as well as of course Ravaisson,[4] was so absent from the curriculums of students studying these later philosophers? This was the philosopher about whom Henri Bergson wrote: 'from the beginning of the century France had a great metaphysician, the greatest she produced since Descartes and Malebranche: Maine de Biran';[5] at whose funeral Royer-Collard remarked, 'he was the master of us all'; and to whom Jules Lachelier referred, in reference to his influence not the character of his thought, as 'the French Kant'.

A lack of translations is surely one of the reasons, but this simply asks once more the question: why has so little of Biran's work been translated into English? As Delphine Antoine-Mahut explains in her preface to this translation, and as Jeremy Dunham also addresses, there may well be other (less friendly) factors playing a central role in Maine de Biran's lack of visibility within the traditions that he influenced. These reasons have to do with the reaction to his work from his younger contemporary Victor Cousin (1792–1867), the first editor of Biran's work after his death. Cousin edited a four-volume edition of Biran's work in 1834, declaring that this edition

---

[3] Ravaisson's seminal essay *De l'habitude* was translated into English in 2008 by Clare Carlisle and Mark Sinclair, and published in a critical edition with introduction and commentary as *Of Habit* by what was then Continuum Press (Félix Ravaisson, *Of Habit*, C. Carlisle and M. Sinclair (eds), London: Continuum 2008). This opened up Ravaisson's extremely influential thinking to English-speaking audiences for the first time.

[4] Ravaisson's indebtedness to Biran is clearly explained in Clare Carlisle and Mark Sinclair's 'Introduction' and 'Editorial Commentary' to their edition of *Of Habit*; see Ravaisson, *Of Habit*, pp. 8–11, 89–94, and in Jeremy Dunham's 'From Habit to Monads: Felix Ravaisson's Theory of Substance'. *British Journal of the History of Philosophy*. 2015–23(6): 1089–1105. In *Of Habit*, Ravaisson affirms what is perhaps the central thesis of Biran's thought, that consciousness is originally always consciousness of effort. He refers to Biran in writing: 'Movement is the result of an excess of power in relation to resistance. The relation and the measure of both power and resistance are present in the consciousness of effort. In the end, if the subject opposed to the objectivity of extension knows himself only in actions that initiate movement, and if motive activity has its measure in effort, it is in the consciousness of effort that personality, in its highest manifestation as voluntary activity, becomes manifest to itself.' Ravaisson, *Of Habit*, p. 43.

[5] Bergson, H. *Mélanges*. Paris: Presses Universitaires de France, 1972, p. 1172.

contained all that was relevant from Biran's posthumous papers. He also wrote a critical introduction to the edition, wherein he declared Biran's philosophy to be limited in its contribution. Cousin's preface is the main focus of Antoine-Mahut's preface to this volume.

As Antoine-Mahut also details, Cousin subsequently used his positions not only as editor of Biran's unpublished work but also as *Conseil supérieur de l'instruction publique, présidence de l'Agrégation de philosophie et de l'Académie des sciences morales et politiques,* and *direction de l'École normale* – roles which led to Cousin being referred to as a 'philosopher king' – to suppress Biran's role and significance in the development of French philosophy in order to prop up his brand of philosophy, 'spiritual eclecticism', which through Cousin's various important political positions was elevated to the status of the official philosophy of the French state. We shall return to that in a moment.

The logistics of teaching Biran to English-speaking students turned out to be no mean feat. The only published English translation of Biran's work was the 1929 translation of *Influence de l'habitude sur la faculté de penser* (1802) (*The Influence of Habit on the Faculty of Thinking,* translated by Margaret Donaldson Boehm with an introduction by George Boas and published in London by Baillière & Co). The only available copy I could locate sat in the British Library. Before simply cutting Biran out of that year's syllabus, I contacted the Bergson scholar Michael Kelly, who had recently edited a collection on the work of Michel Henry, the most Biranian of the French phenomenologists.[6] Kelly in turn suggested that I contact Joseph Spadola, who, while a graduate student in philosophy at the University of Toulouse, had made a translation of Biran's *Sur les rapports du physique et du moral de l'homme* (1812), an essay that Biran wrote as an entry into an essay competition sponsored by the Royal Academy of Copenhagen. Joseph kindly agreed to let me use the translation and I taught Biran that year alongside Ravaisson, Husserl, Merleau-Ponty and Ricœur.

The students were enthralled, drawn into a world of French philosophy and eighteenth-century science of which they previously knew almost nothing. Among the many intriguing aspects of Biran's text for them was

---

[6] *Michel Henry: The Affects of Thought,* J. Hanson and M. Kelly (eds), London and New York: Continuum, 2012. On Henry's Biranianism, see Michel Henry, *Philosophie et phénoménologie du corps. Essai sur l'ontologie biranienne,* Paris: PUF, 1965 (translated as Michel Henry, *Philosophy and Phenomenology of the Body,* G. Etzkorn (trans.), The Hague: Martinus Nijhoff, 1975). There is a very brief discussion of Henry's Biranianism later in this preface.

the fact that in a curriculum of modern European philosophy dominated by the shadow of Kant, the German philosopher seems minimally present in Biran's work. Biran's text seemed to give some indication of what line the history of French philosophy might have taken without Kant, but rather with Hume and Leibniz as the most significant foreign influences on its development. As Dunham points out in his chapter, the first half of the nineteenth century should indeed more properly be referred to as 'post-Leibnizian' than 'post-Kantian'.

Biran was familiar with Kant's work thought primarily through French commentaries.[7] But as Gilson, Langan and Maurer note, Biran's work is also the first entry of Kant into the work of a major thinker in the French tradition.[8] Of Kant, Biran writes: 'I am indebted to Kant for having made a necessary distinction between two terms which all metaphysicians, including Descartes, have confused and which is one of the greatest causes of obfuscation and embarrassment in metaphysics. We feel our phenomenal individuality or existence, but we do not feel the very substance of our soul, no more than any other one.'[9] Biran's praise for Kant's work was, however, limited. Elsewhere he wrote that Kant

mistakenly drew a line between the principles of cognition and those of human morality. He failed to see that the primitive act of willing is at one and the same time the principle of knowledge and the principle of human morality. Without the intimate sense of effort which constitutes the "I", there can be nothing in the understanding, and thus even the ideas of sensation and perception are dependent upon willing.[10]

In short, Kant had 'confused the primitive facts' of effort with 'the first passive modification of sensibility'.[11] Biran's own position contra Kant can be coarsely summarized with a passage from *The Influence of Habit on the Faculty of Thinking* (1802), which also conveys the germ for the central

---

[7] E.g. Charles Viller's *Philosophie de Kant ou des principes fondamentaux de philosophie transcendantale* (Mezt: Collignon, 1801) and J. Kinker's *Essai de un exposition succincte de la critique de la raison pur traduit du hollandaise par J. Le Fèvre* (Amsterdam: Changuion et Den Hengst, 1801).

[8] Etienne Gilson, Thomas Langan and Armand A. Maurer, Recent Philosophy, Volume 2, Hegel to the Present, Eugene, OR: Wipf and Stock, p. 182.

[9] *Ouevres Choisi de Maine de Biran*, H. Gouhier, Paris: Aubier, 1942, pp. 33–35.

[10] Cited in Aldous Huxley, Themes and Variations, 'Variations on a Philosopher', London: Chato and Windus, 1950, p. 5.

[11] Maine de Biran, *Essai sur les fondements de psychologie et sur les rapport avec l'etude de la nature. Oeuvres de Maine de Biran*, Tisserand, Paris: Alcan, 1932, p. 164 fn.

kernel of Biranian thought concerning the absolute facts of the will and what resists it, the body; and effort as the primordial relation between these two absolutes from which all consciousness, perception, knowledge, judgement, and the entirety of the spiritual life of the subject springs:

> Effort necessarily entails the perception of a relation between the being who moves, or who wishes to move, and any obstacle whatsoever that is opposed to its movement; without a *subject* or a will which determines the movement, without something which resists, there is no *effort* at all, and without effort no knowledge, no perception of any kind. If the individual did not *will* or was not determined to begin to move, he would know nothing. If nothing resisted him, he likewise would know nothing, he would not suspect any existence; he would not even have an idea of his own existence.[12]

But the students were also intrigued as to why they had never encountered this philosopher before, if he had indeed exerted such an influence on Ravaisson, Bergsonism, Phenomenology and Post-Structuralism. It seemed important that Biran be made more accessible to English-speaking students, although, again as Antoine-Mahut points out, the question of Biran's importance to the tradition is also being posed in France. I suggested to Joseph that we publish his translation with a group of accompanying essays that would help to situate and indeed invigorate Biran's thought for an English-speaking audience. Joseph kindly agreed and set to work preparing his translation for publication as well as translating two introductory and critical essays from two important French scholars, both working at the University of Toulouse, who agreed to contribute to the volume: Pierre Kerszberg and Pierre Montebello. Jeremy Dunham has been kind enough to contribute to this volume an essay explaining Maine de Biran's important relation to Leibniz. Bloomsbury secured the rights to publish F.C.T. Moore's philological preface to the 1984 publication of *Sur les rapports du physique et du moral de l'homme* in volume six of Vrin's thirteen-volume *Oeuvres de Maine de Biran*, published under the direction of François Azouvi. As mentioned, Delphine Antoine-Mahut has written a

---

[12] Maine de Biran, *The Influence of Habit on the Faculty of Thinking*, translated by Margaret Donaldson Boehm (trans.) with an introduction by George Boas, London: Baillière & Co, p. 58 (*Influence de l'habitude sur la faculté de penser*, Paris: Henrichs, 1803 – a digital copy of this text is freely available for download from the website of the British Library); also cited in Ravaisson, *Of Habit*, p. 92.

new preface (or a kind of counter-preface to Cousin's initial 1834 preface) for this English translation dealing with the intellectual and historical context of Maine de Biran's work, its reception in French philosophy, and its place in the larger current of *spiritualism*.

Readers unacquainted with nineteenth-century French philosophy may be unfamiliar with this term, *spiritualism*. In this context, it refers specifically to a current of thought in nineteenth-century French philosophy that, while traceable back to Descartes or Leibniz (see Dunham's chapter for more on these two lineages), does have its proper origins in Biran's work. Most simply, spiritualism gives both priority and autonomy to the life of the mind or spirit and rejects physicalist determinism. We can see easily how this is expressed in Biran's emphasis on the original and absolute fact of the will as being at the origin of all knowledge. Thus, more specifically, the spiritualist tradition, which originates with Biran and continues through Ravaisson, Lachelier, Bergson, and to a degree into the French phenomenological movement, places emphasis on the power of the will as a counterpoint to materialist determinism. The French spiritualist lineage running back to Biran was to a great extent established retrospectively by Felix Ravaisson's seminal 1867 report on philosophy in France in the nineteenth century, *Rapport sur la philosophie en France au XIXe siècle*. Ravaisson's report is also generally understood as restoring Biran to his rightful place as the founder of spiritualism, after Cousin's attempt to suppress Biran's philosophy and influence. As Dunham discusses, Ravaisson's report was also the final nail in the coffin of Cousin's brand of 'spiritualist eclecticism'.

In a broader philosophical lineage, spiritualism as founded by Biran and continued by Ravaisson can be situated both intellectually and chronologically after the 'ideological' philosophy of Destutt de Tracy (1754–1836) and Cabanis (1757–1808), who befriended Biran in 1801 after reading the first draft of his *Influence de l'habitude sur la faculté de penser*, which he submitted to an essay competition sponsored by the *Institut de France* (in this instance, Biran did not win). 'Ideological' philosophy was concerned with the genesis of ideas. (Marx took over the term from the ideologues, but his usage of it bore more resemblance to Napoleon's attack on 'ideological philosophy' for being unscientific – Marx famously referred to Destutt de Tracy as a '*Fischblütige Bourgeoisdoktrinär*', a fish-blooded bourgeois doctrinaire.) It was a development of Condillac's psychology, and its forerunner Lockean Empiricism, which ultimately sought to reduce or provide explanation of all mental activity by way of experience and observation. For reasons that are made clear in the main text of this volume, Destutt de Tracy and Cabanis saw Biran as a potential ally in the development of ideological philosophy. Biran was, however, going to go in another direction; his philosophy along with suppression by Napoleon marked the end of 'ideological' philosophy in France. Philosophy is a story not only of ideas and friendships, but also of politics and violence.

In understanding the situation of a philosopher historically and intellectually, it is helpful to know something of their lives. François-Pierre-Gonthier Maine de Biran, né François-Pierre-Gonthier de Biran (he picked up the Maine after inheriting an estate by that name, and is usually referred to as Maine de Biran or simply Biran), was born in 1766 in Bergerac in the Dordogne, France. His family was political, but not noble; his grandfather and great grandfather had both served as Mayor of Bergerac. A royalist, he was enrolled in the Royal Guard at the age of eighteen. Following the revolution, the guard was dissolved in 1791, and in 1793 Biran returned to the southwest of France, namely the castle Grateloup, just south of Bergerac. Despite the imprisonment of several members of his family and the exile of four others, Biran was left alone during the Terror. In 1795, he was appointed administrator of the department of Dordogne, and in 1797 he was elected to the Council of 500 (lower house of French legislature during the period of the French Revolution known as the Directory (*Directoire*), which lasted from 22 August 1795 until 9 November 1799). However, due to his anti-revolutionary politics, the election was annulled and he never assumed his post. This drove Biran happily back into philosophy. He continued to hold various relatively minor political posts, which he carried out with rigour: Counsellor to the Prefect of Périgord, Sub-Prefect of Bergerac. Biran's career seemed at risk in 1813 when he was part of a group that publicly expressed opposition to Napoleon. But, following Napoleon's defeat and the restoration of the Bourbon monarchy in the form of Louis XVIII in 1814, Biran's longstanding royalism and opposition to the revolution and the emperor was rewarded. He was made Quaestor of the Chamber of Deputies (something like a financial overseer and auditor). Having made a return to public life, he always felt awkward and ill at ease. Nonetheless, he was friends with the great and good of the day, including such figures as Ampère, Cuvier, Guizot and Madame de Staël, as well as the aforementioned Cousin and Royer-Collard. He died in 1824, before completing the full articulation of his philosophical thought that he had been working towards, earning him the title of 'author of one book that was never written'.

Aldous Huxley wrote a remarkable essay on Biran, 'Variations on a Philosopher', published in 1950, which I have drawn upon for biographical information. The focus on Huxley's essay is not however Biran's public biography, but rather the incredible account of his internal life that he recorded in his *Journal Intime*, edited and published in its entirety in three volumes by Henri Gouhier in 1954–1955.[13] Huxley likely read a previously published version published by Plon in 1927.[14] Biran suffered both physically and psychologically throughout the course of his life, and those sufferings are intimately detailed in his journal. As Huxley points out, this remarkable document allows the reader to contextualize the ideas that Biran grappled with – of particular interest are the central ideas of the will as a hyper-organic force, and effort as the experience of that force as it meets the resistance of the body in its inertia and its material qua physiological determinations – during his life. Moreover, perhaps foreshadowing Merleau-Ponty's emphasis on the philosophical productivity of pathology and illness or Sartre's analyses of shame, anxiety and nausea, the life that Biran detailed in his journal was one lived with a constant sense of unease and being out of place, marked by physical as well as psychological pains and extreme sensitivities. Biran's alienation from the world and his introversion give his descriptions a rare phenomenological depth which accompanies and supports his philosophical writing.

This volume begins with a timeline of the development of Maine de Biran's philosophy and the French spiritualist tradition compiled by Jeremy Dunham. This is followed by F.C.T. Moore's original introduction to volume VI of the *Oeuvres* or collected works of Maine de Biran, edited by François Azouvi and published by Vrin in thirteen volumes between 1984 and 2000 (volumes ten through thirteen are published in two, three, two and three parts, respectively). Scholars who wish to explore Biran's work further, and specifically the text translated here will surely want to consult the original Vrin publication, as it contains many editorial notes that we have not included here for the sake of simplicity and accessibility. Moore's introduction is primarily philological. It provides an account first of Biran's process of writing and refining the text that appears here as *The Relationship between the Physical and the Moral in Man* (*Sur les rapports du physique et du moral de l'homme*). It then details the painstaking editorial work carried out in order to establish the provenance and fidelity to Biran's work in the edition published as volume VI of the collected works. Moore's philological introduction is followed by Delphine Antoine-Mahut's historical and intellectual introduction. She gives a vivacious account of the often

---

[13] Maine de Biran, *Journal*. Édition intégrale publiée par H. Gouhier, Paris: Éd. de la Baconnière, 1954–1955.

[14] Maine de Biran, *Journal Intime* (1792–1824), introduction, translation and notes by A. de La Valette-Monbrun, Paris: Plon, 1927, 2 vols.

treacherous intellectual context in which French spiritualism developed. Antoine-Mahut explains the context of *Rapports du physique et du moral de l'homme* as being 'part of a triptych consisting of two other essays: the essay from the *Institut de France, Sur la décomposition de la pensée*, and a third that was awarded by the Berlin Academy in 1807, *De l'aperception immédiate*'. She then turns to Cousin's infamous preface to the 1834 edition of Biran's work that he edited. She provides the context of Cousin's preface, how it functioned to suppress Biran's thought, but also the response that it received from those loyal to Biran. Finally, she asks if and how rereading *The Relationship between the Physical and the Moral in Man* can help to correct the damage done by Cousin's suppression.

Antoine-Mahut's preface is followed by Joseph Spadola's translation of *Sur les rapports du physique et du moral de l'homme*. A word must first be said about the title. We have translated the French word '*moral*' literally. This may seem like an error, as the function of the term in Biran's title is much broader than the more limited sense of the term in English. Perhaps an adequate rendering would be something like 'life of the mind' or 'life of spirit'. But there was perhaps a reason to leave the term as it was. As Biran notes in his critique of Kant, cited above, he was steadfastly opposed to the absolute distinction between the will, knowledge and morality. For him, the three were originally founded in the primitive act of willing. It could be argued that the use of the term 'moral' in English pulls us closer to that absolute origin that is the will than a more cognitively oriented rendering might.

It is best to let Biran's essay speak for itself, and it is complemented by the contributions which follow it from Montebello, Dunham, and Kerszberg. These chapters contextualize, respectively, Biran's essay in terms of its treatment of the mind–body problem, the selective reading of Leibnizian metaphysics that underpins this treatment, and the phenomenological analyses that support it. The question posed by the Royal Academy of Copenhagen, to which Biran's essay is a response, begins with a rather loaded statement: 'There are people who still deny the utility of the doctrines and physical experiences to explain the phenomena of mind and the inner sense.' The 'still' in the sentence implies a rearguard, futile, and perhaps wrongheaded denial. Nonetheless, Biran makes it clear in his essay that he is one of those people. As Kerszberg points out, what is perhaps most remarkable is the radicality and forthrightness with which Biran denies the utility of the physical sciences in explaining the life and workings of the mind. As such, *The Relationship between the Physical and the Moral in Man* can be considered Biran's most incisive text on the mind–body problem. It is also a mature representation of the philosopher's work and thus suitable as a first introduction to his thought. It is important to note that Biran's work is considered to have three main intellectual phases: his 'ideological' phase, the 'philosophy of the will' phase, and then the 'mystical metaphysical' phase. This work is from the middle of the 'philosophy of the will' phase, seen by many as the most important. One area that is not touched upon in detail in this essay, but which is central to Biran's legacy, is his theory of the lived body. Biran is indeed considered by many to be one of the 'first philosophers of the body' and his concept of the body qua resistance is of course absolutely central to his theory of the self. A self is constituted in its capacity to move and in the feeling of voluntary effort, which can be analysed in terms of the lived-feeling of the force of the will against the resistance of the body and the sensation of muscular contraction.[15] The body as experienced, i.e. the lived body, is a central dimension in Biran's philosophy and one that we hope will be further elucidated for English-speaking audiences in future translations. In the meantime, Mark Sinclair has written a very helpful account of the status of the lived body in the work of the main figures of French spiritualism: Maine de Biran, Ravaisson, and Bergson.[16]

Biran's essay is followed in this volume by Pierre Montebello's Introduction and Commentary on *The Relationship between the Physical and the Moral in Man*. Montebello locates the origins of the modern formulation of the mind–body problem in Biran's 'relationist' philosophy of consciousness. He begins by asserting that Biran's greatest contribution lies not in his development of a philosophy of consciousness, or his discovery of the lived body, but rather in his relational theory, which locates consciousness in the relation between the organic body and the hyper-organic will. Montebello writes:

> Thought and consciousness are born of this *polarity of forces* (resistance and will). This explains why our own psychological reality is never given in the form of an absolute. The absolute designates that which can be grasped in and of itself, in its substantial, objective, exterior unity, without any fissures, whereas the free, conscious, existing subject only perceives itself within a relationship of effort that constitutes it – a relationship that is at the heart of psychology.

Thus, Biran's conception and structuring of the mind–body problem is an effort to give philosophical dignity to the lived experiences of personal

---

[15] See, Dorthée Legrande, 'Phenomenological Dimensions of Bodily Self-Consciousness', in: *The Oxford Handbook of the Self*, S. Gallagher (ed.), Oxford: Oxford University Press, 2011, p. 210.

[16] Mark Sinclair, 'Embodiment: Conceptions of the Lived-Body from Maine de Biran to Bergson', in: *Edinburgh Critical History of Philosophy*, vol. IV, A. Stone (ed.), Edinburgh: Edinburgh University Press, 2011.

existence, but without either ignoring the body or reducing lived-experience to physiology and anatomy – or neuroscience. Montebello argues that this is still the impetus of contemporary versions of the mind–body problem. In doing so, he shows the close similarity between Biran's formulation of the mind–body problem and its development in contemporary analytic philosophy of mind, specifically the work of John Searle. Montebello argues along Biranian lines, which he points out are, almost verbatim, the same as the argument deployed by Searle, for the intractability of the mind–body problem and its continued resistance to physicalist or mechanist reductionism.

The metaphysical underpinnings of these arguments are further developed in Jeremy Dunham's chapter. Dunham illustrates how and where, according to Biran, Descartes' metaphysics led his formulation of the relation between *res extensa* and *res cogitans* astray. Cartesian metaphysics risks collapsing into a form of pantheistic monism where both *res extensa* and *res cogitans* are 'swallowed up' by one 'infinite and active substance' – God. By giving back to the passivity of the body its proper activity, Biran's metaphysics and subsequently his formulation of the mind–body problem evade this trap.

Dunham argues, on the basis of a reading of Biran's 1819 *Exposition de la doctrine philosophique de Leibniz*, that Biran's selective interpretation and adaptation of Leibnizianism was not a rejection of Leibnizian metaphysics, but rather a refinement, an *ampliative* rather than a *distortive* Leibnizianism. He also argues that Biran's apparent critique of Leibniz was operationalized for an (at least initially) unsuccessful intellectual battle against Victor Cousin's spiritualist eclecticism, which would become the official state philosophy of France under Cousin's stewardship of the French national curriculum. Dunham offers a novel thesis concerning the reasons why Biran might publish a critique of Cousin's philosophy under the pretence of a critique of Leibniz. He also deftly demonstrates how this amplification of Leibnizian thought, laid out in 1819, functions to clarify some of the central concepts of the earlier *Relationship between the Physical and the Moral in Man*.

In order to do all this, Dunham first illustrates Biran's development of the spiritualist current of thought against French and British sensualism (Locke, Hume, Condillac), and the rationalism of Descartes, Malebranche and Spinoza. But in doing so, he also highlights the influence of Madame de Staël (1776–1817) and in particular her three-volume work, *De l'Allemagne* (1810), which played an important role in the reception of German philosophy in France and specifically on Biran's understanding and development of Leibnizian thought. Staël's influence is also perhaps important for grasping the relative lack of engagement with Kant in Biran's work. Dunham quotes Staël in arguing that while Kant was indeed the rightful successor to Liebniz, '[n]o one in France would give himself the trouble of studying works so thickly set with difficulties as those of Kant'. Dunham offers Staël's reading of the history of philosophy as 'a major contributing factor for why France's philosophy for the first three quarters of the nineteenth century is better understood as "post-Leibnizian" than "post-Kantian"'.

Subsequently, Dunham shows how Leibniz's concept of force shaped Biran's understanding of self-consciousness or *effort vollu* (willed effort) that is lived-through in relations between the will and the body that resists movement, and which is conceptually so pivotal to the centrepiece of Biranian metaphysics, the hyper-organic force (the will) that is apperceived only in its relation to this body whose inertia resists it. Biranian metaphysics is thus, by Dunham's account, not a retort to Leibniz, but a selective amplification of specific aspects of Leibnizian thought.

From this selective amplification of the Leibnizian concept of force qua willed effort, Biran also derives a theory of the virtual that is one of the lasting legacies of Biran's thought in twentieth-century French philosophy. As Dunham explains, self-consciousness, when lying dormant (i.e. when not felt in the relation between the will and the body manifest as willed effort), does not simply become nothing. Rather, the force of the will shifts into a virtual existence as a *tendency* towards action which perdures as 'half way between power and act' even when not actualized in motility. This will is thus defined by Biran as a '*virtual absolute force* which exists before the manifestation, and which remains the same after, even though its exercise is suspended'.

As stated, Biran's *Exposition de la doctrine philosophique de Leibniz* (1819) was equally a critique of Victor Cousin's emerging position as well as an amplification of Biran's own species of Leibnizianism. Dunham's contribution provides us with further insight into the relation between Biran and Cousin. Cousin, through his role both as the editor of Biran's works after his death and as the administrator for public instruction where he reigned supreme over the national philosophy curriculum, consigned his one-time friend but also critic, Maine de Biran, to the sidelines of official French philosophy, by delaying for ten year the publication and then falsely representing his deceased friend's work. Cousin's spiritualist eclecticism eventually fell, after sustained philosophical attack from thinkers such as Pierre Leroux,[17] Charles Renouvier, and Felix Ravaisson, all of whom 'used

---

[17] See Lucie Rey, *Les enjeux de l'histoire de la philosophie en France au XIXe siècle*. Paris: L'Harmattan, 2012, pp. 410–421.

distinctly Biran-influenced readings of Leibniz to attack the philosopher king'. Despite the huge influence that Ravaisson's *Rapport sur la philosophie en France au XIXème siècle* (published in 1867, the year of Cousin's death) had in terms of its critique of Cousin's reading of Leibniz and its redirecting the course of French philosophy towards a more Biranian spiritualism, the damage to Biran's official reputation had been done. But via Ravaisson's work, Biranian philosophy began to live something of a virtual life within the development of French spiritualism.

As Dunham also points out with the mention of Gilles Deleuze's last text '*L'Immanence: une vie...*' in the intellectual timeline that he has written for this volume, Biran's sidelining is increasingly recognized as erroneous and his influence does indeed rise to the surface at points. Writing of life itself as a 'transcendental field', Deleuze asks: 'Indeed did something similar not happen to Maine de Biran in his "later philosophical project" (which was too exhausted to end well), when he discovered beneath the transcendence of effort *a life*, absolute and immanent? The transcendental field is defined by the plane of immanence, and the plane of immanence by a life.'[18] It is indeed significant that in the last text he composed in his lifetime, Deleuze, himself exhausted, reflecting on the central themes of his life's work, transcendental empiricism, immanence, the virtual, and life itself, turns toward Maine de Biran's own final project.

Pierre Kerszberg turns to Maine de Biran's role as one of the founders, *avant la lettre*, of that other current of twentieth-century French philosophy: phenomenology. As Kerszberg notes at the beginning of his chapter, both Merleau-Ponty and Michel Henry considered Maine de Biran's philosophy to be phenomenological in nature. Between the two (chronologically), Biran's thought also swells the pages of Paul Ricoeur's *Freedom and Nature* (1950). Merleau-Ponty not only considered Biran's work to be a precursor to the phenomenology of the lived body, but he also considered Biran to be an anticipation of phenomenology insofar as he did not acknowledge or was 'indifferent' to the distinction between interior and exterior. As Merleau-Ponty writes in his lectures on 'The Union of the Soul and the Body in Malebranche, Biran and Bergson', given at the École Normale Supérieure in 1947–1948:

Biran did not reduce consciousness to motoricity, but identified motoricity and consciousness. The primitive fact is consciousness of an

---

[18] Gilles Deleuze, 'Immanence: a Life' in *Two Regimes of Madness*, David Lapoujade (ed.), Ames Hodges and Mike Taormina (trans.). Cambridge: MIT Press, 2003, p. 386.

irreducible relation between two terms themselves both irreducible. It's not consciousness becoming movement, but consciousness reverberating in movements. This is neither an interior nor an exterior fact: it is consciousness of self as a relationship between an I and an other term. It's not a question of an empiricist philosophy that would fill consciousness with muscular facts, but of a philosophy that recognizes a certain antithesis, that of the subject and the term that bears its initiatives [the body], as originary.[19]

Biran's understanding of the subject thus bears an affinity to the idea of the embodied subject that Merleau-Ponty had developed in *Phenomenology of Perception* and that he would continue to elaborate throughout his life. We can see why Merleau-Ponty considered Biran's philosophy an anticipation of phenomenology in its 'identification of absolute objectivity with absolute subjectivity'.[20]

Biran's theory of consciousness, which Merleau-Ponty sketches out in his lecture, cited above, is grounded in the observation of the apodicticity of what Biran calls the 'primitive fact' (*fait primitif*): 'I observe within myself a remarkable psychological fact that gives consistency and persistence to the self: voluntary effort, which reveals the indissoluble link between will and consciousness ... voluntary effort is a hyper-organic force to which only inner experience is witness.'[21] Around six years prior to Merleau-Ponty's lectures at the École Normale Supérieure, Sartre had taken issue with Biran's phenomenology of the primitive fact of consciousness as consciousness of effort. In his analysis of the body in Chapter Two of *Being and Nothingness*, Sartre calls into question the very existence of the 'primitive fact' of consciousness qua the effort of motoricity. He writes:

Either it [the body] is a thing among things, or else it is that by which things are revealed to me. But it cannot be both at the same time. Similarly, I see my hand touching objects, but I do not *know* it in its act of touching them. This is the fundamental reason why the famous 'sensation of effort' of Maine de Biran does not really exist. For my hand

---

[19] Maurice Merleau-Ponty, *The Incarnate Subject, Malebranche, Biran and Begson on the Union of Body and Soul*, P.B. Milan (trans.), Amherst: Humanity Books, 2001, p. 64 (Maurice Merleau-Ponty, *L'Union de l'âme et du corps chez Malebranche, Biran et Bergson*, J. Deprun (ed.), Paris: Vrin, 1978).

[20] Merleau-Ponty, *The Incarnate Subject*, p. 83.

[21] Maine de Biran, *The Relationship between the Physical and the Moral in Man*, p. 194.

reveals to me the resistance of objects, their hardness or softness, but not *itself.*[22]

Sartre later continued his critique in writing: 'the famous "sensation of effort" by which Maine de Biran attempted to reply to Hume's challenge is a psychological myth. We never have any sensation of effort.'[23] Hence the fundamental difference between Sartrean and Biranian notions of resistance, each fundamental to their respective phenomenological ontologies. For Biran, the resistance that is partly constitutive of consciousness is on the side of the body, hence consciousness as the sensation of the effort of movement against the resistance of the body. For Sartre, resistance was to be found in the world.

Moreover, as Renaud Barbaras points out, Merleau-Ponty's entire philosophical project, which centred on articulating a philosophy of sensation, the body and eventually the 'flesh', which placed sensation itself within what was sensed (i.e. posited sensing itself within the sensible), also eventually hinged on a rejection of Biranism.[24] At the end of his three lectures on Biran, Merleau-Ponty tells his students:

In conclusion, Biran's importance depends more on certain of his descriptions than on an intellectual grasp of the proper principles of his philosophy. He attempted to move beyond psychologism, to show that a subject's experience is not the simple application of a logos; but he failed to save the particular, to show its movement and transition to the universal. Thus the conclusion of his philosophy sees the problem of the soul and the body posed once more, and in just as difficult terms; he re-establishes the absolute soul facing the absolute body: we find ourselves again where we started.[25]

---

[22] Jean-Paul Sartre, *Being and Nothingness*, H. Barnes (trans.), London: Routledge, 2003, p. 304 (Jean-Paul Sartre, *L'être et le néant*, Paris: Gallimard, 1943).

[23] Sartre, *Being and Nothingness*, p. 324.

[24] Renaud Barbaras, 'The Essence of Life: Drive or Desire?', *Michel Henry: The Affects of Thought*, J. Hanson and M. Kelly (eds), London and New York: Continuum, 2012, pp. 40–61.

[25] Maurice Merleau-Ponty, *The Incarnate Subject, Malebranche, Biran, and Bergson on the Union of Body and Soul*, P.B. Milan (trans.), Amherst: Humanity Books, 2001, p. 85. [Maurice Merleau-Ponty, *L'Union de l'âme et du corps chez Malebranche, Biran et Bergson. Notes prises au cours de Maurice Merleau-Ponty à l'École Normale Supérieure*, J. Deprun (ed.), Paris: Vrin, 1968.]

It is Michel Henry who is ultimately the most Biranian of the phenomenologists and also most insistent on Biran's phenomenological style of thinking. As Barbaras points out, Henry's entire project of rediscovering life as auto-impressionality rests on the Biranian theory of effort as the primitive fact of consciousness feeling itself as the relation between the will and the resistance of the body.[26] In the opening sections of his *Philosophy and Phenomenology of the Body* (1965), Henry writes: 'Maine de Biran's "discovery" of the subjective body was not an accident. His discovery takes place in a context which makes it inevitable and this context is nothing other than that of a phenomenological ontology.'[27] And a few pages later:

> The bringing to light of this sphere of absolute certitude [the ego], which is also a sphere of absolute certitude, presupposes a division be established between that which stems from such certitude and that which rather cannot pride itself therewith, at least in a direct manner. To build a science endowed with an absolute certitude is to effect this division, to reduce the vast field of human knowledge to that of original and absolute knowledge, knowledge which presents itself to us phenomenologically as apodictic evidence; it is in other words to effect the phenomenological reduction.[28]

But Kerszberg focuses not on what other phenomenologists say or have said about Biran's philosophy, but rather on the distinct phenomenological analyses proper to Biran's own work. He begins by noting the radicality of Biran's response to the question posed by the Royal Academy of

---

[26] Barbaras, 'The essence of life', p. 46. Barbaras cites a passage from an older article of Henry's to illustrate the latter's Biranianism. Henry refers to a sentence from Biran, 'there is no force that is absolutely foreign', as one of the most 'laden with meaning the philosophical tradition has ever produced' and then comments further: 'An absolute force, an efficient causality, a power in its efficacy, in the reality and actuality of its exercise, of what it is and what it does, cannot be in the milieu of exteriority, cannot be external to [it] self or as if external to [it]self, cannot be separated from itself and cannot be a stranger to [it]self. This signifies that to all real power a first power is given ... in the immanence of its radical interiority.' The first power is of course, from Biran's perspective, which Henry here affirms, the primordial force of the will. See Michel Henry, 'Le concept d'âme a-t-il un sens?', *Revue philosophique de Louvain* 67 (1996), 26.

[27] Michel Henry, *Philosophy and Phenomenology of the Body*, G. Etzkorn (trans.), The Hague: Martinus Nijhoff, 1975, p. 11 (Michel Henry, *Philosophie et phénoménologie du corps, Essai sur l'ontolgie biranianne*, Paris: PUF, 1965).

[28] Henry, *Philosophy and Phenomenology of the Body*, p. 18.

Copenhagen: 'Biran emphasizes the central thesis of his book, namely that a genuine science of man must become indifferent to causal explanations.' Kerszberg then shows how Biran turns to the things themselves to defend and develop his thesis. It is the phenomenon of hearing that is exemplary in this regard:

> Better than any other sensory event, sound phenomena highlight the theoretically inexplicable yet observed relationship between raw nature and intelligent nature, the feeling world and the thinking world ... Sound experience in its natural state is a reminder that causal explanations are futile in accounting for the disorders and alterations of perception that physiology attempts to explain.

Kerszberg points to timbre as a particularly illustrative example of this. When we attempt to describe timbre, we quickly tend to lapse into mechanical explanation, accounting for tonality as the product of overtones, or use metaphor. The thing that we actually hear, the timbre, is elusive. The phenomenon of hearing is also particularly illustrative of the double nature of the self as passive and active. I am a voice that projects and the ear that hears. Kerszberg writes: 'On the one hand, I have the power to create impressions in myself, since I have the power to give myself auditory sensations, to hear the sounds that my voice produces.' He uses Biran's analysis of the phenomena of hearing and voice to parse a whole constellation of related concepts: memory, attention, *Stimmung* (mood), sympathy, and intersubjectivity among them. Kerszberg ends with a reflection on the value of Biran's phenomenological analyses for future investigation:

> The more the senses feel, the less intelligence thinks and discerns. How do we think about this lived fact that everyone immediately experiences, without relying on a theoretical basis which would be illusory? Maine de Biran's analysis reveals that sound experience offers the most appropriate way to think about this question.

The Relationship between the Physical and the Moral in Man is intended to provide a path into Biran's thought for English-speaking readers. We clearly think that reading and understanding Biran's work is an essential aspect of understanding the development of nineteenth-century French philosophy, the reception of Kant and Leibniz in France, and also the immense influence that the tradition of French spiritualism (of which, properly speaking, Biran is the originator) has had on the development of twentieth-century philosophy, where the problem of the mind–body relation and the question of what dimension of explanation is appropriate to the phenomenon of the will and the experience of effort remain alive and kicking. It also, as Antoine-Mahut points out at the end of her preface, opens up another history of French philosophy, almost totally overlooked, with rich seams for investigation. The accompanying essays from Delphine Antoine-Mahut, Pierre Montebello, Jeremy Dunham and Pierre Kerszberg are meant to provide introduction and critical commentary on *The Relationship between the Physical and the Moral in Man* and on Biran's thought and reception more generally. They are also meant to show the lasting vibrancy and vitality of Biran's ideas and to encourage further investigation.

A last word on the central themes of will and effort is necessary here. The work of the translator can be thankless. Yet to have and to teach a proper history of philosophy, to understand how problems have developed, translations are essential. Joseph Spadola has made an enormous effort, not only in returning to his translation of *Sur les rapports du physique et du moral de l'homme*, but also in translating Montebello's and Kerszberg's essays. To do this, essentially in his spare time, must have taken a monumental act of the will. Thanks.

2 The Development of Maine de Biran's Philosophy and the French Spiritualist Tradition: A Timeline

Jeremy Dunham

1746 Étienne Bonnot de Condillac publishes his *Essai sur l'origine des connaissances humaines.*

1754 Condillac publishes his *Traité des Sensations.* In these texts, Condillac developed a bold empiricist philosophy, the principles of which were the basis for the sensualist and ideological tradition of philosophy. Maine de Biran's first philosophical writings are works of this tradition.

1755 Charles Bonnet publishes his *Essai de psychologie.*

1766 Maine de Biran is born in Bergerac on 29 November.

1785 Biran joins the *Garde du Corps.*

1789 The French Revolution begins. Biran is wounded defending Versailles.

1792 Biran moves to Grateloup to escape from the Revolutionary Wars.

1795 Biran becomes a member of the Council of the Five Hundred in April until the *Coup d'État*, after which Napoleon Bonaparte closed it down. Biran continues to play an active role in politics throughout his life.

1796 The first reading of Pierre Jean George Cabanis's *Rapports du physique et du moral de l'homme* (published in 1802) in front of the *Institut de France.*

1800 Xavier Bichat publishes his *Recherches physiologiques sur la vie et la mort*.

1801 Destutt de Tracy publishes his *Idéologie proprement dite*, the first volume of his *Elémens d'idéologie* (1801–1815).

1801 Charles Viller publishes his *Philosophie de Kant ou Principes fondamentaux de la philosophie transcendental*. This was Maine de Biran's main source for his knowledge of Kant.

1802 Maine de Biran's *Influence de l'habitude* was awarded the *Institut de France* prize. The *Mémoire* was judged by Cabanis and de Tracy, and it is a work representative of their ideological tradition.

1804 Joseph Marie Degérando publishes *Histoire comparée des systèmes de philosophe*. According to Maine de Biran, it is this text that convinces him of the fruitfulness of combining philosophical history with psychological enquiry.

1805 Maine de Biran is awarded the *Institut de France* prize for his *Mémoire sur la décomposition de la pensée*. It is in this text that Biran starts to develop his own unique philosophical position.

1810 Germaine de Staël publishes her *De l'Allemagne*. This text played a crucial role in the introduction of classical German philosophy to France.

1811 Biran starts work on his *Essai sur les fondements de la psychologie*. Although this is the most important of all of Biran's works, he abandoned the project. It was first published, albeit in a much mutilated form, in 1859. A critical edition of this text was published in 2001.

1812 Biran receives the prize from the Academy of Copenhagen for his *mémoire 'Sur les rapports du physique et du moral de l'homme'*.

1817–1818 Victor Cousin gives his lectures on metaphysics and the history of philosophy at the *École normale*. This course was revised and published several times, first in his 1826 *Fragmens philosophiques*, and most famously as his 1854 *Du vrai, du beau, et du bien*. The principles presented in these lectures formed the basis for his 'eclectic philosophy' and these are the founding texts of the eclectic movement.

1819 Maine de Biran publishes his *Exposition de la doctrine philosophique de Leibniz* anonymously. The work is representative of the deeper concern that Biran had for metaphysics towards the end of his life.

1824 Maine de Biran dies on 20 July.

1830 Victor Cousin is made a Full Professor in the Sorbonne, a member of the French Academy, and State Councillor Extraordinaire.

1832 Cousin is made a member of the Royal Council, member of the Academy of Moral and Political Sciences, and the supreme head of the École normale.

1833 Cousin is made a peer of France. This quick succession of promotions gives Cousin almost complete control over the teaching of philosophy in France.

1834 After ten years of having delayed the publication of Maine de Biran's works, Cousin publishes a single-volume collection of his philosophy and claims that it contains all of his important writings.

1838 Pierre Leroux publishes his *Réfutation de l'éclecticisme*, which contains both a critique of Cousin's philosophy and a defence of Biran against Cousin's critiques.

1838 Félix Ravaisson defends Biran's philosophical method in his *De l'habitude*.

1840 Félix Ravaisson publishes an explicit critique of Cousin and a plea for Biranian philosophy in his *Philosophie contemporaine*.

1841 Victor Cousin publishes three further volumes of Maine de Biran's works. Pierre Leroux accuses Cousin of purposely delaying the publication of Biran's work so as not to lose the glory of being the first French philosopher to overcome 'sensualism'.

1841 Jules Simon, a disciple of Cousin, publishes an important critical article on Biran's thought in the *Revue des deux mondes*.

1848 The February Revolution and the end of the Orleans monarchy means that Cousin loses much of his power, although the eclectic school remains dominant in France.

1852 Ravaisson is made Inspector General of Higher Education.

1852 Napoleon III orders the suspension of the *agrégation* for history and philosophy.

1859 Ernst Naville publishes the *Oeuvres inédites de Maine de Biran* in collaboration with Marc Debrit. Although this collection is far from perfect, it provides the reader with a much greater idea of the depth and scope of Biran's thought than any of Cousin's earlier editions.

1863 Victor Duruy reinstates the *agrégation* and appoints Ravaisson as the chair of the committee in charge of setting the examination.

1867 Félix Ravaisson publishes his *Rapport sur la philosophie en France au XIXème siècle*. The text is published in the same year as Cousin dies and is seen to represent the death knell for Cousin's eclectic school and the beginning of the flourishing of the French spiritualist tradition in its Biranian form. Ravaisson becomes the leader of the spiritualist school of which Fouillé, Lachelier and Boutroux are among the most important members. This school obtains many of the most important positions in French philosophy and it maintains powers comparable to Cousin's during the July Monarchy for half a century.

1872   Alfred Jules Émile Fouillée publishes *La Liberté et le déterminisme*.

1874   Émile Boutroux publishes his *De la contingence des lois de nature*.

1876   Gabriel Tarde presents his *Maine de Biran et l'évolutionnisme en psychologie*.

1885   Jules Lachelier publishes his 'Psychologie et métaphysique'.

1888   Henri Bergson publishes his *Essai sur les données immédiates de la conscience*.

1888   Boutroux takes the Chair of the History of Modern Philosophy at the Sorbonne.

1888   Lachelier takes over from Ravaisson as the Inspector General of Higher Education.

1890   Alfred Jules Émile Fouillée publishes *L'Evolutionnisme des idées-forces*.

1899   Tarde takes the Chair of Modern Philosophy at the *Collège de France*.

1900   Bergson takes the Chair of Ancient Philosophy at the *Collège de France*.

1900   Ravaisson dies and Lachelier is appointed the chair of the committee in charge of setting the examination.

1903   Bergson publishes 'Introduction à la métaphysique'.

1903–1905   Émile Boutroux presents his Gifford lecture series *Science and Religion in Contemporary Philosophy* at the University of Glasgow.

1907   Bergson publishes *l'Évolution creatrice*. The text is translated into English in 1911 and this marks the beginning of the 'Bergson Boom' in England and America.

1910   Boutroux gives the Hyde Lectures at Harvard.

1929   English translation of *Influence de l'habitude* published as *The Influence of Habit on the Faculty of Thinking*, translated by Margaret Donaldson Boehm with an introduction by George Boas (Baltimore, The Williams & Wilkins company).

1943   Jean-Paul Sartre Publishes *L'Être et le neant*. Sartre critiques Maine de Biran's 'famous sensation of effort' in the first section on the 'Body as being-for-itself: facticity'.

1947–1948   Merleau-Ponty's lectures on Malebranche, Maine de Biran, Bergson and the union of the soul and the body.

1949   Michel Henry completes his work on his *Philosophie et phénoménologie du corps*. From 1945, Henry's thinking and development of a philosophy of immanence is in large part guided by his reflections on Maine de Biran.

1950   Paul Ricoeur publishes *Le Volontaire et l'involontaire*, the first volume of his *La Philosphie de la volonte*.

1963   Michel Henry publishes *L'essence de la manifestation.*

1970   F.C.T. Moore publishes *The Psychology of Maine de Biran* (Clarendon).

1984–2001   Publication of the complete works of Maine de Biran under the direction of François Azouvi.

1995   Gilles Deleuze writes '*L'immanence: une vie . . .*'

3 Philological Preface to *The Relationship between the Physical and the Moral in Man* by F.C.T. Moore

Translated from the French by Darian Meacham

Moore's preface to the 1984 publication in French of Rapports du physique et du moral de l'homme *(The Relationship between the Physical and the Moral in Man), volume VI of the collected works of Maine de Biran published by Vrin, provides an exemplary philological contextualization of the efforts that went into establishing the text which is translated in this volume. Some of the points made in passing by Moore, aimed at a readership likely to be more familiar with the historical, intellectual, and philological context of the text and Biran's work more generally, are dealt with in more detail by Delphine Antoine-Mahut in her preface, written for this volume. Chief among these is the role played by Victor Cousin in the publication and reception of Biran's work immediately following his death and also the nature of the Mémoires or Essays that Biran wrote in response to questions posed by various academies and institutes around Europe (the Royal Academy of Copenhagen, the Academy of Berlin and the Institut de France, to be precise). These questions were the basis for what we could call essay competitions, which Biran entered and won. The text published in Volume VI of the Vrin collected works, and translated here is a version of the text that Biran wrote in response to a question posed by the Royal Academy of Copenhagen in 1810. The precise question, forming the basis of the competition, was:*

> *There are people who still deny the utility of the doctrines and physical experiences to explain the phenomena of mind and the inner sense. Others instead reject with disdain the observations and psychological reasons in research that have the body as its object, or restrict the application to certain diseases. It would be useful to discuss these two feelings, to show and to establish more clearly to what extent psychology and physics can be linked, and to demonstrate by historical evidence what each of these two sciences has done so far for the advancement of the other.*

The philological detail of Moore's preface may seem somewhat extravagant to a reader coming into contact with Biran for the first time, but we hope that it will serve as a guide to further investigation, should our readers so desire. It also provides an absolutely essential contextualizing of The Relationship between the Physical and the Moral in Man *within the trajectory of Biran's philosophical endeavour.*

– The editors

'Maine de Biran is a man of only one book, and this book he never wrote.'[1] The steps of this unfinished philosophical programme are however apparent in the work that he has left us, of which the majority remained unpublished at the time of his death.

The heritage of these manuscripts is unfortunately no longer intact. Victor Cousin, entrusted by Lainé[2] (the executor of the will) to make an inventory of the manuscripts, arrived too late in Bergerac. 'The pamphlets and manuscripts from the objects left by the deceased were thrown in a basket marked papers without proper discernment and brought to the grocers by one of the servants of the house.'[3] But the manuscripts underwent still further losses after this date: Ernest Naville, thanks to whose work we

---

[1] H. Gouhier. *Les conversations de Maine de Biran*, Paris: Vrin, 1948, p. 6.
[2] Joseph Henri Joachim Lainé (1768–1835), a French lawyer, politician and friend of Maine de Biran – ed.
[3] E. Naville, *Notice historique et bibliographique sur les travaux de Maine de Biran*, Geneva: F. Ramboz, 1851, p. VII.

now have the possibility to proceed with an edition of Maine de Biran's collected works, lent some, which have today disappeared.

It is thus that we lack today several texts and that others contain more and less serious gaps. This is the case notably of the Copenhagen Essay.[4] The details of these gaps will be indicated below.

1. Context of the work

The Copenhagen Essay belongs to the second great stage in the work of Maine de Biran: the properly Biranian stage that began with the Essay for the Institute of France, '*Sur la décomposition de la pensée*' (1804), and continued with the Berlin Essay, '*On Immediate Apperception*' (1807) and the essays read at the Bergerac Medical Society, '*Sur les perceptions obscure ou les impressions génénerales affectives et les sympathies en particulier*' (1807), '*Observations sur les divisions organiques de cerveau*' (1808), '*Nouvelles Considérations sur le sommeil, les songes, et le somnambulisme*' (1809), and finished with the incomplete text '*Essai sur les fondements de la psychologie*' (1812).

During this stage, Biran rethought the notion of reflection or *sens intime*, placed the consciousness of voluntary movement at the forefront of his investigations, and distinguished between 'two lives' in man. Consequently, he was led:

(1) to revise the Lockean empirical psychology that he had inherited; and

(2) to construct a new framework that would reunite the physical sciences, psychology and medicine with this new 'anthropology'.

The essays for the Institute of Berlin aimed especially at the first of these tasks, those from Bergerac and Copenhagen at the second, the *Essai sur les fondements de la psychologie* sought to bring the two together.

2. History of the work

In the 14 May 1810 edition of the *Moniteur français*, the Royal Academy of Copenhagen proposed a question on the relations between psychology and

---

[4] The French word *mémoire* does not really have a direct translation in English. I am translating it here as essay; other possible translations would be report, project or thesis. – ed.

physics. This question reanimated the ideas that Biran had developed in the Essays given at the Institute of Bergerac. The 'new question', Biran later recalled, 'again seduced me and launched me in the direction I was being pulled in . . . by the inclinations and habits of my mind . . .'.

Of this work, we possess today some of the drafts and the official copy (*la minute*) that occasionally refers to other manuscripts where we find passages that we must insert. Biran copied this version and sent the essay to Copenhagen. It was declared the winner on 1 July 1811 and he was invited to publish it. Having been in contact with the publisher Courcier since 1810, Biran agreed a contract in August 1811 for one work entitled *Analyse des faits du sens intime*, and another, *Des rapports de la physiologie avec les connaissances des facultés de l'espirit humain* – versions, clearly, of the Berlin and Copenhagen essays.

Since the official copy can no longer be found at the Copenhagen Academy, and since we have among the manuscripts a fragment of a copy that corresponds very precisely with the official copy, we can conclude that Biran requested his copy from Copenhagen in order to facilitate publication. The Academy would have sent it, with a request that Biran return it to them. We can offer this conjecture in interpreting a note added in parentheses to his *Idea linguae universalis*, written at the time when he read, pen in hand, Leibniz. This brief note indicates: 'before the end of 1811 to Mr Thomas Bugge, secretary of the society, councillor of the state, etc. to Copenhagen.' It seems clear that this refers to the date by which Biran was to return his essay to Copenhagen.

Not only would Biran not send it back, but he also quickly abandoned the project. It is possible that he had the intention to publish the essay as it was or with some small corrections. We can see the trace of these corrections at the beginning of *Rapports des sciences naturelles avec la psychologie*.[5] But soon the corrections would go too far and he concluded that he could not publish the previous essays separately:

> The two essays, from the Institute of France and the Academy of Berlin, were not susceptible to being published separately since, as I had said, they nearly form one theme done in two ways. It was necessary to recast them again in a third, more consistent and careful, composition . . ., But the last work, awarded by the Academy of Copenhagen, having also been thrown into the same mould as the other two and being

---

[5] F.C.T. Moore. *The Psychology of Maine de Biran*, Oxford, Oxford University Press, 1970, p. 192.

composed of a basis of similar ideas; it should also be included in the same plan.[6]

The stage of the essays thus passed, even though Biran continued his voyage in search of his one 'only book'. It is a change that we can easily date since Biran had already written in October 1811, in a letter to Durivau, of his 'complete work'.[7] The story of this work does not concern us here, apart from one important detail that we shall return to later because we must fill a gap in the official copy of the Copenhagen essay with a certain passage from the *Essai sur les fondements de la psychologie*.

But the story of the Copenhagen essay has a follow-up. In August of 1820, Biran wrote in his journal: 'I spent all this month and the end of last month in serious occupations of my choosing. I rewrote my essay to the Academy of Copenhagen with the intention of sending it to the doctor M. Royer-Collard [Antoine-Athanase, brother of Pierre-Paul] who consulted me on a course that he intended to do at Charenton on the subject of mental alienation.'[8] Biran incorporated a part of the original Copenhagen essay directly into this text. He delivered the new essay to Royer-Collard, and in August 1821 deemed it ready for publication. He again established a contract with the publisher Courcier and was ready to deliver the first volume of around 300 pages, entitled, *Nouvelles considerations sur les rapports du physique et du moral*; this would be 'followed by another that would contain a philosophical essay awarded by the Academy of Berlin'.[9]

We cannot see very well, however, what text this was, since Biran spoke of a work much longer than the one edited by Victor Cousin in 1834 under the title *Nouvelles considerations sur les rapports du physique et du moral* (which must be the one sent to Royer-Collard). The idea that Biran thought to add for publication three other texts (two of which had already been published) is unlikely.[10] A simpler hypothesis would be that Biran made use of a copyist who wrote in large handwriting and who left wide margins, like the one he made use of when he was working on the *Essai sur les fondements de la psychologie*. In any case, the publication of the two essays, once more put into process after a delay of ten years, did not take place. But twenty years later, Hippolyte Royer-Collard published, in the second volume of the *Annales*

---

[6] See appendix XX of *Œuvres de Maine de Biran*, V. VI, *Rapports du physique et du moral de l'homme VI* Paris: Vrin, 1984, p. 172.

[7] Moore, *The Psychology of Maine de Biran*, 191.

[8] Maine de Biran. *Journal v. II*, ed. H. Gouhier, Neuchâtel, Éditions de Baconière 1955, p. 287.

[9] Maine de Biran. *De l'aperception immediate*, ed. J. Echeverria, Paris, Vrin, 1963.

[10] Moore, *The Psychology of Maine de Biran*, p. 157.

medico-psycologiques, an '*Examen de la doctrine de Maine de Biran sur les rapports du physique et du moral de l'homme*' (where Antoine-Athanase commented on the *Nouvelle Considérations*), with annotations by Biran himself.

3. Notes on the publication of the text

In his inventory from 15 August 1825, Victor Cousin wrote, concerning the Copenhagen Essay, that it consisted of the 'author's copy (*minute de l'auteur*) and there is a copy in a rather bad state. The work is long and of the greatest importance'. Naville added: 'to print this essay we must also procure a copy of the manuscript from Copenhagen.'[11] But in his catalogue, drawn up after the death of his father, Naville wrote: 'Copenhagen Essay – consists only of a short fragment of the copy.'[12] Without forming a hypothesis about what Naville could have been looking at, I shall summarize the results of my own research on what Naville called the 'chaos' of Biran's manuscripts.[13]

For the Copenhagen essay, we have the following:

(1) *Notes and drafts.* A great deal of this preparatory work remains, especially in BI, Ms 2147. It is sufficiently interesting, but does not serve to establish the text of the Copenhagen Essay.

(2) *Minute.* The minute or official copy is the principle source for the text, but it contains ten gaps, of which eight can be filled in without difficulty.

(3) *The copy sent to Copenhagen* (N). The majority of this copy is lost. What remains consists of a fragment joined to the manuscript of *Nouvelles considerations sur les rapports du physique et du moral* (BI, Ms. 2148).

(4) *Fragments of another copy* (C). This second copy, which contains only eight pages, is sometimes less faithful to the Minute than the first copy, as we can see at the end of the essay, where there is a passage that remains not only in the Minute, but also in the two copies. We can choose between two hypotheses to explain this second copy, most of which is lost:

---

[11] Naville, *Notice historique et bibliographique sur les travaux de Maine de Biran*, p. X.

[12] Naville, *Notice historique et bibliographique sur les travaux de Maine de Biran*, p. XXXIII.

[13] Naville, *Notice historique et bibliographique sur les travaux de Maine de Biran*, p. XXIV–XXVIII.

(I) The essay passed through three stages before being sent to Copenhagen:

   a. the Minute

   b. a first copy (C or N)

   c. a final copy (N or C).

(II) Biran did not make the copy N before sending it to Copenhagen, but in revising the essay in preparation for its (aborted) publication in 1811, he made another copy, C.

Yet what remains of these two copies reassures us about the use of the Minute as the basis for the text (published here), since in the pages that we do have, the Minute and the copy are parallel. The differences between the two are minimal and are due for the most part to the copyists' errors or to their difficulties in decrypting the philosophical writing. In the three cases, the copies also help us to fill in the gaps in the Minute. When it is not the case, there are certain signs that permit us to reconstitute the missing text – for example, where Biran refers very clearly to the manuscript of *Perceptions obscures*, or to the discussion of 'Bichat's division'. In only two cases do the gaps remain irremediable: after M 23 there are several words that we have put in brackets using other similar sections as a guide;[14] after M 28 there is at least a page missing. There was no question of substituting for the author here, so we have merely indicated what could have been the essential content of this passage.[15] The manuscript that properly serves as the reference for this text is thus the Minute (M).[16]

---

[14] See pp. 61–63 of this edition. – ed.

[15] See pp. 65–66 of this edition. – ed.

[16] The final section of Moore's preface has been omitted as it pertained to editorial operations within the translation that we have opted not to indicate for the sake of simplicity.

4 Maine de Biran's Places in French Spiritualism: Occultation, Reduction and Demarcation

Delphine Antoine-Mahut, ENS de Lyon, IHRIM, UMR 5317, LABEX "COMOD"

This volume presents the first English translation of an essay by Maine de Biran (1766–1824), awarded a prize by the Royal Academy of Copenhagen in 1811: *The Relationship between the Physical and the Moral in Man* (*Rapports du physique et du moral de l'homme*).[1] In this sense, it is an editorial event. But it can only be described as such against the background of a historical frame that gives it meaning, precisely because it breaks this framework. This break is also thus the break of a silence or a lack, in any case, an absence. This calls for several remarks and raises questions.

Firstly, it should be noted that if the recognition of Maine de Biran's work in the English-speaking world has been a long time in coming, France also took its time. Not until the 1980s and the titanic effort of the

---

[1] The three essays by Biran discussed here, the 1811 *Rapports du physique et du moral de l'homme* (of which this volume is a translation), *De l'aperception immediate* from 1807, and *Sur la décomposition de la pensée* of 1804 were written as responses to competition questions posed by the Academy of Copenhagen, the Academy of Berlin and the Institute of France (*Institut de France*), respectively. Maine de Biran effectively entered these essay competitions and won. – ed.

publication of the *Oeuvres complètes de Maine de Biran* (Vrin, CNRS), under the direction of François Azouvi, was a synoptic and scientific view of Biran's work possible. Another good indicator of the passage of a 'classic' author towards his integration into comprehensive philosophical training in France is having him appear in competitive teacher recruitment exams. Maine de Biran appeared twice, on the external aggregation of philosophy,[2] in 1996 and in 2014, but only as text from which questions might be referenced during an oral question period, and not as a canonical author and, both times, on the basis of the same text: the essay on the decomposition of thought (*Sur la décomposition de la pensée*), awarded by the *Institut de France* in 1804. While this essay does mark the beginning of Biran's properly Biranian thinking, it does not fully announce itself as such.

Yet if there is a philosophy that we generally label as French, just as idealism or romanticism are designated as German and empiricism is largely assigned to England or Scotland, it is indeed spiritualism that lays claim to Biran: the philosophical current recognizing both of the autonomy and the superiority of the mind (*esprit*) over the body. And although, most often, the genesis of Spiritualism was traced to Descartes, it remains the case that in the nineteenth century, Biran was, chronologically at least, the first of these spiritualists. How, then, can we understand having waited so long before one of the texts that may be the source of a newly deemed national philosophy, or at the very least, one of its designated singular currents, is made known? The first answer that comes to mind is the formula of Henri Gouhier: 'Maine de Biran is the man of one book, and this book, he never wrote.'[3] The text of *Rapports du physique et du moral de l'homme* is part of a triptych consisting of two other essays: the essay from the *Institut de France*, *Sur la décomposition de la pensée*, and a third that was awarded by

---

[2] The external aggregation of philosophy was established in France in 1825. This is a competitive examination for professors of philosophy wishing to teach in the final year at high schools. The competition includes written tests for eligibility (a general philosophy essay, an essay on a theme of the curriculum, and an explanation of text on an author in the programme) and oral admission tests (a general philosophy lesson, a lesson on a field in the curriculum, an explanation of French text on the curriculum – it is within this framework that the essay on the 'decomposition of thought' fits – and an explanation of text in a foreign language). On this French specificity and its history, see the book by B. Poucet, *Enseigner la philosophie. Histoire d'une discipline scolaire (1860–1990)*. Paris: CNRS Editions, 1999.

[3] H. Gouhier, *Les conversions de Maine de Biran*, Paris: Vrin, 1948, p. 6. See also F.C.T. Moore's introduction in this volume for a further explanation of the never-written book. – ed.

the Berlin Academy in 1807, *De l'aperception immédiate*. Biran had proposed to bring together and consolidate these three, but the project was never brought to fruition.

However, the particularity of these texts should be noted. The three essays are answers to competition questions posed by the members of a committee of a given scholarly academy, with the aim of clarifying or resolving a problem specific in a context. In the case of *The Relationship between the Physical and the Moral in Man*, the question posed by the Royal Academy of Copenhagen was to fit into the burning debate between metaphysicians and psychologists, on the one hand, and physicists and physiologists, on the other, by updating the contrasting genesis of relations between these two pairs of disciplines and how each was likely to contribute to the advancement of the science of man.

The exact question posed by the Royal Academy of Copenhagen that Biran would have read in 14 May 1810 edition of the *Moniteur français* was the following:

> There are people who still deny the utility of the doctrines and physical experiences to explain the phenomena of mind and the inner sense. Others instead reject with disdain the observations and psychological reasons in research that have the body as its object, or restrict the application to certain diseases. It would be useful to discuss these two feelings, to show and to establish more clearly to what extent psychology and physics can be linked, and to demonstrate by historical evidence what each of these two sciences has done so far for the advancement of the other.[4]

The writing of a competition essay assumes that it first and foremost is written within the context of responding to a command and not in writing a standalone book. Exterior pressures and demands also played a role in the subsequent revisions and corrections made to these competition texts: prior to the publication of the texts, jury members would demand preliminary alterations. The difficulties encountered by Biran in considering his own work as successful and worthy of being published are therefore derived from the nature and circumstances of this kind of essay. From a certain view, then, to not publish Biran, or to wait to publish Biran and, a

---

[4] On the context of this question, cf. Elizabeth A. Williams, *The Physical and the Moral. Anthropology, Physiology, and Philosophical Medicine in France, 1750–1850*. Cambridge: CUP, 1994.

fortiori, to translate Biran, would be to respect the will of Biran himself. And we would respect this because, implicitly at least, we would prioritize and distinguish different types of writings based on the authorship regime to which they belong. Some rewritten essays are in this sense more esteemed as 'works' than some original essays.

The second possible answer is more general and, in a sense, less generous to Biran. It is rooted in the observation of the philosophical eclipse of the latter by most important masters in the history of the French spiritualist tradition, including the Magisterium Bergsonian[5] or by the perennial success of new branches of this school, such as phenomenology. It would have been expected that before becoming public, because it would be considered a second-order philosophy, or of less important than those of Bergson or Merleau-Ponty, it would have swept away in their waves. Returning to Biran in this sense allows for a nuancing of our understanding of the historiography of this spiritualist current, but without significantly changing the balance. It would only restore a link in a signifying chain, which would, however, remain intelligible without him.

Yet these explanations only intensify the initial question: according to what criteria should Biran be considered a minor author, including within his own camp? We can understand the need to distinguish the historical figure Maine de Biran (and if one were interested in this figure, it would be necessary to provide the full biography; but contrary to other prefaces mentioned here, the aim of this one goes beyond historical and bibliographical details, and focuses on receptions of Biran) from the Biranian figure built by successive readers and receptions, i.e. his historiography, or what one has made of him and said about him. But it is not yet clear in what capacity this historiography carries value as truth concerning the same work, or what, symmetrically, returning to Biran could do to alter our perception of this historiography.

To answer, we need to clarify the nature and purpose of this preface. A preface is a threshold used to carry a link between a context and a text. Biran's text, however, has already been received through three mediations, including two prefaces: one by F.C.T. Moore (1984), translated in this volume; the historical and bibliographical notes on the work of Maine de Biran by Ernest Naville (1851),[6] upon which Moore based his work; and the

---

[5] Cf. F. Azouvi, *La gloire de Bergson. Essai sur le magistère philosophique.* Paris: Gallimard, 2007.

[6] Erenest Naville, *Notice historique et bibliographique sur les travaux de Maine de Biran*, Geneva: F. Ramboz, 1851.

preface by Victor Cousin, in his edition to the *Œuvres posthumes* de Maine de Biran (March 1834). The latter included, in addition to the unpublished text, the *Rapports du physique et du moral de l'homme*, the *Examen de la philosophie de M. Laromiguière* (already published by Fournier in 1817) and the article on Leibniz (*Exposition de la doctrine philosophique de Leibniz*, published in 1819 by Michaud but composed with Stapfer in 1817 for the *Biographie universelle* de Michaud). Rewriting a preface to the *Rapports du physique et du moral de l'homme* thus requires identification of classifications or main hierarchies that were dominant at the writing of these antecedent texts and the imposition of a certain Biranism. In short, it requires us to ask what aspects of Biranism these texts allow us to see and what they consigned to the shadows.

From this point of view, there is one common point in the texts of Moore and Naville: both focus on the difficulties of unifying and establishing a definitive version of Biran's papers, therefore on more philological than thetic themes, and both bypass the polemical dimension of Cousin's enterprise and initial preface.

Yet who is Victor Cousin in 1834? He exercised and in many ways continues to *exercise* all the power: *Conseil supérieur de l'instruction publique, présidence de l'Agrégation de philosophie et de l'Académie des sciences morales et politiques, direction de l'École normale.* He is the 'king of philosophers'.[7] He is the uncontested leader of a new eclectic spiritualist school that is reflected institutionally in curriculum content, teaching and teacher recruitment choices, writ, as the dominant philosophy, or a state philosophy. He is seen as the French founder of a modern historiography placing at its centre a Cartesian cogito designated as the absolute foundation of a psychology both experimental and rational.

Returning to Victor Cousin's preface is thus a way to provide ourselves the means to understand the contours and the figure of the Maine de Biran which was made public and even institutionalized in the vast camp of spiritualists as early as the first third of the nineteenth century. It is a return to the origin of the storylines and background in which the editing and scientific translations of Biran appear as events. It is to produce the reason of an effect, which this volume is the completed expression of and may be

---

[7] 'The revolution of 1830, which had made Louis Philippe king of the French, had made Mr Cousin king of philosophers. But Louis Philippe was only a constitutional King, Mr Cousin was an absolute King' (Jules Simon, *La Philosophie et l'enseignement officiel de la philosophie*, private archives, Fonds Jules Simon, 87 AP 16, cited by P. Vermeren, *Victor Cousin. Le jeu de la philosophie et de l'État*, Paris: L'Harmattan, 1995, chap. 7, p. 176).

so unconsciously. And then, by identifying the problems raised by Cousin's preface, we can restore Biran's voice.

In tracing this genealogy, we shall proceed in three stages:

(1) We shall first discuss the main criticisms levelled at Victor Cousin's edition by Pierre Leroux (1797–1871).[8]

(2) We shall then return to the main arguments of Victor Cousin's preface.

(3) Finally, we shall ask if the return to the text of *Rapports du physique et du moral de l'homme* is or is not likely to correct our reading of the essay.

We can then draw all the consequences regarding the place of Biranism in modern historiography.

1. Mutilation versus occultation: back to the genesis of silence

The decision to make a strong accusation against the person that has identified himself as the father of the great spiritualist family is obviously not a neutral one. It aims to revise (and more than that) Biran's assignment to a subordinate place in this family. It intends to focus gradually on what Biran himself said, rather than on the theses that were attributed to him, or how the editing and the translation of his work appear as a requirement produced by the intrinsic nature of this work rather than as foreign to this work.

The interest in Pierre Leroux's approach lies in the comparison of the treatment of two figures in the history of French spiritualism who both shared an interest in presenting the relationship between psychology and physiology, and whose work was only made public posthumously by Victor Cousin. They are Maine de Biran and Théodore Jouffroy (1797–1842). The

---

[8] Pierre Henri Leroux (1797–1871) was the founder of the periodical *Le Globe*, a journal of young people opposed to the regime of the restoration. Following that, he founded the *Revue Encyclopédique*, then in 1836, with Jean Reynaud, the *Encyclopédie nouvelle*, to which he also contributed over one hundred articles. Directly opposing the official state philosophy of Victor Cousin, he proposed, notably, a history of philosophy that rehabilitated the philosophers of the eighteenth century. On the various aspects and issues surrounding the polemic between Cousin and Leroux, see Lucie Rey, *Les enjeux de l'histoire de la philosophie en France au* XIX*e siècle. Pierre Leroux contre Victor Cousin.* Paris: L'Harmattan, 2013.

argument concerning Jouffroy therefore reflects indirectly on the analysis of the posthumous *Œuvres* of Biran. But while for Jouffroy, Cousin's intervention is comparable to a real 'mutilation',[9] in the case of Biran it takes the form of a deafness to an occultation.[10]

First, a brief introduction. Théodore Simon Jouffroy was a student of Cousin from 1815 to 1822. He worked at *Le globe*, *Courrier français* and l'*Encyclopédie moderne*. He was, successively, lecturer at the *Ecole Normale Supérieure* and then professor of ancient philosophy at the *Collège de France*, and held the chair of philosophy at the Faculty of Letters in Paris, from which he took leave for medical reasons in 1839. In 1833 he was elected to the Academy of Moral and Political Sciences (*l'Académie des sciences morales et politiques*), the Royal Council of Public Instruction (*Conseil Royal de l'Instruction Publique*) in 1840 and president of the Aggregation Jury in 1838, 1840 and 1841. He is best known for having focused on the refutation of materialist physiology from within the French spiritualist school. His ambivalent, near dissident, character, emphasized by Leroux and Giuseppe Ferrari (*Les philosophes salariés*, 1849), stemmed from the particularity of his position: interrogating the advances and scientific demands of physiology upon psychology, rather than refuting them. This is the reason for his close proximity to Maine de Biran and for discussing Cousin's treatment of his posthumous publications alongside his treatment of Biran's.

What happened to Jouffroy? Leroux shows that between the time of its writing and the presentation of excerpts in the *Revue des deux Mondes*, and its posthumous publication in the *Nouveaux mélanges de Jouffroy*[11] in 1842, the text of *De l'organisation des sciences philosophiques* was the subject of a censure or even a rewrite by Cousin. By connecting the mutilation of Jouffroy's texts to Cousin's censorship of Wilhelm Gottlieb Tennemann's work on Hegel in the publication of Cousin's translation of Tennemann's

---

[9] See, P. Leroux, '*De la mutilation d'un écrit posthume de M. Jouffroy*', Revue Indépendante, 1 November 1842.

[10] P-H. Daled studies the efficacy of occultation concerning eighteenth-century philosophers in *Le matérialisme occulté et la genèse du «sensualisme». Ecrire l'histoire de la philosophie en France*. Paris, Vrin, 2005. I show here that this strategy of occultation was applied even within the same intellectual family – spiritualism.

[11] By Jean-Philibert Damiron (1794–1862). Damiron became a member of the Academy of Moral and Political Sciences in 1836 and obtained a chair in Modern Philosophy at the Sorbonne in 1838. He is notably the author of *Essai sur l'histoire de la philosophie en France au dix-neuvième siècle* (1828) and *Essai sur l'histoire de la philosophie en France au dix-septième siècle* (1846). His relation of dependency vis-à-vis Cousin, who secured his post for him, occassionaly placed him in delicate situations like the one concerning Jouffroy related here.

Manuel de l'histoire de la philosophie in 1829,[12] Leroux shows that the 'critical' and censured passages of *De l'organisation des sciences philosophiques* involved, either developments unflattering to Cousin and his courses, or considerations on the philosophical religion or philosophy of religion. To rehabilitate what he sees as the 'true' Jouffroy, Leroux thus brings to the fore writing that appeared in *Le Globe* in 1825, republished with the agreement of Jouffroy in the *Revue indépendante* in 1841, and presents as an Appendix to his 1843 '*De la mutilation d'un écrit posthume de Theodore Jouffroy*' the text titled '*Comment les dogmes finissent*', where Jouffroy incorporates and extends the ideas from his courses of 1830 and 1834. Leroux intends therefore to denounce and correct censorship by Cousin by giving a voice to Jouffroy himself.

Concerning Biran and *Rapports du physique et du moral de l'homme*, the analysis is substantially different. Leroux denounces the 'twelve lost years' between Biran's death and the publication of the posthumous edition (1834). He directly attributes to Cousin a desire for silence about Biran. And by bringing this strategy of silencing together with the mutilation imposed on Jouffroy, he shows how not giving the author his voice amounts to burying him a second time. A delay in the distribution of a work undermines it and destroys its originality. We even gain time to appropriate and to digest it, and then claim the main results – that is to say, to annex it. It is worth reproducing at length Leroux's condemnation of Cousin:

> When Maine de Biran died nearly twenty years ago, he left numerous writings, which fell, after his death, into the hands of M. Cousin. Our late friend doctor Bertrand, who had been closely linked with Maine de Biran, for whom he was the doctor, seeing, after a year or two, that these writings, which he knew where in part ready for printing, seemed not to appear, spoke several times to Cousin to have a sense of this enigma. He did not achieve clarity, and we were handed a letter that we printed in *Le Globe*, where he denounced this fact to the friends of philosophy. He attested in this letter that he had had in his own hands many of these writings completely finished. He attested that Maine de Biran, in his last moments, asked that at his death there be only a short delay for them to be public. Mr Cousin claimed at first that there was no editor: Bertrand found him three; then, that the Biran family was opposed to the implementation of the wishes of the deceased, but he added that these

[12] *Wilhelm Gottlieb Tennemann. Manuel de l'histoire de la philosophie*, translated from German by V. Cousin, Professeur à la Faculté des Lettres de l'Académie de Paris, Paris: Pichon et Didier, two volumes, 1829.

scruples could easily be lifted. In the meantime, he kept for twelve years the manuscripts that had been entrusted to him, without making it known to the public; After ten years he published some, publication which, gave him great honour. But twelve years lost, when it comes to discoveries and a man like Maine de Biran is not nothing. It would seem that he had promised Maine de Biran's writing, like that of Jouffroy, not to the present epoch but to the future.[13]

But Leroux identifies no censorship of the manuscript and pronounces the same interpretation on the same content as that proposed by Cousin in his preface. Therefore, to return to the text of Biran, we must revisit and rediscover important lines and the context that influenced their first reception. We must go back to Cousin.

2. Annexation versus reduction: the battle for the 'true' spiritualism

We can highlight two intellectual mechanisms in Cousin's interpretation of Biran: annexation and reduction. Both mechanisms describe respectively how Cousin appreciates what he shares with Biran in their common cause of a reigning spiritualism, as well as the manner in which he considered it important to distinguish himself from Biran and, if possible, to surpass him so as to maintain his dominant position.

Biran is portrayed above all as the 'first metaphysician' of the modern age.[14] This characterization is both negative and positive. Its negative connotation is pronounced and founded on an opposition against those who are designated by Cousin as the partisans of the school of sensualism and physiologists, or, in other words, those who refuse to recognize consciousness as a distinct reality from sensation. From Cousin's perspective, Biran's contribution consists foremost in undermining any identification of human beings with a product of physiological organization. Claiming Biran as an ally in this way allows Cousin to consolidate his opposition against Condillac's heritage, as represented by Pierre Jean George Cabanis

---

[13] The passage on Biran is located on page 293 of '*De la mutilation d'un écrit posthume de Théodore Jouffroy*'.

[14] *Nouvelles considérations sur les rapports du physique et du moral de l'homme, Ouvrage posthume de M. Maine de Biran*, edited with a preface by Victor Cousin. Brussels: Haumen and Co., 1834, p. 39.

(1777–1808), widely considered to be the principal physiologist of the ideologues, or as represented by Antoine Destutt de Tracy (1754–1836), who was recognized as the metaphysician of this school, or as revived during the early 1830s through the French reception of Franz Joseph Gall's phrenology (1758–1828). Biran is thus brought into the service of Cousin's cause.

But there is also a positive sense to Biran's metaphysics with its reintegration of activity into consciousness. Such a reintegration is based on three compelling ideas: genuine activity is volition; volition is personality and personality is the self (*le moi*) itself; lastly, to will is to cause, and thus the self is the first cause given to us. Biran thus promises a form of spiritualism that is everything except

> extravagant and without relation to the world that we inhabit, since the mind [esprit] that we are, the self, is given in a relation of which it is the first term, but which the second term is [a] sensation, and a sensation is localized at a certain location in the body. In this manner, mind [esprit] is given along with its opposite, the outside along with the inside, nature along with human beings.[15]

Biran's relevance in 1834 is thus foremost as a sophisticated precaution and forerunner of Cousin's spiritualism against the adversary of materialism understood broadly.

The second form of argument mobilized by Cousin's interpretation of Biran concerns the notion of experience. Just as Biran does not deny organic reality and the external world, he does not hypostasize the basic fact of consciousness. In claiming for the basic fact of internal sense – its object of investigation – the same kind of experimental truth as that claimed by the sciences, the new psychology can thus fight on equal footing against the physical sciences. The main contribution of Biran's thinking to spiritualism is thus the displacement of a debate that beforehand experienced difficulty in engaging with its opponent. Combat always aspires to the establishment of a monopoly, but this time on a common territory, namely the experimental territory with the primacy of inner experience. Once again, Biran is called upon as reinforcement in a common struggle.

If this were all, Leroux would be vindicated, since one would no longer understand how Cousin could legitimately remain in the position of the father of the spiritualist school. In order either to return to this position or

---

[15] Cousin, *Nouvelles considérations*, p. 10.

retain it, despite the publication *Rapports du physique et du moral de l'homme*, one must thus reveal the limits of what Cousin called the reduction of Biran's thinking. Reduction thus legitimates annexation in making Biran's contribution a simple dimension of a more encompassing project, namely Cousin's. This runs the risk of appearing like an alternative spiritualism, far more heuristic than Cousin's spiritualism, and yet absorbed by the latter.

Because if Biran has expanded philosophy in enlarging consciousness from the givens of sensation to the domain of active and voluntary experiences, he has equally left a 'massive lacuna':[16] rational experiences in the broad sense. This is not a lacuna among others; it is a lacuna that inhibits that anything can be observed in consciousness. Yet, according to Cousin, this rational substantiality of consciousness is the condition of possibility for all interior experience.

On the metaphysical level, the hierarchy between rational and voluntary phenomena implies a further consequence: it rehabilitates the notion of substance at the foundation of the notion of cause in the sense that if the will causes the act, only reason can provide a cause in itself, or, in other words, substance. Biran's spiritualism is distinct from Cousin's in terms of a different relation to the original categories of thinking; Cousin's choice: the integration of rationality at the foundation of volitional activity grounds and thus surpasses Biran's options.

Equally at stake is another conception of modern historiography.[17] The principal contribution of Biran's thinking consists in a novel interpretation of Leibniz's monadology. In Biran's Leibniz, as interpreted by Cousin, 'the apperception of consciousness provides knowledge of the self, [as] substance and cause together, [as] a simple force [of] the monad, and which is developed through activity that is manifest through effort'. Modern philosophy becomes thus re-centred on the image of a Leibniz who erases by the same stroke the presumptive experimental truths of the so-called philosophers of the eighteenth century. But once again, Leibniz risks eclipsing Descartes, the father of modern rational psychology. To demonstrate how the irreducibility of the self is grounded in reality on its substantiality would at the same time put Leibniz back in his proper place with respect to Descartes.

One can now understand why French spiritualism took its time before becoming finding a home in Maine de Biran. Without a doubt, Biran was not mutilated directly. But maybe Biran was temporarily gagged. In any

---

[16] Cousin, *Nouvelles considérations*, p. 26.

[17] Cousin quite rightly points out that Biran's theory impacts upon 'the history of philosophical systems, I mean, the history of modern systems, the only ones to occupy French philosophy at this time' (Cousin, *Nouvelles considérations*, p. 15).

case, everything was done such that he could be eclipsed in such a fashion that only king Cousin could continue to reign at the institutional court.

The final part of this preface will therefore aim to give a voice back to Biran on those aspects that Cousin had labelled either as problematic or inadequate. This will hopefully leave us in the position – with a proper understanding of the relevant matters – to determine whether Cousin or Biran has the most rightful claim to reign.

3. Rebalancing versus demarcation: the experimental science of man according to Maine de Biran

Reading *The Relationship between the Physical and the Moral in Man* in accordance with Cousin's preface yields two mechanisms, corresponding to those of annexation and restriction, which we shall call rebalancing and demarcation.

From the outset, the rebalancing concerns Biran's metaphysical contribution to the analysis of the duality of the primitive fact of innermost sense in the experience of effort. As regards what was at stake in the question set by the Copenhagen Academy, Cousin made this duality in Biran perfectly clear. Yet he has equally transformed the (thoroughly spiritualist) priority given to mind over body in this relation into an unconditional superiority of mind over body. In other words, Cousin has passed over the vital dimension[18] of the Biranian self in utter silence. It is precisely by way of this dimension that Biran retains a connection to physiology. What Cousin has selected, or indeed isolated, as concerns Biran must therefore be reinstated in reading the latter. Biran opposes 'physiologists become metaphysicians' just as much as 'metaphysicians transformed into physiologists'[19] – in short, he is against those who seek to conflate the irreducible distinction of soul from body with a negation or an absorption of one by the other.[20]

This rebalancing can here be made apparent in three ways.

The first way is in considering a dimension of the reference to Descartes. Indeed, for Biran, it is because Descartes radically distinguished soul from

---

[18] On the vital dimension of the self in spiritualism, see especially Dominique Janicaud, http://www.universalis.fr/encyclopedie/spiritualisme.

[19] *The Relationship between the Physical and the Moral in Man*, p. 80.

[20] F. Azouvi, *Maine de Biran. La Science de l'homme*. Paris: Vrin, 2000.

body that he was able to generate a materialism just as much as he was the contrary position.[21] If the difference is overstressed, we risk producing what we fear. To strengthen spiritualism against its alternative, the physiological dimension of the science of man must not be neglected but, on the contrary, be accorded its full significance.

The analysis of Cabanis in *The Relationship between the Physical and the Moral in Man* confirms this thesis. As Cousin was to remark, Biran clearly emphasizes (as Cabanis puts it) 'the genius of the science of physiology'.[22] But this is equally to explain the profit we may draw from physiology when we no longer claim to make it into the complete explanation:

> This great work seems to me eminently appropriate to make clear, on the one hand, the abuse and the danger of physiological theories in the explanation or deduction of the phenomena of inner sense, and on the other hand, the genuinely useful type of application one may make of these theories to a particular class of sensitive phenomena that take their necessary place in the philosophy of the human mind.[23]

Just as taking spiritualism in the sense of a rationalism risks producing its contrary, so a physiologism properly understood guards against a kind of idealization of inner sense.

The rebalancing that Biran proposes for spiritualism therefore consists in abandoning the sterile struggle with its alternative to the benefit of integrating, in the self, the irreducible phenomena that are the confused perceptions of a living organization: 'Then, doubtless, psychology, to the extent that we include within it this particular species of fact, will find itself bound intimately to physiology.'[24]

We now see where Cousin's demarcating line runs, and in what sense a different form of enlargement might answer the accusation of restriction. For Biran, on the metaphysical plane, it is when psychology seals itself against its other, and restricts itself in this sense, that it risks a suffocating death. To rationalize the self is to lack the interiority of sensations, affects and passions. And to ground the will's causal force by way of substantiality is to sever the vital force.

---

[21] Azouvi, *Maine de Biran. La Science de l'homme*, p. 21.

[22] Azouvi, *Maine de Biran. La Science de l'homme*, p. 144. Biran adds that Cabanis omits 'the entire intellectual and truly *moral* aspects of the phenomena of man *doubled in humanity* [*duplex in humanitate*]'.

[23] Azouvi, *Maine de Biran. La Science de l'homme*, p. 144.

[24] Azouvi, *Maine de Biran. La Science de l'homme*, p. 106.

Contrary to Cousin's historiography, the history of modern thought, according to Biran, must therefore make room for authors such as Thomas Willis (1621–1675), Georg Ernst Stahl (1659–1734), David Hartley (1705–1757), Charles Bonnet (1720–1793), François Gigot de Lapeyronie (1678–1747), Marie François Xavier Bichat (1771–1802), Philippe Pinel (1745–1826) or further Franz Joseph Gall (1758–1828) – that is, those whom dominant or institutional thought strives to expel from the corpus of 'philosophy'. In contemporary terms, we could say that Biran is one of the first defenders of the fertility of an interdisciplinary approach to the human being, and that this interdisciplinary approach is for him the only measure of the scientific status of the psychology he promoted.

Yet a question remains. If Biran indeed proposed an alternative to Cousinism, why was his voice not heard once his writings were published? Why did no school issue from him? Why did he not introduce a clear line of demarcation at the heart of French spiritualism?

We could answer that, each in their own way, authors such as Théodore Jouffroy, Félix Ravaisson (1813–1900) or Francisque Bouillier (1813–1899),[25] drew precisely on the threads that tightly bond psychology to physiology (for Jouffroy), habit (for Ravaisson) or even to a form of vitalism (for Bouillier), which issued directly from Biran's canvas. We could equally consider Bergson's élan vital and Merleau-Ponty's study of perception as singular, new grafts onto unnamed Biranian roots.

That these roots remain unnamed may then be interpreted in two ways. We may note the perennial force of authoritarian thought that makes it risky to take sides with this alternative voice. But we may value the power of this voice, despite institutional pressure, and let it resonate in other bodies of work in order to test its capacity to intervene in turn.

We began with an idea according to which this first English translation of Maine de Biran would be an event. It has now become one of the first nodes in the network of a history other than the authoritarian. In its turn, it could therefore make an intervention.

---

[25] On Ravaisson, cf. Dominique Janicaud, *Ravaisson et la métaphysique. Généalogie du spiritualisme français* (Paris: Vrin, 1998). On Francisque Bouillier's place in the French Spiritualist stream, and on the role granted to the history of philosophy, and particularly to Leibniz, in Bouillier's strategies against Cousin, cf. D. Antoine-Mahut, 'Reviving spiritualism with Monads. Francisque Bouillier's impossible mission (1839–1864)', *British Journal for the History of Philosophy*, Special Issue, *300 Years of Leibniz's Monadology*, ed. Pauline Phemister and Jeremy Dunham, 2015. 23(6), pp. 1106–1127.

5 *The Relationship between the Physical and the Moral in Man: Copenhagen Treatise 1811*

Maine de Biran

Programme

(Extract from *Moniteur français*, 14 May 1810)

Some still deny the utility of physical doctrines and experiments in explaining the phenomena of the mind and of internal sense. Others on the contrary disdainfully reject psychological observations and reasons in investigations whose object is the body, or restrict their application to certain illnesses. It would be useful to discuss these two sentiments, to show and to determine more carefully to what extent psychology and physics may be linked to one another, and to demonstrate by historical proofs what each of these two sciences has done for the advancement of the other.

Introduction

'Corporeae machinae mentibus serviunt, et quod in mente est providentia, in corpore est fatum.'[1]

To observe or to collect phenomena, to *classify* them, to posit *laws*, to *seek out causes* – such are the regular procedures that alone can lead to truth in the sciences of fact.

It is by following this path traced by Bacon, and never allowing themselves to invert its order, that the promoters of the natural sciences managed to erect, in the interval of one century, an edifice as imposing by the solidity of its mass as by the beauty and regularity of its proportions.

The first step, which consists in observing and collecting the facts of nature, is founded upon the regular exercise of the first and simplest faculties of the human mind – the *senses*; it thus supposes the reality of an ancient and famous maxim, *nihil ist in intellectu quod non prius fuerit in sensu*,[2] a controversial maxim, so often contested in the theory or the science of *principles*, and so obviously justified in practice, or in the science of results. The action of walking thus serves to refute those who deny the existence of movement.

But this word 'sense', as simple as it at first seems, has itself a rather wide latitude of meaning: beyond the *external senses*, whose number, functions and range are rather well determined, there is one or several internal senses, whose nature and derivative faculties are not equally nor as unanimously recognized.

Sight and touch, which put man in direct communication with external nature, are the truly predominate senses in the human organism (*l'organisation humaine*), and since we attach a far greater importance to studying and knowing things than to knowing ourselves and to studying ourselves, so it is upon the relationship between these first senses that our attention first fixes – it is under their tutelage that the observer is trained. The most extensive, the most influential branch of his education, consists in clarifying, comparing and rectifying their testimony; and all the ideas to which he attains while raising himself up to the highest degrees of the

---

[1] 'The bodily machines are at the service of the minds, and what in the mind is providence, in the body is fate.' Leibniz, *Epistola ad Hanschium de Philosophia Platonic sive de Enthusiasmo Plantonico* (1707).

[2] 'Nothing is in the intellect that was not first in the senses.' Leibniz, *New Essays on Human Understanding*, II, I, §2.

intellectual scale, all the *abstractions* that his practised mind can grasp or create, always conserve some imprint of this origin.

As for the internal sense that is hidden within us, whose development is most belated, whose cultivation most rare and difficult, it emerges only in the silence of all the others. It is appropriate only for a unique and simple subject, whose study at first offers nothing attractive, and which most men seem more disposed to flee that to investigate. It is, however, through the cultivation of this internal sense that man enables himself to satisfy the oracle's precept, *nosce te ipsum* [know thyself].

Internal observation is nothing other than the present application of this sense to that which is in us, or which properly belongs to us, and whatever idealism may say, it is by focusing upon its testimony, and not by raising ourselves up to the *heavens* or by descending into the abyss, on the wings of the senses or of imagination, that we may contemplate our thought and know our nature.

Here, right from our first step, as from the first advancement of the sciences of fact, we encounter two orders of phenomena that are distinct and even opposed, and hence two kinds of observation, which have nothing in common as to their means, or their object, or their aim – and even seem most often mutually to contradict themselves, one tending to take flight far away from us, the other staying as closely as possible to the *self*, seeking only to penetrate into its depths.

It is perhaps by paying heed to this conflict between the two sciences' tendencies and means that Newton, hitting upon the core of the question with which we are occupied, cried out, 'O physics! Preserve thee from metaphysics!' It is also by heeding the necessarily double observation of two classes of phenomena, which when mixed up and conflated produce so many errors and illusions and misunderstandings, that we may cry out in turn: 'O psychology! Preserve thee from physics!'

Let us recognize at present, pending further developments that constitute the object of this treatise, that it is not possible for the two sciences in question to have more necessary ties with one another than the external senses of touch and sight have with a sense that is wholly *internal*, or that the object of an external representation, variable and multiple, has with the subject one, simple and identical, that represents itself. Let us add that the way one observes or collects external and internal phenomena differs for the two cases as much as the imagination or intuition of outside things differs from *concentrated reflection* – a first result that would seem to remove any idea of utility or propriety from applying the facts of physics to those of psychology.

The object of the first part of the proposed question, it seems to me, turns mainly upon the last two methods of science, the *positing of laws* (which does not essentially differ, as we shall see, from the regular classification of phenomena) and the *search for causes*, and upon the application that is permitted or possible to make, in these two respects, of the physical sciences to psychology … Below we present the layout and division of our work:

False application of the relation of *causality*;
subject of discussion and misunderstanding in the application of physics to psychology.

'How,' says Mr Dégerando quite rightfully, 'could physiology, which cannot explain physical life itself, explain feeling and thought?'

An impatience and a precipitation all too natural to the human mind cause it almost inevitably to seek out *causes* or to establish general laws for phenomena that it did not take the time to observe or to verify; and imagination, the first faculty to be exercised, takes hold of these phenomena even before the senses are accurately applied to them. If this is true for a science whose object is palpable or immediately accessible to the senses, how much more so shall it be for one in which the external senses have no use, or for which one has long believed that any direct *observation* is impossible!

It must therefore have happened that after imagining *causes ex abrupto*, or feigning explicative hypotheses within a wholly corpuscular philosophy – one extended these same explanations, these hypotheses, to the most obscure phenomena of the mind and the soul, whose nature one did not yet know how to evaluate, nor whose succession how to observe.

Here we encounter all the hypotheses that align with the atomists' most ancient systems, from Democritus, Leucippus and Epicurus, to Descartes and Gassendi, hypotheses with which they claimed to explain the workings of the senses and imagination through *impressional species* (*espèces impressionnelles*) that emanate from objects themselves – *tenuia rerum simulacra* [thin images of things]; animal spirits; vibrations or vibrationcules produced in infinitesimal nerve fibrils, etc.: all explicative hypotheses created before the nature of each type of sensation or idea was investigated, and before their similarities and their differences were established.

The philosophers of antiquity, following a path contrary to that of induction, which modern physicists since Newton have so successfully practised, put themselves at the source of everything, and imagined general causes to *explain* everything; their method, which had created nothing but vain systems, did not have more success in Descartes' hands. In Newton's time, Leibniz, Malebranche and other philosophers used it to as little advantage – ultimately, the useless hypotheses that were thought up on account of this method, and the progress that the sciences owe to the contrary method of induction, have brought back around all right-thinking minds.

The physics of Descartes, not very rich and especially not very solid as regards *details*, is scarcely anything other than a collection of hypotheses used to explain poorly observed or unverified facts.

The constant aim of this philosophy is not only to establish the existence of a cause, of a general law experienced in its applications to particular facts falling within its domain, but to state or imagine *how* such and such a simple nature, such and such a supposed *impulsive force* acts upon matter to produce such and such effects.

'Give me *matter* and *movement*, and I shall *create* the world.' Such is the spirit of *Descartes*' philosophy: with certain principles or simple natures that he draws from the depths of his thought, he will indeed create a living nature, as well as an inert nature, while believing he is *explaining* its laws; he will state how the various whirls of subtle matter are formed, how each of them circulates by flushing towards its centre all the bodies that are placed in its sphere of activity and that rotate with it; he will explain magnetic attraction and all the phenomena of elective affinities as another interplay of subtle matter that penetrates into the pores of certain bodies, always travels through them in a certain direction, enters and exits in a certain direction, etc.

Likewise he will explain how the animal spirits, set in motion in different parts of the body, come and agitate the *pineal gland*, and awaken certain sensations or material images, or determine certain muscular movements by the reaction of this gland, etc. Thus, nature will have no more impenetrable mysteries; there shall exist no phenomena for which the human mind cannot only designate the general cause or the individual productive force, but also know how they are *produced*.

These illusions, too flattering, too seductive for the imagination that conceived them, dissipate like vain shadows before the torch of reason, or rather the true spirit of the physical sciences, which was reignited by Bacon, and in whose glow a multitude of bright minds are paving the way, and marching with assurance on a course to which the spirit of observation not only opened the way, but also for which it traced the line of circumvallation and set the limits. They return to the study and simple analysis of the phenomena of nature, which alone should serve as a foundation to science. They advance prudently, using induction and analogy, in the classification of these phenomena, which are carefully verified in their details by observation and by the experience of the senses or of the instruments that extend their scope. They strive to posit general *laws*, whose reality, on the one hand, is established by experiments repeated a thousand times over, and whose value and limits, on the other, are established by the perfected methods of calculation that are brought into harmonious accord with the phenomena observed. Lastly, they abandon the *how* of things, whose secret the great architect of the universe has reserved for himself, to dedicate their efforts to the *how much*, which falls within the province of man, and is the end point of his efforts, in the science of fact, of external nature.

Such was the spirit of this wise and luminous method, worthy to serve as the interpreter and support of *Newton*'s genius. Thus did this audacious search for causes find itself confined within the most narrow limits; Cartesianism's vain hypotheses had already themselves contributed to discrediting this search to so great an extent as to exclude it from the realm of philosophy, and if it was able thereafter to find a place within this realm, it did so under another name or by following a wholly opposite tendency or direction.

Let us dwell a moment upon the foundation of this reflection on the search for *causes* or the explanation of effects, such as our modern physics may have conceived or practised them.

We have already noted that the explanation of a physical phenomenon in the Cartesian doctrine consisted not only in determining the natural *cause* on which this phenomenon depends, but furthermore in demonstrating or imagining in detail *how* this cause acted to produce the effect in question; suppose, for instance, we wish to *explain* the interplay of affinities or the phenomena of electricity, of magnetism, etc., a Cartesian would feel compelled to indicate the figure or form of the fluid molecules that are considered to be the immediate or occasional *cause*, or of the *pores* of the body in which it penetrates or circulates, the movement or the direction that it takes on there, etc., all things that the imagination can conceive but that neither the senses nor experience can verify.

A physicist of Bacon or Newton's school, on the contrary, will first attempt to analyse all the phenomenon's sensory circumstances; he will try various experiments to ascertain whether it has some analogy with other facts whose *laws* are known: and if he succeeds in placing them under these laws, and in showing by observation or by calculation that it depends on them or that it is a particular function of the same cause (x), whatever may be the nature of this cause, he will feel he has given all the *explanation* desirable of the particular phenomenon at issue. It is thus that instead of imagining hypotheses to explain the phenomena of magnetism, of electricity, of galvanism, today we put our efforts into verifying the analogies that these three orders of phenomena may present between one other, into demonstrating experimentally the laws governing their action by moving further from the centre point (as the physicist Coulomb did). It is thus that Franklin explains the phenomenon of thunder, by establishing all the sensorial analogies that exist between this phenomenon such as it appears in a storm cloud, and such as it appears in the apparatus of our electric batteries. It is thus, lastly, that we would feel we had sufficiently explained the *chemical affinities* if we succeeded in verifying Buffon's conjecture that the laws governing these particular phenomena and the more general laws of the attraction of masses are identical, by placing in the expression of these first laws, as an infinitesimal function, the figure of the chemical molecules brought together until they are in immediate contact.

We can thereby see how our modern physics, which has become more modest, more reserved and more circumspect, perhaps excessively so in certain respects, aspires to understand the system of nature without attempting to *explain* it, and even dispensing with imagining *explicative* hypotheses to account for the facts ... *hypotheses non fingo*, said the great Newton; and, indeed, *attraction* was never anything other for him than a *general* fact with which a series of analogies successively came to align; never did he pretend to turn it into a real *explicative* principle of *phenomena*.

We can also see how this latest intellectual development in the sciences of fact, which we characterize under the heading *search for causes*, does not prevail, strictly speaking, in the current method of our physicists. Indeed, this search reduces to a simple generalization or classification of natural phenomena, that is, to moving from effect to effect until it reaches the most general effect from which the particular ones derive and in which they are assumed to be contained. But, in this ascending scale of effects, the mind's whole task consists in perceiving the ever more extensive relations between the phenomena that it is comparing and whose ideas or signs it links together in accordance with the real order of the successions or of the analogies it succeeds in discovering; as the number of these perceived analogies increases, that of the formerly separate categories diminishes; the various series diverge and tend to meet up at their summit. It is thus that the real *causes*, the true *productive forces*, withdraw to the rear of our minds and are said to be simplified possibly even to the point of systematic unity. But the secret return of the mind towards some absolutely unknown, efficient cause (x,y), which we no longer even attempt to determine in itself, is not less compelled by the nature of our minds; and whatever care is taken to remove the *unknown*, or to conceal its name or distinctive functions, still it subsists in the secret confines (*dans l'intimité*) of thought, which pursues it and vainly seeks to grasp it externally.

Such a method seems quite conducive to cutting out from the root all the systematic illusions of which the imprudent investigations on the nature of forces, and the modes of their action, or on what we can truly call *explicative* hypotheses of *phenomena*, are so often at risk; this method, however, has its own illusions and chimeras, if not in its way of observing the various orders of phenomena, at least in its way of classifying and generalizing them according to feigned or assumed analogies, which it often seeks to establish between facts that by their nature are entirely heterogeneous.

This last reflection brings us back to the more precise object of the proposed question, which consists in examining first to what extent the opinion of those who currently deny the utility of physical doctrines or experiments to explain the phenomena of the *mind* or of *internal sense*, can be justified.

Whereupon I shall observe, without further delay, and in accordance with all that precedes, that the type of *explanation* discussed here can be taken in three main different senses, namely:

(1) the sense in which the physics of the ancients and of Descartes *explained* phenomena through their *causes* by seeking to determine how a given cause, whether *material* or *immaterial*, acted to produce these phenomena – the question here is to what extent any given physical explanation of the facts of internal sense or of the workings of the mind can be useful or justified;

(2) the type of explanation that consists in reducing to one and the same class both the phenomena that reveal themselves (*se découvrent*) only to internal sense, and the strictly *physical* facts, such as they might appear (*se représentent*) to the external senses or to the imagination; this reduction or assimilation being founded upon analogies or identities believed to be observed between the two types of facts in question, considered in their order of succession, subordination or reciprocal dependence – this mode of explanation would seem to be the only one in keeping with our current mode of philosophizing in the positing of laws and the search for causes;

(3) in the sense in which the word *explain* means simply to make *clearer* things or ideas that are obscure by their nature, by comparing them to other tangible (*sensible*) things or ideas that are as it were their *illustration* (*figures*). One could thus seek to

represent the internal phenomena in question by certain external or physical movements that are produced in the body (*l'organisation*), and that, presumed to correspond to the sensations or ideas produced in the mind, may serve as their symbols or natural signs, without at all being connected to them by any relation of identity or even of resemblance, it not being necessary for *signs* to have any resemblance with the things or the phenomena signified, in order to express or represent them to the mind as regards their real properties, their succession, etc. The explanation in question would thus be purely *symbolic*.

An analytic examination of these three systems or modes of explanation will be the object of the first part of this treatise.

Part one

Of the misuse and futility of physical doctrines and experiments in explaining the phenomena of the mind and of internal sense. Analysis of the various systems of explanation.

First article

Of physical and physiological methods of explanation.

In returning all the way back to ancient philosophy, one finds these purported physical explanations of the senses and of the mind's ideas first introduced by the *Eleatic physicists*, and then more or less accredited by the various Greek and Latin schools ... Or better put, these first philosophers, having not yet risen to a clear distinction between the two orders of phenomena or operations, one of which relates to the properties of matter and the other to the functions of the mind and of the soul, were not yet really concerned with determining what their mutual relations, their means of correspondence, and the ties that unite them, may consist in. They could even less consider *explaining* the phenomena of the mind or of internal sense with physical doctrines in that these phenomena themselves were mixed up in the physical systems of those times and were presumed to be part of them. Who indeed could recognize today the makings of an explanation, however probable or specious, in these thoughtless doctrines that took the *ideas* of the mind for the shadows or faint images of objects – *tenuia rerum simulacra*? – or that believed that these simulacra detached from objects at various points, readily penetrating the pores of coarse bodies by their tenuousness and coming and striking the *mind*, which itself was but a more thinned out body, over whose composition and form solemn discussions would arise, to determine whether it was made of fire, of air, of water, or whether it did not participate in the nature of all the elements and contained in its composition something similar to what we perceive in each of them; if its form wasn't spherical, the most perfect of forms, or a composite of all the forms, which makes us able to perceive and imagine all those that are outside of us, etc., etc.?

We do not think it necessary to insist further on these first illusions of the childhood of philosophy, where metaphysics, yet to be born, found itself confused and identified with the most crass physics, a physics abundant in explanations as haphazard or ridiculous in their means, as they were audacious in their objects, or their goal.

To find some regular theory on the respective functions of the soul and the body, and on the relations of causality or dependence, of analogy or dissimilarity, which may exist between the phenomena of the mind and those of matter, it is necessary to traverse the various eras of philosophy successively occupied by the doctrines of Plato, Aristotle, Epicurus and the Peripaticians, before arriving at Descartes, who was the first to deal a fatal blow to ancient philosophy, in a manner that we must now consider.

Descartes must be considered the true father of metaphysics. He is the first philosopher who established an exact dividing line between the functions that belong only to the soul, and the properties or qualities that can be ascribed only to bodies. He was the first, as observes a profound and eminently judicious writer,[3] to employ the only appropriate method for precisely studying the operations of the mind, that is, proceeding by way of *reflection*, and not by way of external or tangible (*sensible*) analogy; an example that no philosopher had given before, and that very few followed after him. In this way, he realized and established that *thought*, *will*, *remembrance* and all the other attributes of the mind having no resemblance with extension and *figure* and all the other qualities of bodies, knowledge of them can only emerge from reflection or from intimate sense properly consulted, and that the exact notions that can be formed about them can never be gleaned from external objects, the existence of these objects and that of our body being liable to doubt, whereas we have the immediate

---

[3] Thomas Reid, *An Inquiry into the Human Mind.* (Note from the author.)

certainty or positive evidence of the existence of the soul, or of the thinking self, even in our very doubt of all the rest.

By starting from this principle, and proceeding by way of *reflection* to investigate the phenomena of internal sense, one could not imagine – I shan't say the *utility*, but even the possibility of adapting any physical doctrine or experiment whatsoever to the explanation of phenomena so conceived. Nor is this all: from the point of view centred on the intimate reflection of the self, it appears just as difficult to grasp the object of a physical science, to lay its base, as it was from the external or material point of view of the imagination to arrive at the subject of a purely psychological science and to lay its foundations.

But doubt about the existence of the body is just as impossible for the very fact of consciousness as doubt about the existence of the soul or of the thinking *self*. By returning to this first truth by another indirect route, by seeking to found it upon vain artificial or logical methods, or upon the intervention of God himself (*tamquam deus ex machina*), Descartes' system seemed to open up two opposite routes, one of which led directly to a true idealism where the mind draws everything from within itself, and applies its laws and forms to external nature, and the other of which tended to lead, by another order of considerations, to a kind of speculative materialism, where purely mechanical laws, used first to explain all the phenomena of organized, living and perceptive nature, as well as of dead matter, are later illegitimately extended, to the point of invading the very domain of the *soul*, which was initially circumscribed within very narrow limits, so it could preserve its independence, and remain in an isolation equally forced, equally contrary to the testimony of intimate sense.

Nothing, indeed, is closer to the soul than the particular intimate modifications that stem directly from the dynamics of life (*jeu de la vie*), those appetites, those affections[4] or determinations of an instinct wholly blind in its principle, which *Descartes'* system claimed to explain in detail, by the laws of a true mechanism. If a multitude of organized, living beings, to whom we are naturally inclined to attribute the faculty of feeling, of spontaneously moving and of imagining, can exercise these faculties according to purely automatic laws, why, putting feeling and thought aside, or even placing them under mechanical or organic laws, does one not seek

---

[4] Biran uses the word '*affection*' – which in French has a somewhat broader range of meaning than in English – to refer to the various impressions and modifications of sensory experience. For lack of a satisfactory equivalent in English, I have opted to translate the word directly as 'affection', with the caveat that this word is used here as a term of art rather than in its ordinary sense. (Note from the translator.)

to explain, by the action of matter or the interplay of certain *spirits*, all those particular operations Descartes attributes exclusively to the soul, of which a number of philosophers deny, moreover, that any idea can be formed, only recognizing as idea the *image* depicted in the *imagination (fantaisie)*? I indeed know not whether these supposed mechanical explanations such as are found in the volumes of Descartes or of Malebranche on the passions and imagination have not contributed more to confirm certain rather unreflective minds in the standpoint of materialism, than to extend, accredit or justify the contrary opinion.

What is certain is that by claiming to reduce the explanation of the phenomena of organization and of life to the ordinary mechanics of brute bodies, and by confusing two types of laws kept quite separate by nature, Descartes' doctrine, in addition to holding up the progress of physiological science and falsifying its theory, also did harm in certain respects to the philosophy of the human mind, which its method of reflection otherwise tended to direct in such a fine and useful direction.

If indeed everything operates in living bodies by the mere laws of mechanics, there is no admissible intermediary between pure automatism and pure intelligence; nor as a result is there any tie, any natural means of correspondence between thought and extension, between the soul and the body. A relation, a reciprocal *action* of one upon the other could only take place by a perpetual miracle, or the intervention of the supreme force, which alone is truly productive, the unique and exclusively efficient cause. The material impressions of bodies being nothing but *occasional* causes, will nonetheless be *necessary* occasions or conditions for the affections or representations of the soul, since these will occasionally and necessarily determine the consecutive and automatic movements of the body; whence it follows:

(1) that intimate sentiment or fact of consciousness, which constitutes the *self* (as) real cause, or immediate productive force of the movements brought about by the will, is but a mere *illusion*, and that the criterion for truth no longer being in this internal testimony upon which all science is founded, can no longer be anywhere ...

(2) that there being no intermediary between thought proper and the blindest mechanism, we must choose one or the other, or fit into thought's domain a multitude of affective impressions, of penchants, of appetites, of obscure sensations, which, though never appearing to the consciousness of the *self*, nonetheless affect a being in its purely sensorial capacity, by becoming the basis of the

immediate and unreflecting sentiment of existence; or again mix up all those functions of life and of physical sensitivity among the properties and movements of brute matter; in both cases, alter the nature of the most well established phenomena, assimilate the most obviously opposed classes, close our eyes on an entire class of facts that are an essential part of the complete knowledge of man, to which one perhaps cannot attain except by raising oneself up through the numerous degrees of the animal scale, from the most obscure nuance of a sensitivity that is not yet thought, to that elevation that is the station of the reflective and enlightened contemplator of the works of creation.

The doctrine of Descartes immediately produced the sect of mechanical physiologists, who by working with mechanical explanations and with the laws of organization and of life, end up failing to recognize the fundamental principle of the mother doctrine and the great distinction established between extension, figure and movement, which can be represented, and the indivisible subject (*le sujet un*) of sensation, which can only reflect on itself. Once this dividing line was removed, the explicative physical hypotheses of the senses and of ideas could henceforth go unchecked.

One thus ends up asserting that the efficient *cause* (and no longer just the *occasion*, or the necessary condition of sensation) is none other than the object that presses upon the organ. This pressure penetrates all the way to the centre of the brain by way of the *nerves*. The brain then reacts outside itself upon these nerves and thereby upon the representations or images of external things, or upon the *heart* and muscular organs, and thereby upon affective *sensations*, movements, *animal attractions* or *repulsions*, etc.

Such is the substance of all those physical explanations that various authors since Hobbes have modified and developed in an infinity of ways, but that on the whole are summed up in these few words.

These physical explanations share with Descartes' physical hypotheses the common vice of being purely gratuitous products of the imagination, impossible to justify by any kind of external or internal observation, and even of being in opposition to the facts of intimate sense, which they pretend to explain. But they have in addition a character of absurdity that is quite particular to them. It is by excluding any participation, even passive, of a feeling subject, or of a hyper-physical substance, superior to material organization (such as Descartes conceived the soul, and which the authors of these hypotheses persist in disregarding or expressly denying) that they posit a relationship of hypothetical resemblance first between external mechanical movements and purely organic impressions, and a still more illusory and obviously absurd identity between the same movements or impressions and the *feelings, perceptions, ideas* or operations that the *self*, the indivisible and simple subject of thought, perceives in itself and attributes to itself in the ineffable fact of consciousness.

Whence a revolting opinion that was suggested by Hobbes and that certain physicists have since not feared to profess expressly: that all matter essentially and in its nature has the *faculty to feel*, as well as that to *attract* or to move – that all it needs are *organs* and a memory like animals in order to manifest its obscure affections, etc.

It is useless to insist upon such opinions, as well as upon the physical explanations of the senses and of ideas that pure materialism has claimed to deduce from them; we only needed to mention them in order to foreshadow the illusions and dangers attached to such explanations, even when (like Descartes and Malebranche) one wishes to reconcile them with the metaphysical theories most solidly established upon the facts of intimate sense.

Second article

Of the systems of physiology, and of their use in the explanation of the phenomena of internal sense.

The real test of a hypothesis lies in the details of the phenomena they are used to explain. It was by pushing to the limit the supposed explanations of the physiological mechanists, who saw in the body a mere *hydraulic machine*, or a composite of levers, cords and instruments intended to transmit and carry on the movements of fluids or solids, etc., that philosophers finally realized, owing to the incompatibility of the results, both with each other and with nature, that it was necessary to give up hypotheses that the imagination alone could still foster, but that experience and reason repelled at each turn.

If the goal of such haphazard hypotheses had not first been to explain the senses and the imagination, which by their nature are inaccessible to all observation or experiment, perhaps their reign might have been longer. But as soon as one tried to adapt these hypotheses to the laws of organization and of life, there was a kind of experimental *criterion* to which to compare them. To demonstrate that they could not be reconciled with the facts of physiology was to lessen and annihilate their value with respect to another order of much more obscure and much more uncertain explanations. It cannot be disputed that, in this respect at least, the better-conducted research that ruined the *mechanists'* system usefully served the interests of the philosophy of the human mind.

Stahl was the first to take a stance diametrically opposed to those who claim to apply purely mechanistic laws to the functions of the organism and of life. He was also the first to eliminate the barrier erected by Descartes between the *reflective* consciousness of that which belongs to the soul and the representative science of that which pertains to the body; and since, before him, physics had been *transported* into *metaphysics*, by restricting ever more the domain of the soul, he sought on the contrary to transport metaphysics into physiology, by giving to this hyper-organic force, to this principle of feeling and thought, the most unlimited dominion.

An attentive and scrupulous observer of the phenomena of organization and of life, Stahl quickly recognized the signs of a distinctive activity, an activity that to a certain extent is independent from externally prodding objects (*objets d'incitation extérieure*), over which it prevails, rather than being absolutely and constantly subordinate to them, as the movement of a body is to that of another body that strikes it.

He recognizes an inexhaustible variety of means appropriate to a multitude of particular accidental goals, guided with an evident intention tending towards one single regular and constant end – the preservation of the organized being amidst all the possible causes of alteration, the endurance (*durée*) of life amidst so many causes of death!

He compared the phenomena of animate and inanimate bodies: on the one hand, he found movements that are always exactly proportionate to the quantity of matter and to the force of the shock and impetus involved, and that consistently reproduce themselves under the same physical circumstances: which gives rise to the possibility of finding the expression of those mathematical laws that apply without exception to all the physical facts of the same order, which would be expressed therein and precisely calculated in advance. On the other hand, he found variable movements that are now persisting, now stopping, now resuming and now breaking off again with no external cause, by the mere spontaneity of their internal productive force, or at times by an existing cause that, slight though it may be, on one occasion produces the most vigorous effects, and on another occurs over and over again, each time with renewed intensity, yet does not produce any perceptible effect.

The great laws governing the *habits* of organized machines, those habits that are exclusively particular to them, such as the periodicity of the vital or animal functions of wakefulness and sleep, of growth and deterioration: the seemingly intentional efforts of living nature to remove causes of illness, to fight against them, or to return to a healthy state – a host of other phenomena, which this is not the place to evoke, revealed to Stahl's genius a marked opposition between the laws governing the motion of brute matter, and those governing the dynamics of living bodies. These latter appeared to him attributable only to an intelligent driving force superior to matter; and finding within himself, in the testimony of intimate sense, in the production of voluntary movement and of effort, the unique original prototype of such a force, considering that it is not an essential feature of this active and intelligent principle to know itself or to have *consciousness* of its own *acts*, in order to *be* and to *act*, he felt no qualms in attributing to it everything truly *hyper-mechanical*, or hyper-physical, that takes places in the living and feeling being. Thus, the soul is posited as the unique subject and the exclusive efficient cause of the most obscure *vital* movements, of the impressions or affections most foreign to consciousness, as well as of the acts that are brought about by a free will, and that an internal light envelops with its lustre.

This identity or this systematic unity of principle could perhaps still rely on the Cartesian doctrine that had partitioned all the beings of the universe into two broad classes that are mutually opposed, as are the incompatible attributes of thought and extension: whence it followed that if an order of phenomena could not be attributed to one of these classes, it necessarily had to fit into the other, or in other words, if it escaped the physical laws of bodies, it had to belong to the metaphysical laws of the mind.

By attributing the phenomena of the mind to these latter laws, Stahl thrust himself into the opposite extreme as the mechanical physiologists. He forced all his hypotheses; he did a kind of violence to the facts, established various assimilations, or illusory analogies, between things that are heterogeneous by nature. However, it was nonetheless a great step forward for the science of bodies and one cannot fail to see today that this great line of circumvallation traced around physiology, in preventing that science from henceforth being confused with ordinary physics, prepared the way for all its subsequent advances.

Let us observe that the system of explanation that was discussed previously presents itself here from a rather different point of view. Before, it was a matter of starting from physical theories or experiments, or properties of bodies, to explain the phenomena of the mind or of *internal sense*. Here, the goal would seem to start from the facts of consciousness as given and thus to explain the functions and movements of the organic body, an explanation perhaps equally illusory, equally impetuous in its goal. Nonetheless, the question is not, as in the preceding system, to determine *how* the effect is produced by its cause, but only to ascertain this nominal cause by the analogy, real or assumed, between the effects to be explained and another class of effects recognized as depending on the cause in question. As a result, this mode of explanation falls under the second division that we established, and whose advantages and disadvantages we are currently discussing.

The doctrine known by the name of animism, pretending to assimilate, by their cause, two orders of phenomena as distinct and separate as the organism and simple vitality on the one hand, and thought and will on the other, was founded upon a physiological observation as certain in the fact of intimate sense as hypothetical in its consequences. These consequences turned out to be foreign to the very thing claimed to be deduced, namely: that the operations of *sensation* (*sensibility*), of the will and of *thought* can gradually become more and more nebulous as a result of habit or the frequent repetition of the same acts or movements, to the point that they no longer even scratch the surface of internal sense, and disappear altogether from consciousness's view: the same clouding over (*obscuration*) can be produced by the inattention of the mind when it is preoccupied with other impressions or congenerate movements, but in either case this does not prevent these *unperceived* impressions or movements from belonging to the same soul, which is still their cause and identical subject, even when it moves, or when it receives an impression unaccompanied by consciousness or the sentiment of the *self*. One thus concluded that the vital movements, or the internal impressions that correspond to them, were in fact originally true sensations, acts accompanied by consciousness, but somehow ceased to be so, either as a result of habit or due to those continual distractions that are occasioned by forceful external perceptions; to this we reply (and this is the strongest objection that can be made against this system):

(1) that *consciousness* being the chief and sole characteristic of the operations attributed to the thinking soul, all that takes place in the body [outside of its participation can only be attributed to it by a feigned analogy; and

(2) that a doctrine that reduces] the phenomena of the organism or of pure vitality, and of sentiment and thought, to the *systematic* unity of a subject or of a common cause, offends all the laws of wise observation, and all the exact procedures of the sciences of fact, where identity of cause can only legitimately be concluded from the resemblance or homogeneity of the observed facts that one seeks thereby to unite into a single class and to attribute to the same nominal cause.

But what resemblance, what homogeneity can be established between a mode or movement perceived internally as being brought about by the will and accompanied by effort, and an organic phenomenon devoid of all consciousness and foreign to the *self*...?

Considered as the cause or *unknown* productive force behind all the movements and functions that take place in the various parts of the organism (*l'organisation*), Stahl's *soul* is thus distinguishable from the *self*, which resides entirely in the consciousness of its own acts or modifications; in this respect, this force could be classified as one of those forces of the external universe for which, strictly speaking, there is no *science*, outside of the effects in which and by which they appear (*se représentent*) to the senses or imagination.

We are thus brought back to a physicalist standpoint by the very doctrine that seemed the most likely to stray from it, as if it even the most spiritualist doctrines could not end up elsewhere; indeed just as Descartes' system begot that of the mechanists and resulted in spinozism, so Stahl's system produced another kind of materialism, which one might call *organic*, in which all the phenomena of the mind and of internal sense are attributed to the laws of vitality and of a wholly physical sensitivity. What does it matter whether it is the soul or the organs?

The soul, according to *Stahl, feels* or *perceives* all the various impressions; it alone executes the various kinds of movements that take place in the body; it unceasingly acts or is on the lookout (*activas excubias agit*), putting the organs in contact with one another and with the objects or occasional causes of impressions. These causes or objects do nothing except, as it were, give the initial *warnings*; the soul does all the rest. It forms its sensations on its own, exalts or tempers them as need be. It acts now to concentrate, now to spread out (*épanouir*) the organs. It is true once again that the self, often a stranger to these kinds of warnings and to these supposed *sensations*, is just as completely unaware of what its soul is said to *feel* or perform as it would be if this principle operated or felt in another being. But at least it is established in this system that there exists in living organized bodies an acting force that governs them according to its own laws, and thus shields them to a certain extent from mechanical agents. Given that foreign objects cannot be considered the *efficient* causes of *sensations* and of acts of consciousness, but rather that the soul creates them or contributes essentially to their creation through an activity that is particular to it, and also takes the initiative in the particular phenomena of sentiment and movement – an infinitely valuable point of view, which suitably restricts, or as we shall put it later on, better serves to trace the dividing line between the domain of the soul or of the *self* and that of the organism, overturns all the vain material explanations of the phenomena of the mind, and assigns to those explanations that it is permitted to use, the proper limits within which they must be contained, in order to illuminate certain essential parts of the science of man, without usurping it altogether.

I have said that in the absolute, and too exclusive, meaning of the animists, the hypothetical unity of the principle or of the productive force of sensory and intellectual vital phenomena tended to lead back, by another route, to a sort of organic materialism; indeed the mysterious unspecified agent that by the name of soul sets in motion all the organs required for ordinary life, feeling and thought, as soon as it operates unbeknownst to the self, or as soon as it is separated from it, is no longer but an *immaterial* force as it were, in a certain sense foreign or objective with respect to the *self*, to the individual subject of thought. Since any method wisely adapted to the physical sciences utterly excludes all useless notions or investigations such as might be concerned with the essence of the productive *causes* of phenomena (let us express these causes arbitrarily as (x,y,z), which is nothing other than a mere formula, an abbreviated sign with which all analogous phenomena of *similar kind* are aligned), it will appear quite indifferent whether we call the unique force in question *soul*, *arché*, *enormon* or *vital principle*, especially insofar as it is distinct and separate from the *self*. The only thing that must be considered, and that is truly characteristic of the system in question, is the unity of class under which one claims to place the phenomena of life and of *thought*, by starting with these latter as *givens* of intimate sense, so far as their principle or subject of inherence, the *self*, is concerned, and then by assimilating them, as required by hypothesis, with phenomena that would otherwise seem to belong to a foreign principle or have a foreign *subject*, the *non-self*. But as soon as one has accepted this assimilation or analogy between phenomena, the nature, the essence of the cause, whether real or nominal, is now but a matter of logic: it is thus permissible to rename or even completely disregard this cause in order to embrace the effects themselves.

Thus, just as Stahl had said that an animal's nutrition, growth and vegetation are acts or particular modifications of the same principle that makes man think or that thinks in him, one will feel justified in saying that the principle by which man thinks or feels is but a particular modification of the same principle that makes him vegetate.

Just as Stahl would say that the soul, simultaneously present in each part of its realm, whose needs it anticipates, whose forces it directs, activates and primes; secretes in the liver, the spleen, inhales and exhales in the lungs, contracts and dilates in the heart, digests in the *stomach*, thinks in the *brain*, feels in the nerves, and in all the areas that it animates, so one might feel justified in saying that it is the organs themselves that, each imbued with its ineffable portion of life, and endowed by nature with different vital properties that we distinguish by their effects without tracing their cause (one or multiple), secrete, digest, move, feel and think. Who would have thought that we would go so far as to state this principle that appears so extraordinary and so bizarre when it is taken *literally* rather than figuratively, namely that the brain produces the *organic secretion* of thought, and digests it, like the stomach secretes gastric juices and digests *food* (Cabanis)? Stahl's simple and individual unity is thus replaced with a kind of collective and artificial unity, to which the same functions are assigned. It will be the totality of the living parts collected into one system, and pertaining to a common centre, which will be

[*A page is missing from the manuscript here. In the missing page, Biran might have shown how Stahl's system leads, by logical extension, to materialism, and how, in both cases, it is one and the same mode of explanation, which consists in assimilating two classes of heterogeneous phenomena. The titles of the third article and of §1 are ours. (Note from the editor.)*]

Third article

Of symbolic explanation. How one has claimed to explain the facts of internal sense by attributing them either to hypothetical nerve firings (ébranlement nerveux) (Hartley, Bonnet), or to the organic centres (Willis, Gall). Deviations from this method of explanation.

§1 Of the systems that explain psychological phenomena by the interplay of nerve fibres. Of Bonnet in particular

As we have already stated in the introduction to this treatise, the senses of sight and touch predominate in the human organism (*l'organisation humaine*), along with a system of representations that is founded almost exclusively on their primitive use. These senses, however, are as it were entirely in their objects; they reach only what is external or foreign to the *self*, and therefore physical and material. Thus, if one reduced our whole system of knowledge to our objective *representations*, any given *idea*, of whatever nature it may be, could necessarily be reduced to some perceptible image of shape, *extension* or movements represented in space. Otherwise, it would not be, strictly speaking, an *idea*, a conception of the mind, but merely a word, an *empty* sign. This, it seems to me, is how several philosophers understood it, and particularly those who, habitually engaging in physical investigations, thought they could attribute everything to the object of their favourite science. Thus, ever since the great restoration of

Bacon, physics seems ultimately to have usurped the entire realm of human understanding.[5]

Faithful to his principles, Ch. Bonnet does not conceal, at the outset of his analytic investigations of the soul, that it is not in the soul itself, or the self, that he will study the phenomena of the mind and of internal sense. 'I have undertaken to study man,' he says naively at the beginning of the preface to his *Analytical Essay*, 'as I have studied insects and plants ... Physics is the mother of metaphysics.'

Who could believe this? Let us nonetheless see what we can say about it, and examine just what the daughter of such a mother may become.

'*There is no reasoning in perception*,' says a psychologist whom we have already cited.[6] 'Nature ordains that certain means and instruments shall intervene between the object and our perception of it, and these means and instruments limit and regulate our perceptions.'

Any means or instrument that intervenes or is supposed to intervene between the *object* and the perception that represents it does not enter into this perception itself. It can thus be considered as falling solely within the domain of physics, which can indeed only extend as far as the external means that preceded the sensation or perception without at all being part of it. Thus, the way in which beams of light move, by *emission* or *vibration*, from the luminous body that is their source, to the surface of the opaque body that reflects them towards the eye, the mode of this reflection, that of crossing in the pupil, refraction in the different humours of the eye – essentially all the phenomena that precede the immediate impression of these beams on the retina – belong to pure physics and, being outside the act of perception, can in no way serve to *explain* it. But these beams then produce an *impression* upon the *nerves* or the fibrils of the retina, and a change occurs in the nerve endings of this organ. What is this change, or of what does it consist? We have not the faintest idea, and it does not appear to fall within the domain of physics or of ordinary mechanics.

Could the beams indeed be considered as acting by *impulse*? But what relationship can we establish between this supposed shock, or any

---

[5] The preeminence that Bacon gave to the physical sciences finds itself aptly expressed in the remarkable passage of the book *De Augmentaris* [*Scientiarum*, I. 31]: "the human mind, if it acts [upon matter, and contemplates the nature of things, and the works of God, operates according to the matter, and is limited thereby: but if it works upon itself (like the spider weaving its web) then it has no end, but produces cobwebs of learning, admirable indeed for the finesse of the thread and of the work; but of no substance or profit."] (Note from the author.)

[6] Th. Reid. 'Section 21: Nature's Way of Bringing About Sense Perception', in *An Inquiry into the Human Mind*. (Note from the author.)

transmitted movement, and the phenomena that follow? Is it a kind of electric attraction or a chemical affinity that occurs even prior to the contact between the beams and the fibrils of the retina, endowed by nature with a mode of sensitivity or affectability that is particular or specific to it? That may be, but it is not yet quite clear. The most obvious result that can be drawn here, from physical or physiological experience, is that in order for visual sensation to take place, there must always be *continuity* and integrity of the nerves themselves that extend from the retina to the cerebral pulp in which they penetrate and disappear, although the scalpel has till now not been able to follow their tracks back to a unique central point where it was long thought they would converge.

The least obstacle that obstructs this continuity of the nerves seems to destroy the sensitivity of the retina, and prevent or annihilate perception.

But again, what happens along the nerves of the retina from the extremities covering the back of the ocular globe to those that are routed in the brain? Is it a vibration or an infinite series of vibrationcules passed on to the nervous fibrils and transmitted all the way to the cerebral centre? Is it an impulsive movement instantaneously communicated to the animal spirits that flow in each of these fibrils? Is it an electric phenomenon that occurs between the luminous fluid and the fluid of the nerves? etc. etc. You can choose the hypothesis you like, but in each case you will only imagine or picture (*se représenter*) outlines of movements or arbitrary modes of movement that have no relationship with the sensation or perception of the self, nor with any phenomenon of internal sense. It was long thought that to explain *vision*, it sufficed to say how the image of the external object formed itself in miniature on the retina by the passage and crossing of beams in the pupil, their refraction in the aqueous humour of the cornea, etc.: all purely physical facts, such as those that explain the workings of the darkroom. By imagining that the soul did nothing more than contemplate such *images* or unite itself with them, one created altogether *imaginary* difficulties as to what causes us to see objects *right side up* whose images are upside down on the retina, or to see one object though there are two images. But a more healthy psychology evinces the insufficiency and emptiness of these explanations. As it has been quite rightly said, images do not really exist anywhere, and those that are assumed to be traced on the retina in order to explain *vision* or the representation that is produced of an object in the soul have no more substance than the vain simulacra or flickering shadows of bodies, the *tenuia rerum simulacra* of Lucretius and Epicurus.

All the physicist's investigations are thus restricted here to determining or to conjecturing that:

(1) there is a change, or rather, a certain movement produced in the nerve fibres of the *retina*, and propagated by the effect of the initial contact of light beams, or by a particular fluid, to an indeterminate point in the brain;

(2) corresponding to this change is an immediate particular impression or affection that is scarcely noticed, because it is ordinarily very weak when the light beams act upon a healthy organ;

(3) corresponding to this immediate impression wrought upon the nerve fibres of the retina and transmitted, either by these fibres or by a particular fluid, all the way to the brain, is an external intuition of the colour spectrum, in addition to the image of an extended object with a certain shape and colour, in accordance with the hyperphysical laws coordinating the senses of sight and touch.

Here we have three correspondent facts whose intimate connection we can observe, deduce or foresee by a kind of habitual reasoning, but without being able to establish or conceive of any type of relation between them other than that of succession or simultaneity, and not of analogy or resemblance, nor of causality or necessary dependence.

Who indeed could say what type of analogy or dependence exists between the movement of the luminous fluid, and that of the nerves, or between the latter and the more or less perceptible impression that the eye experiences due to the contact of the beams, or between this contact and the external intuition of colour, or between this intuition and the perception of the coloured object? Who can *explain* how one of these effects can bring about or produce the other?

Observe that the only fact that is clearly and immediately known here, is the representation or the intuition itself of a coloured object; or rather in certain cases, the sensation of *light*; all the rest is not known as a part of perception, but rather deduced from certain experiments or external observations, from certain arguments whose principles idealism denies, though it is forced to acknowledge representation itself as a phenomenon of the mind.

How, then, shall we explain the primitive fact by the deduced fact, the certain from the uncertain, the clear from the obscure? And yet this is what all the authors of the physical explanations that we are presently discussing claim to do. Now this is how they justify, if not their success, at least their attempts.

We do not know what an *idea* in the *soul* itself is. It is thus not at so obscure a source that we should study the phenomena of the mind with a view to forming *clear ideas* of it,[7] and the most uncertain hypothesis on the mechanical workings of the brain to which these phenomena are linked will always teach us more than even the most concentrated, the most thorough internal observation, since otherwise we would be like the spider of which Bacon speaks: *tamquam aranea texens telam* . . .[8]

Now, since it has been clearly proven that our ideas originate in the *senses*, and that there is no difference between the *senses* and the *organs*,[9] we need only focus all of our attention on the *latter* and *study* what happens in the organ when it transmits to the soul the impressions of objects that produce ideas. All that can happen, however, in the organs (external and internal), in the nerves and in the brain, are movements. It is quite true that

> we do not know how certain movements can produce certain sensations and *ideas* in the soul, but we *know*[10] *at least that we only have ideas in consequence of the movements that are aroused in certain fibres* of the sensory organs and of the brain, and this is enough to justify hypothesizing about these fibres and about their *movements*, as well as about *ideas*, in order to see them as *natural signs* of *ideas*; thus we can study these signs, and the result of their possible combinations; and we can then legitimately deduce from them the order in which these ideas were generated in the *soul*. Indeed, as soon as it is proved that the ideas are linked to the movements of sensory fibres, then the type of *fibres* in question, the order in which they are agitated, the relationship, the connection we can establish between them, the physical effects that the more or less repeated action of objects can work upon them, will give us the origin of all that the soul experiences.
>
> Preface to the *Analytical Essay*

Such is the substance of a hypothesis that, once we admit its first principle, is perfectly coherent in its consequences, and will truly seem to convert and to translate the internal science of the ideas and of the faculties of the human mind into a sort of external dynamic, or theory of the movement of the brain's fibres.

I shall make several remarks on this bold transformation, remarks that can be extended to all like systems of explanation.

---

[7] Ch. Bonnet, preface. (Note from the author.)

[8] 'Like the spider weaving its web'. See supra note [5].

[9] False identity perpetually supposed by those who engage in *physical* explanations, the source of all the deviations and illusions of these systems. (Note from the author.)

[10] How do we know? And with what kind of science are we dealing? (Note from the author.)

(1) I shall first ask how we know so positively that such perceptions or ideas only take place in the mind in consequence of certain movements aroused in *certain fibres* of the brain. And upon what experimental or observational truth, either external or internal, can this correlation or essential dependence be grounded? We know by intimate sense and by consciousness that there are within us sensations, perceptions, ideas, various intellectual acts that the mind performs upon the raw material given by the external senses. These facts of intimate sense can receive no higher degree of elucidation than what they already enjoy at the source where they must necessarily be studied and distinguished, in order for us to form truly reflective ideas of them.

We know on one the hand, and by a rather roundabout route, namely the anatomical dissections performed on the dead, that in our organized machine there are a *brain* and *nerves*, and the experiments attempted upon the living have shown that these nerves and this brain collaborate as instruments or as organic conditions to create animal sensations, and even, albeit more indirectly (see the preceding article), to create the regular and complete perceptions of the thinking being. But anatomy and physiology have not discovered anything in the brain resembling those fibres that can be divided into an infinite number of types and arrangements and are capable of an infinite variety of movements. These extraordinarily numerous *traces* that are said to form and remain in the cerebral pulp utterly escape the scrutiny of the eye and the most delicate investigations of the observer.

(2) But let us assume that the fibre movements in question are such as they are assumed to be, and that they correspond exactly to the phenomena of the mind; this correspondence can only be admitted as a kind of *pre-established harmony* between the movements of the fibres and the ideas or operations that they are supposed to represent or exhibit (*figurer*). For no matter what we do, there will always be absolute heterogeneity or complete want of analogy between the two orders of facts. But since it is not necessary for there to be any resemblance between the *sign* and the thing signified, this heterogeneity will not prevent us from taking certain fibres or movements for symbolic or figurative, if not natural, *signs* of the corresponding ideas.

It will follow from this harmonious connection that if a superior intelligence were to read the brain from the outside in, and knew *in advance* the secret relations these organic movements have with ideas, or merely their parallelism, it would discover the whole series of the latter by the representation of the former, just as we penetrate into the secrets of an author's thought by means of the written or printed characters that represent it. However, there are a number of essential distinctions that must be made.

First of all, the organic signs in question could teach the superior intelligence what is happening concomitantly in the interior of the feeling and thinking organized being only by placing it as it were in the shoes of this being, by making it feel and think like it, by a form of imitation or of sympathy; and such, to our thinking, is indeed the chief effect of natural as well as artificial signs. But when it is a question of what is happening in ourselves, of those modes, ideas or even operations whose internal apperception or immediate feeling we have or can have directly, independent of any imaginary conception of the interplay or movement of fibres, what need do we have to resort to these means? When we have the thing signified, what use is the sign? When that which is represented (*le représenté*) is right there, why go so far seeking after that which represents it (*le représentant*)? When we are able to communicate immediately with our thought, why call on the aid of a foreign intermediary who may be unfaithful?

But is it a question merely of the external communication of the phenomena of a wholly internal sense, whether one wishes to express or manifest them on the exterior or to *explain* them, as it were, with tangible natural or symbolic signs? I would like to observe that the expressive *sign* of an idea or of a fact, in order to fulfil its role, must suggest to the mind how this idea or fact was conceived, without altering or changing its *nature*. If instead of directing our attention towards that which is signified, it does nothing but turn away or distract our attention from it, either by making us focus on the sign itself or by directing the mind to another altogether different type of idea, it will no longer be a mere true representative sign: it will itself be the principal object, or a subject of diversion and of transformation, converting one system of ideas into another.

Such precisely is the role that fibre movements play when they are substituted for ideas, which they are supposed to represent, and when one seeks to reason about them as if they were the ideas themselves. When we are thinking about these movements or when we are laboriously following all the hypothetical details of so complicated a machine, it is indeed quite difficult not to forget that in all this, we are only dealing with *tangible* signs intended to represent reflective operations or internal phenomena, and the mind, which the signs ought to guide towards these phenomena, after dwelling so long on the former, ends up losing sight of the latter. After reasoning so long upon the movements of fibres, as if they were feelings or ideas, we end up convincing ourselves that one represents the nature of the other and does not differ from it, as the habit of spoken signs often convinces us that words express the essence of things.

In consequence, the object of psychology, when completely distorted in this way, will appear identical to that of physics or of a psychology of the brain and of its nervous fibres. And in virtue of this complete transformation of one system of ideas into another altogether heterogeneous one, we end up wondering whether all these operations of the soul are anything other than movements, series or repetitions of movements.[11]

What! Are there only movements or repetitions of movements in those intimate acts through which the *self* wills, acts, recognizes himself as the *same*, remembers, judges, reflects? And shall we ever be able to acquire the ideas pertaining to these acts, like the idea of the *self*, of its unity or identity in time, by seeking them out in external space, by imagining movements, vibrations of fibres, etc.?

It is indeed only by seeking within itself, as Leibniz understood quite well and supremely expressed,[12] it is only in the intimate sentiment of its own acts, that the soul finds the *idea* of *substance, force*, cause and identity, which, when transposed onto the phenomena of external nature, establish between one another those forms of coordination or of connection through which they appear to us.

Indeed, there is another who also thought that we can know the nature of certain ideas in the soul, where we should exclusively study them and search after their source: that philosopher, as wise as he is profound,[13] who expressly stated that we have just as clear knowledge of reflective ideas, such as *willing, judging, remembering*, etc., as of any *sensory* idea. But what indeed are reflective ideas if not ideas whose exclusive source is the soul, the *self*, and that can only be conceived there? It is true that there are two different kinds of *clarity*, and the one that pertains to the facts of internal sense is not the same as the one that hinges on the external senses, to which one attempts to reduce everything.

Ch. Bonnet, along with all the other authors who apply physical doctrines to psychology, does not tire of saying that the soul does not know itself, and that, as a result, it cannot know all that is distinctive and exclusive in it, unless it has the proper means or signs to represent it, or to throw it into a sort of relief outside of itself in organic objects or instruments, etc. Again, he confuses

---

[11] Bonnet, *Elements of Psychology*. He states in his *Analytical Essay* §75: I declare 'that I do not claim to equate the *idea* with the *occasion* of the idea: but I do not know the idea at all, and I know somewhat the occasion of the idea'. Surely we know an idea in our mind by intimate sense or reflection better than we know the occasion of the idea or the movement of fibres by representation. (Note from the author.)

[12] "It is not less natural to the mind to exercise reflective acts or to contemplate itself than to perceive things outside itself; or rather, it does not know external things except by the knowledge of things that are within itself." Leibniz. *Animadversiones Circa Assertiones Aliquas Theoriae Medicae Verae Clar, Stalii; Cum Elusdem Leibnitii ad Stahlianas Observationibus Responsionibus*, Dutens. II, 2, 145. (Note from the author.)

[13] Locke, *Essay on Human Understanding*, [book II, ch. 6]. (Note from the author.)

objective knowledge with internal or subjective knowledge, the *image* with the feeling or *idea* proper, external intuition with the immediate internal apperception, the symbol or *schema* with the reality of *signified* thought.

Perhaps the soul does not know its nature or its essence as object or as *noumene*; and what are we given to know in this manner? But far from not knowing itself as *ego*, as primitive thinking *subject* of consciousness, on the contrary it can have no clearer apperception, no more evident knowledge than this, and without it nothing can really be perceived or known in the outside world.

But it was not my task to establish any particular doctrine on the origin or the reality of our knowledge. I only had to point out the basis of a necessary distinction between two systems of knowledge or ideas, one representational and the other reflective, a distinction that is too often ignored, and whose neglect could alone have brought about the physical explanations that I have sought to analyse as to their means and their aim, and upon which I ask to make yet one last observation.

It has been said[14] that all the ideas or operations of the mind are *subordinate to the interaction* and movements of the organic fibres in the senses and brain, as these movements themselves are subordinate to the action of objects. For this principle to be true, or even probable, it was necessary to reduce the whole of psychological phenomena to *passive* modifications of our sensitivity, to ignore completely all the truly *active* faculties of intelligence and human will ... This is what the authors of the physical explanations whom we are discussing did, to the extent that they could and indeed they would have had more difficulty employing these explanations in the general and exclusive manner that they propose, if they had given full consideration to the *initial action*, which is born out of hyperorganic force, and of the intimate sentiment that by essence accompanies this action, or to its most *immediate results*, which can only be conceived or reflected upon in the very bosom of the subject from which it emanates.

The entire system of human understanding is reduced, under Hartley's view, to associations of ideas or of images that come directly from the *senses* or can be reduced to them. These connections between ideas, however, are all represented by mechanical associations between vibrations and vibrationcules that are produced in the sensory or cerebral fibres corresponding to these ideas. The physical laws that preside over these series of vibrations are the same as those that regulate the phenomena of

---

[14] See Ch. Bonnet, *Analytical Essay on the Faculties of the Soul*, and Hartley, *Physical Explanation of the Senses*. (Note from the author).

the mind. The will finds itself enveloped in them, and in all the circumstances of this *fatum* of the body, one seeks in vain what might be due to the foresight or activity of the *mind*.

Ch. Bonnet, like Condillac, seeks to deduce everything from a simple passive sensation brought about by the action of an external *object*. He makes no distinction between purely affective *sensation* and *perception*. Under his view, these two modes only really *differ* in *degree*, more or less as we have seen, from the two types of *sensation* that are physiologically distinguished under the names of *organic* and *animal*.

Whence it follows that, *sensation* being merely the most immediate result of the object's initial action, that is, an *impression* received by the nerve endings and propagated all the way to the brain, the internal perception of a passive modification that the soul (or self) experiences and with which it is assumed to be identical, will itself be nothing other than a circumstantial result of the same movements and will be *explained* in the same way.

All the rest is but a consequence of this first step or of the hypothetically posited identity between sensation – or a certain passive modification due to a foreign action – and the perception of the *self*, which distinguishes itself from this *modification* and discovers it only through an action that it controls. To confuse two things that are so different, is it not to confuse the object with the light that illuminates it?

As a result of the first principle of identity, the reproduction of the same sensation in the absence of the object is again nothing more than the same fibre movements reproduced either spontaneously or by some intestinal organic cause. Memory and imagination differ only by the magnitude of the shock received by the fibres in the brain.

Remembrance, which constitutes the first of these faculties and distinguishes it essentially from the second, and which is nothing other than the identity *recognized* by the *self*, is a repetition of the same modification at two different moments. This purely intellectual or reflective faculty, which all physical explanations fail to explain, is itself nothing but a result of the movement of these same fibres, whose state and disposition, having changed as a result of the initial impression, will transmit a *weaker* impression to the soul when they are put in motion the second time. It will make it think or feel that the sensation is not *new*, that it was already present,[15] as if there were some relationship between an impression – or an attenuated movement,

---

[15] I will not get into the details of this explanation, which seems to have caused the author of the *Analytical Essay* much trouble, and ask the reader to consult the work itself to judge the insufficiency of physical explanations when it comes to truly intellectual or purely reflective phenomena. (Note from the author.)

or even a sensation that has become less lively – and the wholly reflective act through which the *self* recognizes the identity of the repeated modification by recognizing its own identity, as if it were sufficient to determine the conditions or laws of this sensory attenuation (*dégradation sensitive*) in order to explain those of intellectual remembrance.

In the same way, the passive habits of the organs are confused with the *active* habits of the motor and thinking subject, and as a result of this confusion they are given similar, equally mechanistic explanations, although in fact everything is contrary in these two systems of habits.

The same repetition that imperceptibly attenuates, alters and erases passive sensation and all the subordinate faculties that originate in it serves, on the contrary, to perfect, illuminate and develop the *perception* of the mind, as well as all the intellectual operations whose true principle or source is the soul's motor activity – a supremely fitting proof of the essential difference or even the opposition between the laws that govern living and feeling (*sensible*) organized beings on the one hand, and moral and intelligent beings on the other.[16]

One might think that Ch. Bonnet very clearly recognized this activity of the soul, and that he attributes to it the greatest influence possible over all the operations of thought and even of sensitivity. But I do not know to what extent we ought to consider *active* (at least in the sense reflection attaches to this word) that force of the soul that is otherwise considered as always and essentially *subordinate* to the action of external *objects*; which only acts upon the fibres as a result of the movements that have already been transmitted to them, and which in sum does nothing but *react* and thereby increase the intensity of these movements, never acting to produce them by its own laws or decisions.

No one admires more than I the depth and intellectual force of Ch. Bonnet; no one respects more the feelings and intentions of so supremely moral and *religious* a philosopher; and the importance that I have given to examining his doctrine sufficiently proves the rank it holds in my thought, and the felt esteem that it inspires in me in many respects. However, I shall observe in conclusion that the number of great and beautiful truths spread throughout the psychological writings of this philosopher is altogether independent of the physical hypotheses regarding the movement of the brain's fibres to which he felt obliged to attach his ideas. I feel justified in asserting that there is not a single one of these important truths that the author did not

---

[16] Only active and intelligent beings have a force in them that enables them to break free from the sphere of habits, etc. (Note from the author.)

find within himself, by personal reflection, independent of all mechanical considerations, and that he would not have expounded upon just as well or better in the ordinary language of reflection, free from all those complicated and symbolic signs that he so patently abused.

If these hypotheses, which seem to explain everything, do not in fact explain or illuminate anything, and if they are of no direct use in discovering psychological truths or expressing them precisely and correctly, we may conclude that they are truly useless to the science of the phenomena of the human mind. I shall add that they are illusory and dangerous, when one seeks to base the foundations of science upon them. The example of Bonnet is supremely fitting proof. Without the obsession of physical *explanations*, he would have certainly given more weight to the activity of the soul; he would not have reduced the faculties to passive functions; he would not have gone astray in a labyrinth in which it is futile to seek to reconcile human liberty with the necessity of organic laws; in sum, he would have had a better conception of all the phenomena in question by studying them at their source, rather than by transforming or distorting them to fit into his system of physical explanations.

§2 Of a system of explanation based upon the location of the faculties of the mind in the particular organic centres, and of the craniological hypothesis in particular

Nature itself seems to have divided our *sensations* pertaining to the outside world into *five* classes or types circumscribed by equally many separate organic seats or instruments, where they seem in some sense to be located: the sensations of *touch*, sight, hearing, taste and smell. Thus, the type of decomposition or analysis representative of that faculty which is expressed in physiological language under the general heading *external sensitivity* is indicated and set out in advance.

This analysis is indeed based solely on circumstances that, appearing automatically to the senses or to the imagination, do not require a reflective return to the act of perception itself, or to the variable role that the individual subject may play in it, passive when it feels, active when it perceives and judges.

Considered in this last respect, the sensations that are grouped together into the same class or type because they are located in the same place would perhaps exhibit notable differences if they were subjected to another, more profound analysis, although this analysis, it is true, would no longer be illuminated by that direct light particular to things that can be represented *spatially* or that have an effect on definite points of *external* space.

Space and location (*l'espace et le lieu*) being after all, as a famous school argued, the *forms* of our *sensory* intuitions, we are naturally and almost inexorably inclined to dress up in these *forms* even our most intellectual ideas or notions, and it seems as though the mind cannot conceive what the imagination cannot locate. Language and popular opinion, no less than the systems and prejudices of philosophers, sufficiently justify the generality of this observation. Since sensations and images are more or less sharply distinguished from one another in proportion as the organs they affect are naturally separate or circumscribed, and since in this case it is not difficult to circumscribe the proper domain of the faculties to which they are attributed, why should we not seek to imitate nature itself in some fashion, or to follow the path that it indicates to us, by founding – upon the division established between the organic sites attributed to the various faculties, whether this division be natural or hypothetical, real or probable – the distinctions or classifications established between these faculties themselves, both those whose object can be represented externally in space, and those whose subject, hidden in the depths of the self, reveals itself only to intimate sense? And would that not be the most appropriate means to pass on to the latter the degree of apparent clarity and facility that purely reflective ideas seem to borrow from the sensory (*sensible*) images with which one manages to align them?

But if we immediately recognize the real division between our *external* senses by their use or the application of one of them, such as touch or sight, to the others, we have no such direct or certain means of recognizing or assessing the degree of separation between the various sites that must be attributed to more hidden faculties, or to phenomena of internal sense, whose division into types or classes can be established in advance by altogether different considerations or from altogether different points of view.

Let us see how one goes about compensating for this lack of natural immediate and tangible natural data, and ascertain what more or less plausible reasons might justify a division between the cerebral organic sites assigned to the faculties or phenomena of the mind, whose distinction is claimed to emerge from this very physiological division, and to be confirmed and verified by this means alone.

We have already seen how in the systems of Hartley and Ch. Bonnet the analysis of the ideas and of the elementary faculties of the understanding is reduced to an almost anatomical decomposition of the fibres and fibrils in the senses and brain, to which these authors claim to ascribe each elementary mode or phenomenon of the mind.

The number of sensory (*sensitifs*) or intellectual *elements* has no other bound, as it were, than that of the elements of the nerve fibres. Each idea, each complete sensation, which only affects the soul in a certain state of complexity, is represented by a *bundle* of fibres, each animated by a movement or a *vibrationcule* that is *particular* to it. Thus, not only are there as many distinct and separate organs as there are *types* of sensations, but further still, each specific sense, such as sight, touch, etc., allows within its composition for an equal number of small distinct organs, each separate and suited to an individual sensation or to an elementary impression. The smell of a rose, for instance, has a fibre expressly distinct from that suited to the carnation; furthermore, each of these fibres is itself composed of fibrils, each appropriate to a particular odorous molecule; and so on ad infinitum.

These fibres or fibrils, uniting together from all different parts, converge at the *seat* of the soul, which they form through their union, and which is thus nothing other, as Ch. Bonnet puts it in his picturesque language, than a *miniature neurology* (*neurologie en miniature*); just imagine the extraordinary composition of this little central organ in which the soul is supposedly present in its own special way! Within this central organ, organized in such an admirable way that nothing gets mixed up in it and everything manages to reach it and stay preserved as distinctly as attested by the phenomena of imagination, memory, remembrance, comparison, etc., we can thus posit as many particular divisions not only as there are specifically distinct external senses, or *types* of sensation, but even as there are fibres and fibrils suited to each elementary sensation or impression, respectively, and therefore as many special faculties of *perception*, *memory*, *imagination*, etc., as there are partial organic divisions in the general seat of the soul.

Thus, the perception of colour will be carried out in a different *location* in the central organ from the perception of sounds. Since each sensation must afterward be *transformed* into an *idea* or a memory image (*image souvenir*) or a judgement, etc. in the cerebral division where it was received or transmitted, in this same seat of the soul there will be not only particular districts for memory, imagination and comparison, considered as *general* faculties or faculties common to all the types of sensation for which they can be used, but also as many circumscribed divisions corresponding to the special faculties of memory, imagination and judgement, as there are sensations or impressions, either specific or elementary – for instance, the remembrance or the imagining of odours, as distinct from the corresponding faculties sharing the same name.

If I have stopped a moment here to develop this part of Ch. Bonnet and Hartley's systems, of which I had already so extensively spoken before, it is merely to point out how this distinction between special faculties, with which a currently famous doctor has been almost exclusively credited, is already contained in very familiar doctrines, of which it is an immediate consequence, and how it contains all the difficulties and objections we had already raised against these doctrines.

It is true that the division of cerebral seats such as we have just set out, and the localization of the special faculties purportedly ascribed to them, here requires, as it were, the eyes of faith or imagination. This division does not reveal itself by any tangible sign taken from inside nor a fortiori from outside the organism (*l'organisation*), and what scalpel would be delicate enough to reach that *miniature neurology* and penetrate such an infinitesimally small order? Thus, the divisions in question were only presented in theory as a probable hypothesis or as a mere induction from experience or indeed as symbols suitable for representing to the mind or explaining the corresponding distinction between internal phenomena; their authors never pretended to make them into direct objects of experience or into a means of recognizing or visually representing the thinking being's most intimate abstract faculties, the mind or heart's most secret dispositions. This attempt was reserved for our times, and the honour belongs, I believe, quite entirely to Doctor Gall.

But before moving on to an abridged examination of this particular system, we shall make a few observations applicable to all the hypotheses regarding the localization of the soul and its faculties.

The oldest system of this kind, as well as the most widespread and most probable, appears to be that which only admits of one common centre or *sensorium commune* for all the intellectual modes or acts attributed to the same thinking subject, a *single* seat for a *single* and indivisible soul or *self*. But when it comes to assigning this true seat a definite place in the *brain*, all opinions diverge, and the physiologists turned metaphysicians agree no more among themselves than the metaphysicians transformed into physiologists. Descartes housed the soul in the *pineal* gland in view of the thinking subject's unity, given, he argued, that all the parts of the brain are double, and that the gland is unique.

Lapeyronie and Lancisi drew on recent experiments to modify this seat and transport it to the *corpus callosum;* this opinion was itself overturned, and the soul was sent travelling to the different regions of the brain successively, until finally it seems to have settled down in our time in that sort of collar that joins the *medulla oblongata* to the cerebellum, where injuries are always fatal, and seem to whisk away feeling and life in one single blow. We may nonetheless rightly doubt whether new experiments or new facts from physiology or comparative anatomy will not again destroy this latest opinion. 'Anatomy,' wrote the illustrious Haller to Ch. Bonnet, at a time when this kind of investigation was much more common than today,[17] '*anatomy is mute as to the soul's proper seat.*' It is indeed probable that it will forever remain so, at least in the sense in which one has so vainly attempted to make it speak.

It would perhaps be desirable that, by more clearly distinguishing the domain of reflection, or what pertains to our own subjectivity, from the domain of imagination and all that *exists* for us only by objectifying itself externally, it would be desirable, I say, for us to recognize: (1) that the *metaphysical* simplicity of the *self* that exists and perceives itself as *one* in the act of thought (from which we deduce, by an ontological principle, the *absolute* simplicity of a noumenal force, of a *lasting substance*, even outside the exercise of thought) has no relationship, no essential analogy with the type of physical simplicity we objectively attribute to an atom or an indivisible point taken to be the soul's *location* or the seat from which it carries out all the operations whose distinct ideas are given to us by a wholly intimate sense, where in sum it perceives, believes, incites, judges, remembers, etc.; (2) that the more or less narrow bounds assigned to the *sensorium commune*, even supposing that they were as well established by physiological experiments as they are now *uncertain*, could not in any way enlighten us on the ineffable link that indissolubly unites – in the same act (*fait*) of consciousness and from the very origin of any possible perception – the two elements of the primitive duality: the subject and the object of thought; the living force and that to which it is applied; *effort* and *corporal* resistance; the *self* and the *non-self*; in sum, in a more common and less dogmatic language, the *soul* and the *body*; (3) that these same physiological experiments and all the considerations and facts of this order will thus necessarily be unavailing when it comes to establishing a relationship between the multifarious and diverse internal phenomena and one or several equally variable and multifarious seats, not only with respect to their succession in *time*, but in a very different respect – their simultaneous coordination in *space* or in the *cerebral expanse* (*l'étendue cérèbrale*).

A similar relation will indeed always be, by virtue of the laws that define our thinking nature, the stumbling block of all the theories and hypotheses whose objective it is to define or explain this relation, and which will only

---

[17] Physical sensualism and transcendental idealism must equally repel this kind of investigation; according to the former system, sensation is everywhere and the soul nowhere; according to the latter, material organization is but a pure phenomenon, a figment of the imagination, and the soul cannot be in a corporal place, since this place has no reality. (Note from the author.)

serve to prove the weakness of the human mind, to lay bare its necessary limits, and in sum to make even clearer the absolute heterogeneity separating the two orders of ideas and facts that only the most complete ignorance or thoughtlessness could attempt to equate.

Surely the unity of the centre at which all the sensory-motor nerves converge, or the unity of the organic seat where the soul supposedly carries out all its particular operations, is no better proved by physiological observations or experiments, or is not more susceptible to being so proved, than is the *multiplicity* of centres; but it must be admitted that this first supposition, admitted though not proved by Haller and Bonnet, has the advantage of establishing a certain harmony between the separate points of view of imagination and reflection, by representing to the imagination – through the figure or tangible symbol (*symbole sensible*) of a unique centre to which the acts of the intellect are ascribed – what reflection conceives as the authentic individual unity of the same *self*, whereas in the contrary system there seems to be a kind of discordance between the sign or symbol and the thing signified or represented, between separate organic seats that are so inappropriately and in such a roundabout way said to perceive, judge, remember, each in its own way, and the individual, precise, unequivocal meaning that reflection attaches to each of these intellectual signs.

Thus, wise minds, on their guard against precipitous inductions and rejecting hypotheses that no direct experimental fact or fact of intimate sense could confirm, have agreed throughout the ages to classify among the most haphazard conjectures, and the most disavowed, as it were, by common sense, any system that attempts to locate or *disperse*, as it were (as if they were physical objects), the phenomena of the mind, between which only simple metaphysical distinctions can be established or imagined.

When Willis, among others, attempted to assign separate divisions of the brain to the various intellectual faculties by housing the imagination in the corpus callosum, memory in the *cortical substance*, judgement in the *corpus canalis*, the wisest physiologists and metaphysicians joined in rejecting such a hypothesis as devoid of any plausibility and as being unsupported by observation. They objected that, far from being able to establish some precise relationship between the functions of the brain taken as a whole, or certain parts of its substance, and the perceptions, sentiments, intellectual or moral acts, of which it is considered to be the *unique instrument (instrument propre)*, we are not even able to determine all the relationships of simple organization and the necessary or subordinate role that the brain plays in the functions of physical or *animal* life; that most direct observations or experiments are often in this last respect uncertain and misleading; that the anatomist's scalpel, liable to go astray in that pulpy mass, has difficulty unravelling even a few distinct parts, and leaves veiled not only the existence of various others but above all the usage for which nature might have intended them; that all the real discoveries made upon the anatomy of the brain can scarcely have any other goal than to determine a small number of new circumstances pertaining to the form, connections and tissue of certain parts of the brain unknown to previous anatomists and that each time we think we are moving further ahead or especially each time we pretend to establish some determinate relationship between details of physical organization and facts of sentiment or internal experience, we merely wander in the vagueness of these hybrid hypotheses (*hypothèses mixtes*), which, attempting to embrace two sciences, accord with neither, and are rejected by both at once.

It is upon the confusion or the false identity established between the operations of the intellect[18] and the material they are exercised upon, between the active faculties of thought and the passive functions of sensitivity, between the images that are dependent on the nature of received impressions or modifications and the ideas or acts of the mind that are in no way dependent on them, remaining the same whatever may be the nature of these variable and multiple impressions; it is, I say, upon such a confusion of ideas and principles that any hypothesis is founded that attempts to locate or disperse various cerebral seats, those faculties of the mind that, by the nature of their use and above all by the nature of the purely reflective ideas that correspond to them, can have no relationship to *space* or *location*. It will thus suffice to re-establish the essential distinctions that were erased by these false assimilations in order to make all hypotheses of this kind vanish like shadows.

These arguments, which were, I believe, victoriously brought to bear against Willis's and other similar systems, could be applied with renewed force to a recent hypothesis of Doctor Gall's pertaining to the same subject.

This author has exhibited two quite different types of genius, that of the physiologist, who instructs and astonishes us by the sagacity and depth of his observations on the nerves and the brain, and that of the superficial and systematic metaphysician or moralist, who surprises us in another fashion with his casual assertions and inductions, his illusory analogies, and his frivolous explanations.

---

[18] 'I believe,' says Dr Hufeland quite rightly in his remarks on the system of Dr Gall, 'that one must carefully distinguish between the intellect (or that which *represents*) insofar as it relates to the external world and must be put in contact with it, and the intellect (in the strict sense), which has consciousness of its own operations, which reflects upon them, etc.' (Note from the author.)

He would perhaps have caused less ado in certain circles, but would also have called to his hypothesis more serious attention on the part of those whose chief study is man in his intellectual, moral and physical dimensions, had he more solidly connected this hypothesis to his fine physiological doctrine, or rather had he been able to derive, from the experimental or observational facts of the latter, data suitable for establishing the former, or for providing it with the degree of coherence or plausibility that it lacks.

But Doctor Gall's doctrine on the distinction between certain so-called *special* intellectual *faculties*, which he claims to link to equally many separate divisions or seats distributed throughout the entire expanse of the cerebral mass ... this doctrine, I say, which seems to me in contradiction with all the real data of a healthy psychology, is no more capable of being justified by direct physiological experimentation; and however great the author's sagacity, however great the dexterity and finesse of his scalpel, he seems indeed to have sensed that such means abandoned him, when it came to assigning separate organs to various intellectual and moral faculties, and to establishing or explaining the divisions that might exist between these latter, by appealing to the separation of the organic seats attributed to them.

He thus does not seem at first to have bothered to go digging into the depths of the brain to distinguish each of the divisions in which a given corresponding faculty was to be housed, and one can see from the treatise he bequeathed to us that his anatomy of the nerves and brain has an altogether different goal, and takes a more useful, less uncertain and less vague direction.

The craniological hypothesis rests entirely on purely external signs, which do not require the scalpel's aid to be recognized, which show themselves to the simple touch, and which thus have a usage that is much easier, more general, and more suited to the taste and dispositions of the multitude.

These signs and their practical use are not established by reference to any scholarly *theory*. In any case, their establishment does not suppose any *knowledge* about what underlies the relationship that connects signs to the objects signified, namely a certain distinct protuberance of the skull and the *faculty*, the disposition of the mind or heart that is supposed to correspond to it. This relationship is thus at first presented solely for what it is, namely a mere hypothesis, which may be impossible to verify *a priori* by any kind of direct physiological or psychological observation, but whose legitimacy one claims to establish (a posteriori) by the invariable correspondence existing between certain protuberances on the skull, which can be perceived through the senses of sight and touch, and certain special faculties characterizing individuals, whether men or animals, in whom the same protuberances are observed. Whence it follows that one can continuously adjudge the hidden faculties by the pretty bumps that can be seen; and by extending these empirical results to the theory of the human mind, one can also determine that there are *special* faculties that are distinct and separate from one another, in their use, as are the cerebral centres and organs in which and by which they are exercised, etc.

The craniological doctrine rests entirely upon the most absolute empiricism. The reasoning that follows from it, or the consequences that can be deduced from it, do not change its substance, and are external to it. It is simply a question of *fact*, or a mere relationship between *facts*.

All individuals, then, whether man or animal, whose skull presents a visible protuberance at a certain place, is of such and such a disposition of mind or of character: he has a good memory, or a lively imagination, or talent for a certain art, or courage, etc. For the contrary disposition, the skull will exhibit an indentation rather than a protuberance.

Here we have a new and perhaps quite remarkable connection between the physical structure of the cranial bone and the intellectual or moral faculties.[19] But does this relationship exist in nature, or is it but a figment of imagination? Is it a positive and real fact founded on an adequate number of sure observations constantly verified across the immense variety of cases or circumstances in which it is applicable, or rather a mere hypothesis founded upon a few particular inductions precipitously or erroneously generalized? It is either one or the other. In the first alternative, craniology or the art of knowing man's intellectual and moral faculties by the skull's protuberances is a de facto certainty (*une certitude de fait*), though it is not founded upon any physiological or psychological theory, and remains beyond all explanation; and how many physical truths, the very ones whose practical function or application is most useful or most extensive, fall into the same category? In the second alternative, the hypothesis, presenting no justification for its current acceptance, must be, if not outright rejected, at least put on hold pending further information, and until it has in its favour that mass of probabilities on which physical or purely empirical certainty is founded, when reasoning cannot fill the gaps left by observation, and attach an isolated branch to the totality of the immutable laws of nature.

We would thus have nothing to say about this doctrine, considered in its relation to the subject of this treatise, if Dr Gall had thought fit to confine himself to the empirical point of view or the mere factual relationship that

---

[19] Such is the relationship assigned by Camper between the obtuseness of [an animal's] *facial angle* and its degree of intelligence. This relationship, which it seems one can verify exactly by ascending the animal scale from fish to men, can nonetheless only be established empirically and is not thereby more certain. Perhaps one should have stopped there. (Note from the author.)

links the protuberances of the cranium to so many special faculties. But in presenting to the common eye *bare* facts or signs (which are alone within his competence), he felt he could not go without engaging in a more in-depth debate with scholars, the purpose of which is perhaps to align so far as possible his craniological hypothesis, his physiological doctrine, or his partition of the nervous system and brain, with his system of special faculties, which are supposedly divisible in proportion to the seats to which they are hypothetically ascribed.

Without wishing or pretending to undertake the detailed examination of these explanations that by itself would provide the subject of a long treatise, I shall merely refer to the preceding reflections and limit myself below to summarizing all that is most directly related to my subject, observing: (1) The general and external structure of the solid skull, being entirely molded after the internal form of the pulpy cerebral mass, which is housed in it as in its container, all the details concerning the contained substance's shape and form correspond exactly to the cranium that contains it (*la boîte osseuse contenante*); therefore, there are as many swellings or tubercles spread out on the surface of the brain, as there are visible protuberances on the skull; the bone protuberances act as a casing for these swellings, which are housed in them more or less as the soft organized substance of madrapora and coral are housed in the solid and scaly offshoots that represent the zoophyte body to us in the form of a branchy plant; but continuing this comparison, which seems to conform quite well to Doctor Gall's point of view, just as each polypus arm or entire polypary branch is by itself a tiny, complete organized machine that can live and function separately from the common stem or the whole animal, so each one of the tubercles housed in the bone protuberance is a particular small organ acting as the seat of the faculty whose natural predominance or habitual use gave it a sufficient degree of development to make it sensorial (*sensible*). This special faculty is determined in just this way, and it can be observed, studied in its sign as well as in its isolation from all the other faculties.

Here we begin to see how the (craniological) hypothesis tends to link the psychological division to the physiological divisions previously established by direct observation or by the anatomical dissection of the brain. This dissection, carried out in a new way and begun at the base of the encephalon, teaches us, according to Doctor Gall, that the nerves, instead of descending from the brain, which is considered as the common stem or matrix, towards the spinal cord and the lower organs, on the contrary head upward from these organs towards this same spinal cord, which forms the chief and sole line of communication between the different parts of the nervous system. This system is not, as had been thought, like a tree whose roots form a single stump and branch out in various offshoots and ramifications; it is rather a network whose separate parts each enjoy their own particular functions but at the same time participate, in proportion to their value, in the organization and functions of the whole. The great spinal cord acts all along its length as the meeting point for the threads of the network that lead to it, and thus enables them to communicate with one another. Mr Gall (and this is the novel part of his system that is most important for the main purpose he has in view) has observed a series of swellings along this cord, from which an equal number of pairs of nerves emerge, each forming an individual system. The brain or the cerebellum itself forms one of these swellings, which is merely bigger and more considerable than the others, having its own partial tubercles or protuberances, etc.

This new physiological system may be well founded; and although the direct dissections or observations upon which it rests do not yet seem to have been generally accepted by physiologists on all points, no one denies that they are quite ingenious and conducive to extending the boundaries of science; but even if their physiological results were proved with the greatest certainty, we would still need to close the immense gap that shall forever separate this order of facts from the phenomena of the mind and internal sense. The division of the general nervous system into small individual systems, each originating in a *tubercle* of the spinal cord, would prove nothing about the division of the special faculties of the intellect, and might even have no relation to it, and the craniological hypothesis would forever remain a hypothesis.

But one can see by this broad and imperfect presentation of the new system how it is the prelude to the psychological consequence that there is no longer a unique centre for the functions of organic or animal life, nor for those of intellect life and thought; or how, since each function has its own particular protuberance in the spinal cord that acts as a little brain, we must conclude by analogy that the special faculties are also dispersed or separated without regard for the unity of the self. Here, then, everything is less subordinate to a single power, less *united* in every sense of the word, than in other systems.[20]

---

[20] Dr Gall also seems to consider the real or absolute unity of the *self* as a simple abstraction of the mind, when he expressly attributes the particular sentiment of *one's self* to the organ of each special faculty. And he indeed needed to do so in order to be able to reconcile the separation of these special faculties with the intimate sentiment that is linked to the exercise of each of them. It follows that the *self* is nothing more than a composite sentiment, or a sort of *derivative* of all the other individual sentiments, which indeed amounts to annihilating its individuality, or real unity, which is the basis of all *metaphysics*. (Note from the author.)

(2) The parallel divisions of organic centres and of intellectual faculties, which one tends to prove reciprocally, by applying one to the other, refers directly or indirectly to some internal classification of the phenomena of intelligence; for since we have a vulgar language to express these phenomena, since we speak of memory, imagination, judgement and reasoning before establishing any systematic division between these faculties, or before even seeking to carry out any regular analysis, and since we are understood by others by *more or less* understanding ourselves, it must be that we already have in our minds some general and more or less reflective notion of the internal phenomena expressed by the habitual terms of language; which supposes pre-established divisions and well- or poorly made classifications of this order of facts.

When we later come to establish a doctrine whose purpose is to find or to recognize the organs or seats of certain faculties and thus to distinguish them by material signs, our starting point is necessarily the classifications of language, whose signs we borrow.

(1) Now, it can happen that we use these signs such as we find them already established, without seeking to analyse their foundation or reflective value; this is what the authors of the physiological hypotheses have often done, such as Willis and others, up to and perhaps including Doctor Gall, who, thinking they are capable of designating the seats of the various faculties in the brain, assumed without further inquiry that this real diversity corresponded to the conventional terms of our languages, as if nature had proportioned the number of cerebral divisions to that of the artificial and purely logical distinctions that we fancy to establish, in considering a single subject often from various *abstract* points of view, in examining one single capacity or faculty of the mind, one single disposition of the heart in those delicate and subtle nuances relative to given fortuitous circumstances, customs, mores and habits of our societies.[21]

(2) It could happen, on the contrary, that before founding a system of physiological division between cerebral centres assigned to various faculties, we borrow the foundations of an artificial classification of these faculties from some system of metaphysics, that we seek out the groundwork of a regular and truly analytic classification of the phenomena of the mind or of the operations of the intellect, either in our own reflection or in some scientific theory we are determined to adopt.

---

[21] Is it not peculiar, for instance, to see Dr Gall seriously claim to assign separate organs and as a result special faculties to flirtation, guile, vanity, pride, hypocrisy, dishonesty, as if all these artificial products, born of certain forms of society, were stamped with *nature's* seal? (Note from the author.)

For instance, when Mr Pinel attributes to a madman the ability to exercise certain faculties nominally classified as *attention*, *meditation* and *contemplation*, the exercise of which is, he claims, separate from that of certain others, his base or his starting point is the conventional classification of these phenomena such as they are deduced in the particular theory of Condillac, where all the faculties of the intellect, considered from a solely *passive* point of view, are taken, as it were, from within *sensation*, or are nothing other than sensation itself, which purportedly transforms itself to produce them;[22] and it is in this sense alone that Mr Pinel was able to claim that a madman contemplates, meditates, judges, compares, etc., whereas in fact he merely *feels*. But it seems obvious to me that taking another less arbitrary, more real basis for his classification, or one more consistent with the facts of *human* nature, Mr Pinel would have found that these hyper-sensory faculties such as contemplation and attention could in no way be truly separate, neither from one another, nor from the fundamental apperception (of the self) or the *conscium sui*, which is the basis for all intellectual and moral existence, nor therefore be attributed to a true madman.

Here we have a firm example of what happens when one tries to combine these two diverse doctrines or hypotheses. The physiologist, obliged to build on the more or less indeterminate signs of a language that is not his own, or looking to some metaphysical system for support, will feel he must follow its path, and adapt to it the investigations or facts that fall within his domain. As the number of classes and signs of arbitrary division and subdivision increases in the pre-established system, the systematic physiologist feels obliged to increase the number of cerebral centres in order to house each supposedly elementary faculty, each form, each category, etc.; and indeed, if Dr Gall had adopted the metaphysical doctrine of his illustrious compatriot *Kant*, would he not have had to multiply the skull's protuberances in proportion to the number of theoretical divisions in which this system abounds? But what actual utility can there be in grafting, as it were, a physiological hypothesis onto a hypothesis of another order? In what way can these artificial means really advance the science of intellectual and moral man, by appealing to the science of physical man, or advance this latter by appealing to the former? Does one not see that by seeking to bring together two *sciences* in what is most arbitrary, most uncertain, most obscure in them, we are merely adding artifice upon artifice, uncertainty upon uncertainty, obscurity upon obscurity? And how, from

---

[22] See Condillac's *Logic*. (Note from the author.)

the heart of darkness in which nature appears to have wrapped the functions of the nerves, can we hope to borrow a few rays of light to illuminate the phenomena of internal sense, which in any case already bear within them their own kind of light – *non ex fumo dare lucem*?[23]

Indeed, if, necessarily building upon the classifications of a pre-established language, the mind first seeks to link the signs that express its various faculties to so many truly distinct phenomena of its intimate sense, or if a given purely psychological division of these phenomena of the mind were fixed once and for all by reflection and justified by the use of a suitable *criterion*, wouldn't psychological science's goal be perfectly met? And what more could one look or ask for? What new light could come from the outside? It would perhaps be peculiar and maybe even useful to a certain extent, from a social or external point of view, to be able, as it were, to make perceptible to the eye, or to make palpable to the touch, those phenomena that belong to a wholly internal sense, just as we illuminate or confirm the testimony of an external sense by that of another. But we have sufficiently seen how deceptive and illusory the means used to perform this sort of transposition or symbolic interpretation are, how liable they are to alter, to distort everything they portray, similar to those curve-faced mirrors that stretch, separate, transpose the parts of the object presented to them, disfiguring it to the point that it is no longer the object we see, but something else altogether.

Let us conclude from all that precedes:

(1) that craniology[24] and all similar systems, whose purpose is to establish and explain the psychological distinction separating the

---

[23] "[Not] to give light from smoke." Horace. *Ars Poetica*, verse 143.

[24] Having only had to consider Mr Gall's doctrine with respect to the hypothetical *explanations* that I set out to combat, I was not able to expand upon the objections to which I think this doctrine is susceptible, chiefly with respect to the localization of the faculties, affections, and passions, instincts, animal appetites, etc., whose particular seats it claims to assign to certain protuberances of the brain. Although it is acknowledged that many headless creatures exhibit faculties of belief, etc., I shall confine myself here to an objection that, I believe, attacks the craniological hypothesis in its most immediate consequences, just as everything we have seen in the text radically attacks it in its principle or at its base.

Animals, he claims, have the same organs as we have relative to external sensations. In most animals, several of these organs are even more refined and unrestricted than ours; why then do they not have the same moral or intellectual faculties, if not because in the interior of our brain there are particular organs that we have and of which they are devoid?

This argument, well founded insofar as one uses it as factual proof to establish a general relationship such as the one Camper founded upon the obtuseness of the facial angle or the contraction of the cerebral cavity; this argument, I say, proves nothing in favour of faculties of the intellect, by a parallel division of the cerebral centres physiologically assigned to these faculties, can only be founded on a sort of hidden relationship, or on an altogether illusory empiricism, which no direct experiment nor legitimate induction from any order of facts can justify;

(2) that the hypothesis of a multiplicity of seats attributed in a cerebral space to intellectual acts that by essence bear the seal of thinking unity (*de l'unité pensante*), offends the laws of psychology and the primitive facts of intimate sense;

(3) that such doctrines continually confuse the *fatum* of the organism with the foresight of the mind, equate the *active* faculties of intelligence with the faculties or functions of passive and animal sensitivity, which, not having the same necessary relationship to personal unity or individuality, can to a certain extent be studied or observed in its organic signs, as we shall have occasion to point out;

(4) that each time we attempt to assign organic centres to certain intellectual faculties, we must assume that these faculties are *given* previously in number and in kind, by virtue either of an analysis or a true, reflective division or of a purely logical and artificial division that physiologists adopt temporarily, claiming to verify it, to explain it, or in sum to give it a surer grounding in the facts of organic nature; but that such a classification, instead of molding itself, as it were, to the positive facts taken from this organic nature, merely passes its artificial imprint on to these facts, and forces them to conform to its hypothetical divisions – a general result that, although more directly applicable to the particular systems of explanation with which this article is concerned, ought also to be extended to those systems that we examined prior.

Gall's hypothetical division, and can even be turned against his system advantageously. Indeed, one could say to him: man having several faculties that animals have not, it follows, on your account, that the organization of the human brain must include various parts that are foreign to an animal's brain; but men from all countries, from all ages, must have and must have had these organs you speak of, and, quite certainly, the same man has them at all times; why then is there so extraordinary a difference between individuals of our species who are subject to various accidental circumstances concerning country, climate, institutions? How is it, above all, if the superiority of the faculties depends solely on the multiplicity of cerebral organs, that any given man finds himself so different, according to the climate, season, temperature, etc. (Note from the author.)

In going all the way back to the common principle or source of all these systems that attempt to give a physical or physiological *explanation* of the phenomena of the mind, in seeking to show that they are all founded on an illusory assimilation perpetually established between the phenomena of the individual *self*, which are misunderstood with respect to their nature, their character, and their particular meaning, and another order of facts completely foreign to the *self*, we have perhaps made several useful steps for the science of man.

It is perhaps only given to the genius to blaze new trails and to bring light to the darkest regions of science; but being incapable of so lofty a flight, we have merely sought to dissipate certain illusions or false shadows, liable to lead us astray from the outset, and to send up, as it were, a few of those signals that indicate perilous waters from afar, and preserve travellers from them.

Conclusion of the first part of the treatise and introduction to the second part

We felt the need to insist somewhat expansively and with all the necessary details on the motives that might win acceptance for the opinion stated at the beginning of the illustrious academy's programme. Those who *currently deny the utility of physical doctrines or experiments* used to *explain* the phenomena of the mind and internal sense are fully justified.

Their denial is justified in perhaps a rather curious way by the history of that infinite multitude of haphazard and strange systems that, from Democritus through to Dr Gall, have attempted to found – upon the anatomy of the nerves and the dissection of the brain – knowledge of the soul's seat and of the immediate instruments of its intimate operations, as well as the interplay and functions of these instruments.

But this denial can be confirmed, I believe, in a still more useful and instructive way, by deducing the uselessness and emptiness of the explanations in question from the very nature of things or from the nature of the absolute heterogeneity separating the two orders of facts that are compared and applied to one another, and that is perhaps the only way to protect the mind from overly futile attempts; that is, to close off the entrance to a dangerous maze, and to redirect the time and energy being wasted in search of *impossible explanations* towards the quest for new facts or the laws governing them.

In moving on to the second part of the programme, in which we must discuss the inverse opinion, held by those who think it necessary to *reject psychological observations or reasons in investigations whose object is the body* or who restrict the application to certain pathological alterations of the living organic body, I shall first note that if by this expression – *psychological reasons* – what is meant is some system of explanation of organic or vital activity by the direct influence of the soul or thinking subject, as if we wanted, for instance, to link the vital functions, such as the various secretions of the liver, spleen and lungs, the pulsations of the arteries, the beating of the heart, and all the regular or abnormal circumstances of the dynamic (*jeu*) of life, to a certain class of phenomena of the *mind*, which by essence fall within the domain of consciousness and which can only be given to individual internal sense, we see clearly that all that was observed previously with respect to the heterogeneity of these two orders of facts proved in advance the uselessness and emptiness of this second inverse mode of explanation, or in other words that it is equally impossible to find the cause (*raison*) of the phenomena of the living body in those of the mind as it is to explain the phenomena of the *self* by the properties of *living* or animal organization. The reciprocity between the principles and the consequences of these two propositions is so evident that it is enough simply to state them. In fact, it follows from all that we said previously, and we need not dwell upon it longer.

But if, putting aside all systems of explanation founded on illusory analogies or comparisons, we limit ourselves to asking to what extent the observations or investigations that have as their *object* certain functions characteristic of the organized body or the living animal, can be linked to certain psychological investigations that have as their *object* certain *affections* or passions of the soul or of the self-same subject who feels or suffers (*pâtit*), and thinks, wills or acts; that is, to what extent and in what precise type of phenomena any given branch of *experimental* – as opposed to *rational* – psychology, might come in contact with some given branch of animal physics, again experimental and not speculative or hypothetical, in the search for causes; to what extent a double experience can illuminate these two factual branches by their parallelism or even their correspondence; in sum, what one (of these branches) has done or can do for the other, then the question changes: it is no longer a matter of *explaining* or of *seeking out hypothetical causes*, but merely of *observing types of simultaneous facts*; and this connection, which is truly inexplicable in theory and completely transcends our theoretical outlook as well as our vain hypotheses: is it anything more than a *fact* of a particular hybrid kind, in which two different types of observation, which are situated, as it were, on their common limit, coincide? And this very connection, so observed, either in its regular state or in its abnormalities, will all the more deserve the philosopher's attention in that it unites the most important and fundamental laws of the science of man, considered as a *hybrid* being, *living, feeling* and *thinking*. It is no longer a matter of the theoretical relations that two sciences so different in principle may bear to one another, but only of the homologous points, as it were, on which a certain practical part of one might be compared with a certain equally practical part of the other.

All our encyclopaedic divisions of the sciences, as well as all the classes into which we sort the things and beings we need to study or wish to expound upon, are more or less arbitrary products of man. It is quite rare for them to express, interpret or imitate perfectly the work of nature itself. The scope of our intelligence or the limits of our knowledge grow or shrink successively, whereas nature is fixed, always consonant with itself, throughout the immense variety of its simultaneous or successive productions, coordinated in time and space.

In the current state of our knowledge, we are justified in distinguishing three sciences whose respective objects are the properties or motion of brute bodies, the functions or phenomena of living organized bodies, and lastly the phenomena observed in beings endowed with intelligence and will, that is, physics, physiology and psychology.

But it is striking that, as we rise higher in the hierarchy, these three great divisions or classes of properties and phenomena seem, as it were, to encroach on one another and tend to make each other more complicated, first by uniting two by two, as in animal existence, then three by three, as in the human constitution.

The laws of physics steadfastly and uniformly govern brute bodies, which are exclusively subject to these laws; the laws of physiology are distinct but not *separate* from those of physics in every living organized body, which in addition has its own particular laws as a *living* being; lastly, all the intelligent beings we know have organized bodies that, as living beings, participate in the laws of physics and physiology while at the same time having their own truly hyper-organic as well as *hyper-physical* laws.

A certain wholly systematic philosophy only recognized two classes of beings: machines or pure automatons, and thinking beings. It did not therefore recognize an intermediary science between *physics* or mechanics and psychology, or between the science of bodies and the science of minds. Psychology was therefore the exclusive science of the phenomena of the *mind* and of *internal sense*; all that did not emerge immediately from this *internal* sense, or that was not a thought, had to be a mechanical effect that could and should be *explained* by the laws of motion or the properties of material shapes (*l'étendue figurée*), whereas the phenomena of the mind could only be *explained* by themselves or by their own laws (from which, in passing, the faculties and ideas innate to the soul necessarily derived, for where else would they have come from?). We have seen the troublesome consequences of this too absolute point of view exhibited in Descartes' doctrine.

But as soon as we have recognized the laws specific to living bodies, which are distinct and separate from those of brute matter, another kind of assimilation opposed to that of Cartesianism tended to occur between the phenomena of life and organics (*de la vie et de l'organisation*) and those of sensation on the one hand, which did not seem to differ essentially from them, and those of thought on the other hand, which were said to originate exclusively in sensation, according to the famous axiom: *nihil ist in intellectu* ... Physiology has had the fate of being dragged along now by physics, now by psychology: it encompasses a subject that belongs also to psychology. This second assimilation was chiefly favoured by Stahl's doctrine. This philosopher doctor, adopting Descartes' exclusive principle, according to which there can only be two kinds of beings – bodies and minds – was naturally forced to conclude that the vital and organic functions belong to the soul, solely because they could not be attributed to material bodies, which are governed by altogether different laws. Thus, physiology proper, whose foundations Stahl was the first to lay down as an independent science distinct from physics, was now, inversely, to be identified with psychology, or to become an essential part of the *science of the mind*, as it was before of the science of bodies.

Just as a small intermediary state between two others that are stronger than it is often at risk of losing its name and existence, if the more powerful states do not feel the need to respect its limits out of their own self-interest, so was the domain of physiology bound to be invaded successively, first by physics, under the rule of a wholly mechanistic doctrine, and next by psychology, extended more than fortified by the system of the animists.

But to follow through with our comparison, if the intermediary state succeeds in gathering enough strength to win its independence, it can then in turn usurp one of its two neighbours by forming a coalition with the other; is this not what happened to physiology, which, urged on in its progress by the successors of Stahl, and bolstered by the new discoveries that enriched the physical sciences, has seemingly sought to invade the entire domain of the soul, and push its conquests all the way to the phenomena of the mind and of internal sense?

It would be curious and interesting to follow in detail all the circumstances of this mutual action and reaction between the three sciences, which converge on one and the same object, namely man, considered in relation to the three principles or elementary forces that constitute his complete being.

May the reader reflect for a moment on the immensity of research, the degree of methodological perfection, and in sum the force of genius that was needed to recognize the two forces, one tangential and one attractive, that contribute to the trajectories and elliptical motion of the planets, and to assign to each their respective contribution; and the problem of determining the relationship between the forces that reciprocally compound or cancel one another in the same thinking, moving and feeling organic whole, to how superior an order of difficulty does it belong! On how different a combination of faculties – both rarer and more difficult to exercise – is it founded! What depth of reflection, and more, what finesse and tact, what immensity of acquired knowledge, what acquaintance with a double observation, in sum what *philosophical talent*! All too conscious of all that we lack to venture to solve so great a problem, let us confine ourselves here to analysing its main parameters.

First, there is no doubt but that the living body gives rise to various purely physical phenomena, such as the decomposition of atmospheric air in the lungs, the interplay of elective affinities among the different humours that form and unform within the organized machine, the refraction of light beams as they pass through the three humours of the eye before arriving at the retina, the way in which the sonorous fluid makes its way to the eardrum, and makes the spiral lamina vibrate, the way in which the sapid molecules are dissolved by the saliva, the way in which the bone parts arrange themselves into all manner of levers to execute and transmit movements, etc.

But these phenomena become more complex in living beings when combined with those specific to (vital) organization, such that in any resulting physiological product, it is very difficult to separate out the contribution of pure physics, and we expose ourselves to the gravest of errors by claiming to ascertain the order of succession between movements, to evaluate the absolute *quantity* of the movements and phenomena observed in the *living* being when assimilated to *dead* matter. Second, the distinction between various vital properties unequally distributed among the different organs, the order of subordination and dependence established by nature between the functions of the same organic whole, lastly the regular classification of phenomena of this kind, necessarily lead the physiological observer to establish certain relationships that may exist between these properties, these organic functions and activities, which fall strictly within the domain of his science, and facts of another order that he can neither see nor imagine, nor verify by any sense or external instrument, but that he is at times obliged to integrate into his results or in the aim of his experiments. If his goal, for instance, is to recognize whether a certain part of a living being is, as we say, *sensitive* or non-sensitive to the impression of a particular stimulus, the experiment will have to take into account phenomena that can scarcely be grasped other than by a wholly internal sense, or by a sort of sympathy that temporarily places the surgeon in the patient's shoes – phenomena that can never be captured by direct observation. It is thus that the varying degrees of sensitivity present in animals are not perceived, but rather concluded or inferred, with greater or lesser certainty, from certain contractions or movements with which the observer associates them.

But how to distinguish precisely between the impression that proceeds from the external stimulus and that which is added to the total sensory product by the internal disposition of the animal, such as the general state of distress the organism is in, the current degree of nervous excitability of the irritated organ or of the whole system, various internal conditions that can absorb or divide and distract its sensitivity, such as the fear with which it is gripped during the operation, etc.? To avoid this complication, an analysis of which would be quite difficult to perform, it is well known that physiologists, severing the knot they cannot untie, find it simpler to cut or detach the nerve stems through which the irritated organ communicates with the brain. But then, the integrity of the system being broken, the sensitivity that was before *animal* becomes purely *organic*, or rather, there is no longer sensitivity in the strict sense, but rather a simple vital property, which under any given heading, *irritability* for instance, can thus be studied in its binary combination with some physical force as in the previous case.

Third, let us add a *will* to that sensory motor force characteristic of *animals*, which by its action alone so alters and complicates all the results of the physical experiments in which it appears, and in which it occasions so much variation and uncertainty. Here we have another yet higher degree of complication and another cause of disturbance and anomaly, no longer solely with respect to the physical and vital effects, but also with respect to the products of animal sensitivity and contractility. What legitimate conclusion, for example, could one draw from the immobility of Scévola's arm on the burning coals, in evaluating the degree of pain that he is experiencing or in judging his insensitivity? This experience, which has already been cited and through which we can summarize all those that repeatedly take place (perhaps in a less emphatic and striking fashion) in the depths of our consciousness each time the *law of the mind*, in opposition to *the law of the body*,[25] stops or changes the

---

[25] "But I see in my members another law waging war against the law of my mind." [Saint Paul, *Letter to the Romans*, 7:22–23.] (Note from the author.)

fatum,[26] – does this experience not seem to cancel out the effect of any organic or animal force or property? On the contrary: these forces subsist in a subject exceedingly worthy of our admiration; they are merely subordinate to a superior power, which, unable to destroy or modify them in themselves, changes and stops all signs of their manifestation. Annihilate this force created by a sublime act of will, and the arm retracts by mere instinct, which is sensitive to the initial impression of pain. Cut the brachia, and the arm remains immobile, but here it is the immobility of death, and there, that of life, of moral life, far superior to that which produces the movement of animal retraction. Who would dare posit between these antagonistic facts an assimilation or identity contrary to the facts of external or internal sense? Who would dare say that the will is not an autonomous force (*force propre*), a force *sui juris*, but merely an effect (indeed well hidden and very complicated) of the *affinity* connecting all the parts that compose living machines, combined with the central *force* of the globe and the action of all external objects?

I am assuming here that the reader acknowledges the three divisions established by Bichat between the different modes of muscular contractility and the physiological foundations of these divisions. I am not speaking of non-sensory organic contractility, which does not concern our purpose; nor do I have find that there is any difficulty on the subject of sensory contractility (*la contractilité sensible*); to this contractility correspond the special sensations of a movement devoid of effort that the *self* does not attribute to itself as cause.

But it seems to me that Bichat confused the most distinct ideas and facts by identifying animal contractility with voluntary contractility in the last of his categories, and I feel I must call attention to this inaccuracy by distinguishing two modes that he confounds either inadvertently, or with a view to conserving a certain symmetry between his divisions, although he was led by his own principles to separate them.

'The locomotive muscles,' he writes (p. 123 of his excellent work, entitled *Physiological Investigations on Life and Death, etc.*):

> can be activated in two ways: (1) By the will; (2) by the sympathies. This latter mode of action occurs when an internal organ is aroused (*affection*), the brain is also aroused (*s'affecte*) and brings about involuntary movements in the locomotive muscles. In this way, a passion bear its influence on the liver; the brain, sympathetically aroused, arouses the voluntary muscles; it is then in the liver that the underlying principle

---

[26] "That breaks the laws of destiny." [Lucrelius, *De Rerum Natura*, II, 251–287.] (Note from the author.)

of their movements is found, which movements, in this case, belong to the class of those of organic life; so that the muscles, although always set in motion by the brain, can nonetheless, by their functions, belong in turn to both *lives*.

We can now conceive what the movements of the fetus are. They belong to the same class as several of those of the adult, which have not yet been sufficiently distinguished; they are the same as those produced by the passions on the voluntary muscles. They resemble that of a man sleeping who, although no dream agitates his mind, moves more or less vigorously. For instance, there is nothing more common than violent movements during sleep following laborious digestion; here, the stomach, working vigorously, agitates the mind, which in turn sets the locomotive muscles in motion.

In this respect, let us distinguish two types of locomotion during sleep: one, as it were voluntary, produced by dreams, is a derivative of animal life; the other, resulting from the internal organs, finds its principle in the organic life to which it belongs: this is precisely the life of the fetus.

I could find various other examples of involuntary and therefore organic movements, carried out in the adult by the voluntary muscles and apt to give an idea of those of the fetus, but these suffice. Let us simply note that the organic movements, as well as the sympathetic disturbance of the brain, which is its source, slowly dispose this organ to perceive sensations and the muscles to carry out the movements of animal life that begin after birth.

Once these distinctions, established with such accuracy, sagacity and depth, have been posited, why confuse this mode of contractility carried out by the sympathetic reaction of the brain with that which is performed by its own direct action? Why not organize into two different classes: (1) animal contractility, determined by that sympathetic reaction of the brain that is the most general cause of the movement of animals, who are subject to the influence of their needs and appetites; and (2) the contractility specific to man, who, directed by a self-moving principle, or a hyper-organic force, can emancipate himself from the chains of affections and passions? By distinguishing these two classes or types of contraction, Bichat could have escaped a difficulty that he creates for himself and that he confesses he cannot resolve.

Why, he asks, does sensory organic contractility never transform into animal or *voluntary* contractility, whereas nervous organic sensitivity becomes animal as it increases by degrees (pp. 103 and 104)? This difficulty alone should have made the author notice the fundamental flaw of his classification and the gap that exists in his symmetrical division of the modes of contractility. Indeed, to preserve the analogy between the classes of various modes of sensitivity and contractility, he had to link organic sensation to organic contraction, and therefore imagined that the latter becomes sensory in the same way the former becomes animal – that is, by increasing by degrees. But by linking voluntary contraction with animal sensation, all analogy fails; one ends up comparing heterogeneous things, for we are no longer dealing with nervous or muscular impressions, both of which are felt when they attain that degree at which they can be transmitted to the brain, rather than remaining concentrated in their particular organ; but on the one hand, it is an impression transmitted to the centre, and on the other, a willed action and a movement transferred, inversely, from the motor centre to the muscle for which this centre is the sole principle of its contraction. Sensitivity and will, analysed according to two opposing physiological principles, are thus heterogeneous and incomparable elements.

Why be surprised, moreover, that a simple muscular sensation does not turn into an act of will and that the sensory contractions of the heart and stomach cannot enter into the realm of this power, given that we have established that these .mechanisms of organic life do not communicate directly with the unique centre of voluntary contractility? What absurdities can one be led into by this obsession to generalize and to reduce everything to the systematic unity of a principle! Surely someone who explained gravity by attributing an express will to heavy objects that tend towards the centre of the earth would be no less absurd than he who pretends to explain the will by a central force or interplay of affinities.

Where did one ever see a better application of Cicero's perspicacious remark: *nihil est tam absurdam quod non dictum sit ab aliquo philosophorum*?[27]

Let us move past these uncertainties, and in the successive encroachment on each other's limits perpetrated by the three sciences we have been comparing, we can nonetheless see that the realm belonging to physics proper has remained the best circumscribed of all, and that the most important conquests achieved by contemporaries in physiology as well as in the analysis of human faculties have contributed to restricting this science within the proper limits in which it should henceforth remain enclosed.

But the two new perspectives from which the two essential components of the *science of man* have been conceived, the comparisons that the great observers have claimed to make between them, the kind of analogy or

---

[27] "Nothing so absurd can be said that some philosopher has not said it." Cicero, *De Divitatione*, II, LVII, 119.

identity of object to which they have claimed to reduce them – in sum, as we have already seen, the common classes and divisions in which they enveloped the phenomena of life and of animal sensitivity, and those of life and of internal sense – could only increase our uncertainty as to their respective limits, or even make us doubt whether these limits really exist in organized, living and thinking nature, or whether the totality of all these phenomena, different from one another solely in the degree to which they possess one single like property or faculty, rather in fact constitute one single science, that of the functions and laws of *sensitivity*, where the general expression *sensitivity* or *faculty of feeling* would receive that unlimited range of meaning that certain modern doctrines have attributed to it, where *living* is *feeling* or thinking, *willing* merely *feeling*.

Without reproducing here the objections already made against this unity of divisions and classes, against the particular system for the derivation of faculties in which the physiologist and the metaphysician concur, in appearance, in a certain commonality of language, explanation and phenomenic point of view, I shall merely summarize the above by observing that man quite certainly unites within him two kinds of faculties that we cannot refuse to *distinguish* when considering the facts of intimate sense, even though we would equate them, as to their *principle*, with the *absolute*, *productive* force; that in man, there are or seem to be two kinds of laws resulting from the double relation that he bears, on the one hand, as a living being, to objects, by the impressions they produce on his various organs, and on the other, to himself, or to his own modifications as *thinking* subject, capable of reflecting, acting and *willing*.

In virtue of these first laws, the total life of the organized being is a kind of *derivative* of all the passive impressions simultaneously received by the various organs, whence there arises that multitude of obscure affections that incessantly modify the animal and push it in a blind direction, without the least participation on the part of the person or *self*.

In virtue of the second laws alone, which are truly hyper-sensitive, man is endowed with a life of relation and *consciousness*. Not only does he *live*, and *feel*, but in addition he has the *apperception*[28] of his individual existence; he has the *idea* or consciousness of his sensation. Not only does he *have* or *bear* relations to the beings surrounding him, but he also *apperceives* these relations; far more, he extends them, incessantly changes them or himself creates new ones, in the exercise of his activity, of that free power of *effort* or of will that constitutes his personality and characterizes his nature.

---

[28] I always take the word *apperception* in Leibniz's sense: *apperceptio est perceptio cum reflexione conjuncta* [apperception is perception joined with reflection]. (Note from the author.)

Indeed, everything this power accomplishes is duplicated as it were, as apperception, in the consciousness of the same *self*; everything that is done outside it, or outside its participation and collaboration in the purely sensory being, is there merely as *affection* or *obscure* immediate simple perception. In the latter case, the animal is devoid of self (*sans moi*); only in the former case do we find a person constituted as such for itself and therefore the exclusive origin of all intellectual faculties, or of all phenomena of the mind or of internal sense.

Now, suppose we restrict psychology to being merely the science pertaining to these latter intellectual phenomena, of the laws of their succession or of their derivation from the primitive fact of consciousness, of the conditions under which they are carried out, of the means and signs through which they appear in a wholly internal experience, etc.; in this case, I persist in maintaining that psychology is completely external to physical and physiological doctrines and experiments, and that there is no intelligible connection between them, no theoretically admissible explanation, and I prove this by all that was said in the first part of this treatise.

But suppose we give the science called psychology an *extension* that indeed seems attributable to it, understanding by this term not only the phenomena distinctive of the *self* and *internal sense*, or the products of the activity of willing and of thought, but in addition all the passive affections of animal sensitivity, which precede, prepare and perhaps bring about the constitution of the person in time (*amènent dans le temps la constitution personelle*), the *obscure perceptions* that only need a ray of light of *consciousness* to illuminate, develop and rise up to the height of the *idea* – these appetites, penchants and determinations which, it is true, are still blind and subordinate to the *fatum* of the body, but which, falling under the rule of an enlightened power, can become the auxiliaries, the instruments and the motives of its activity and unite itself with the most elevated sentiments, with the most noble passions of the human heart – finally, suppose we include in psychology all that *touches* as it were the self, without being the self nor belonging to it, all that which, though it does not yet fall within the domain of *internal* sense, of our reflective individuality, can become the object of a sort of immediate internal tact that in certain individuals is chiefly linked to the most simple affections and the most fugitive impressions, indeed to organic activity or to the most obscure products of the animate machine's dynamic (*jeu*).

Suppose finally we understand the term psychology as that important branch of the science of man that endeavours not only to recognize, to establish the very important and numerous phenomena of this class of obscure perceptions, to distinguish them at their source, or by the signs announcing them in the living organism, but moreover that studies their relationship or their de facto connection (*liaison de fait*) with the products of another order, with the direction and form of the ideas of the mind, and the development or the mode of exercise of higher-order faculties.

Then, perhaps, psychology, insofar as we include in it this particular order of facts, will be intimately tied up with physiology, and although unable to borrow from it, nor to provide it with any of those supposed explanations that are never more than *vicious circles*, each science will glean useful data from the other, in order to obtain the most complete knowledge possible of a subject that to a certain extent is common to them both – that is, *internal man* considered solely as *feeling*, or as susceptible to *affections* or *passions* (this last word being taken in its full *range*).

This being established, in the second part I shall seek to analyse all the modes of passive sensation that psychology and physiology grasp each from the point of view specific to it; from there we shall determine their common relations, the kind of link that unites them, and the kinds of reciprocal aid they can lend one another.

Second part

Of an order of sensory phenomena considered from the double perspective of physiology and psychology, and of the common relations of these two sciences and of the reciprocal aid they can lend one another.

The light distinctive of and *internal* to consciousness does not suddenly illuminate man as soon as he is born into the world of phenomena, and the constitutive fact of personal individuality, truly first in the order of facts pertaining to apperceived or reflective existence, is not first *absolutely* in the order of time, or in the succession of phenomena of purely *animal* or *sensory* life.

Man begins to *live* and to *feel*, without knowing his life (*vivit et est vitae nescius ipse suae*).[29]

This multitude of affections and secret impressions, of *appetites*, of penchants and of determinations that appear in the awakening animal, constitute sensory life and form the particular domain of *instinct*, blind in its principle, and necessitated in its acts.

Born and carried out outside of the *will* (*vouloir*) and of thought, these first *determinations of sensitivity*, having not yet received that imprint or intellectual

---

[29] "He lives and is unconscious of his own life." Ovid. *Tristia,* I, III, 12.

form through which they are adapted to internal sense, remain forever removed from it, and cannot be duplicated there in the form of apperceptions, nor reproduced in the form of memories or remembrance; thus, animal or purely sensory life is always in the *present*. We never fall back into it.

In the development and full exercise of all our faculties, if a purely affective sensitivity comes to operate at that superior degree of energy that blinds the mind and subjugates the will, we exist without *consciousness*, without *self*, or without the possibility of going back to these same sensations, which all the more defy remembrance in that the *person* has more completely identified himself with them or absorbed himself in them.[30]

But these *animal* sensations, devoid of consciousness or *personality*, or reduced and gleaned from that state of *simplicity* that I express by the term pure *affection*, seem to me distinguishable only in one of the following two ways, either (1) insofar as they are grasped by a certain internal tact, or secret and natural sympathy, foreign to all reflection, which makes us *feel* or *sense* it immediately, first within ourselves, then in organized beings like us; or (2) insofar as they are to a certain extent represented in certain signs that the observation of living nature provides, or in the study of the functions and conditions of the dynamic of life and of the most immediate organic impressions, of which the affections seem to be the most immediate result, even if they are not completely identical to them.

But in the implementation of these two means of distinguishing and noticing the pure phenomena in question, the psychologist and the physiologist obviously can and ought to help one another and illuminate one another on a subject of study or of observation that is common to them both.

Perhaps this internal tact we are speaking of is not less necessary to the physiologist doctor than to the moralist metaphysician – and after all, isn't this the first and the chief tie that unites them, that inspires in them that particular attraction that each feels for the science of the other, that constant need they experience to communicate with one another and to agree?

Perhaps this affective state, considered in that kind of *native simplicity* conceived and expressed so well by a certain philosopher doctor, when he said that man, simple in vitality, is double in humanity (*homo simplex in*

---

[30] Condillac and Bonnet in their common hypothesis of an animated statue seek rather vainly to deduce all the intellectual operations from a simple sensation that the statue's soul *becomes*, or with which it is said to be *identified*. How did Bonnet in particular not see that this complete identification of the soul with each of the successive or simple modes of passive sensation radically destroys the personality and prevents it from *arising*, far from being its source, as these two metaphysicians concur in supposing? (Note from the author.)

vitalitate duplex est in humanitate[31]) – this state inherent to the very act of living, and variable like the modes of this act, which necessarily precedes, in the order of time, the birth of the *self* and the development of any thinking faculty, while being the most important subject and an end in itself for physiological studies, provides the physiologist with an essential starting point, and with data he cannot go without, if at least he does not want to begin or end up with the gloom of certain *innate ideas*: if he is convinced that the mind can conceive nothing absolute, he seeks to grasp or better fix his subject by comparisons and contrasts, and to trace more exactly the contour separating light from darkness, and the *self* from that which it is not.

From this point of view, then, the physiological considerations concerning all the phenomena prior to the *self* and independent from individual apperception, would be, as it were, the essential prolegomena to any complete analysis of the phenomena of the mind or of internal sense; indeed, all that is subordinate, in the same living, feeling and thinking being, to the exclusive laws of vitality or animal sensitivity, and therefore all that is outside the laws of intelligence, enter into psychology's particular domain. It would therefore fall to psychology to determine, by way of *external* observation, all the organic circumstances that may be ascribed to these modes of exercising a *passive* and, if I dare say so, impersonal sensitivity, to those *obscure* affections or perceptions that subsist and manifest themselves by certain signs while the self is asleep or thought is absent. Psychology would seek to ascribe them to their source, to their respective instruments or determinant causes, to designate their effects or their characteristics in the regular or altered order of the vital functions that fall directly within its immediate domain; lastly, in determining these phenomena in their physical aspects, it would prepare us better to evaluate the degree of influence they can have in the moral sphere.

It is in this way that, starting from the first determinations of sensitivity, or of animal instinct, physiology could perhaps succeed, by an alliance propitious for the progress of the science of moral man, in shedding new light upon the hybrid phenomena that constitute the passions of the intelligent being and, drawing still nearer to the physiological object, to fix to a certain extent the organic conditions that correspond to the spontaneous production, the

---

[31] "We have thus succeeded little by little in distinguishing the nerves; we have found that some nerves, enabling sensation and movement, derive from the brain; and that other nerves, serving no such function, have their origin in the cerebellum. Suppose that we conserve all the sensitive parts of the human body, but that we remove the heart." Herman Boerhaave, *Praelectiones Academicae De Morbis Nervorum,* Lugduni Batavorum, 1761, II, 496–497.

persistence, or the forced return of certain persistent images or spectres, which appear to be the products of certain alterations or pathological states whose seat is the brain or the nervous system, or sometimes certain internal organs. Finally, exploring the domain of physical sensitivity in its full extension, and above all adhering to that class of obscure vital impressions whose difficult analysis still remains rather imperfect, physiology could manage to circumscribe its own limits: by helping us better to know man as a sensory being, simple in *vitality*, it would lead to, but necessarily stop at the sphere of the thinking and willing being, double in *humanity*.

To this general picture of the precious data with which physiology could provide the science of intellectual and moral man, if we now contrasted the services that the science of the phenomena of the mind and of internal sense could in turn render to that of the functions of sensory life (*la vie sensitive*), we should see that they are not less important nor less numerous; and internal observation teaches us first that the regular exercise of the operations of thought, promoted by a certain mode of the vital functions or by certain dispositions inherent to the nervous system and to passive sensitivity, in turn influences these dispositions extraordinarily, and can bring about changes sometimes advantageous, sometimes detrimental.

Who is not familiar with the organic effects due to imagination and to the passions, which contribute in so remarkable a fashion to the foresight of the mind and to the *fatum* of the body; which arise successively now in one, now in the other; now leave the mind to reach the organs, now leave the organs, where they originate, to act upon the mind and to disrupt and modify it so profoundly? Who is not familiar with the admirable effects the moralist doctor produces by the sole art with which he seizes the imagination, the sentiments, and the ideas of a patient? And who does not bless in his heart the name of that benefactor of humanity who by the sole application of these psychological views to the treatment of the insane, by administering a purely moral therapy, still manages each day to uplift these degraded beings deprived of the greatest prerogative of their nature, to save them both from manic furies and from bouts of melancholic apathy, or from so many other total or partial eclipses of the intelligence, which aggrieve the heart and shame human reason?[32]

Considering the connection and mutual relations between these two sciences from these two points of view, we shall divide the second part of this work into two parts. The first will include the analysis of the phenomena of the organism, or of *passive* sensation, external or internal, which are linked to certain *ideas* or feelings of the soul, correspond to them, or

---

[32] See *The Treatise on Mental Insanity*, by M. Pinel. (Note from the author.)

contribute to bringing them about. The second will treat of the influence that certain ideas of the mind or sentiments of the soul may have upon affective phenomena and the workings of the organs.

Section one

Abridged analysis of the phenomena of animal sensitivity; of the immediate affections *or* obscure perception, *which arise in the body, and directly or indirectly influence the phenomena of the mind.*

I divide these phenomena into two classes, one of which is composed of all the immediate impressions received by the nerve endings of the organs of the external senses, and the other of impressions immediately received or produced by the very dynamic of life (*le jeu même de la vie*), at the centre of the internal organs; this division of facts is essentially related, as one can see, to physiological considerations or observations.

Here and in all that follows we shall assume a well-founded distinction that is recognized today by the most profound psychologists,[33] although disregarded and concealed by those who have claimed to deduce all the phenomena and powers of the *human* mind from passive sensation: namely the distinction that exists between the purely *affective* part and the *representative* part of any single *perception* or external sensation. I cannot stop here to prove what has been shown elsewhere, in an analysis (*ex professo*) of the *human faculties*, namely that any *clear* or *complete* perception, which indivisibly contains the two halves of the primitive *duality*, the subject (*self*) and object (*non-self*), is essentially founded on the combination of the motor activity of the soul and of the hyper-organic force; that the organs on which and through which this force is exercised are mere organs or instruments of representation, whence it follows quite clearly, contrary to Locke and his disciples, that the first ideas of *sensation* are neither *simple* nor *passive*, and do not derive ready-made from the external world through the channel of the senses.

As for the organs that are situated outside the motor force's domain, they can be nothing other than the seats of passive affections, which are immediate products either of the contact of bodies, or of those intestinal and spontaneous movements of which the dynamic of life is composed: affections merely *felt*, in a more or less obscure way, by the animal, without any apperception of the self, nor any representation of foreign existence.

---

[33] See Th. Reid. *An Inquiry into the Human Mind*, Dugald Stewart, Degérando, etc. (Note from the author.)

This being established, we see clearly: (1) how these impressions or obscure affections are, by their nature and their particular character, as well as by the organic seat in which they arise, situated outside of the mind's sphere of activity and of knowledge's circle, and how by their mode of production or receptivity they enter into the domain of the science that studies these very functions of organic or animal sensitivity, of which they are the elements or raw material; (2) how the psychologist can be led by a more complete and developed analysis of the *total* phenomenon of sensation, or of perception, which for him is no longer simple (*le simple*), to a truly simple element (*un simple véritable*) of instinctive affection, and to find natural elements or signs,[34] in a science that ends where consciousness begins.

Let us endeavour to study these little known signs, perhaps too often neglected by metaphysicians.

Article one

External affective impressions.

§1 The affections of external touch

By including under this heading all the affections whose seat is spread out along the entire surface of the human body, we shall find that these immediate impressions are far more varied and numerous than the

---

[34] Th. Reid in fact considers the immediate affections we are discussing as signs instituted by nature to induce the mind to perceive or represent completely external objects. He notes quite rightly that impressions of this kind, which have few or no proper names in our habitual languages, are often non-sensory, and always unperceived or *imperceptible* by themselves, the *natural sign* thus disappearing before the *thing signified*. It seems to me that in this part of a work full of the most astute and judicious observations, Reid falls into the mistake common to metaphysicians of too precipitously generalizing particular facts, or of supposing that what pertains to a given external sense, such as sight for instance, indiscriminately applies to all the other senses or to all the sensory and intellectual products that may be attached to them. Reid holds, for instance, that any immediate, more or less affective, impression made upon any given external sense, naturally suggests to the mind the perception or the idea of the object, or of the external cause of which it is the sign; but even supposing that this were true (which I do not believe) of the immediate impressions made upon the retina by light beams, we would be fully justified in doubting, and in my opinion in denying, that such is the case for the impressions of hearing, smell, taste, which by essence are purely affective and are linked only secondarily, or in virtue of our habits, to the phenomena of objective representation.

imagination can conceive and, above all, that the resources of our languages, which are only rich in signs designating *objects*, and quite poor in signs designating the modifications relating to *ourselves*, do not enable us to express them.

To these impressions we must ascribe a multitude of sympathetic influences, exerted by various ambient fluids on the absorbing pores of the skin and by these latter on the various internal organs, whose functions, now invigorated, now impaired, bring about an immediate sensation of well-being or discomfort in the sensitive being, and a host of variable affections still more obscure in themselves than in the external causes or agents to which they are linked.

Whence, in part, the successive variations we experience in the sentiment of existence due to changes in habitat, climate, season and temperature;[35] whence, too, the sudden effect that the actions of certain contagious miasma have on our sensitivity, and that are hidden principles of a multitude of illnesses, now transmitted by immediate contact, now transported from place to place on those invisible and airy fluids that at times create a nefarious solidarity among the inhabitants of the most distant regions of the globe.

To obscure impressions of this kind, we must ascribe, in large degree, the source of that secret sympathy or antipathy operating between individuals that attract or repel one another at first sight, perhaps according as their vital atmospheres are in harmony or opposition in their reciprocal contact. Is it indeed not probable that several extraordinary phenomena of this kind would tend to make us believe that in each living organism there exists a more or less marked power to act from afar, or to create an influence outside itself in a certain sphere of activity similar to the atmospheres surrounding the planets?[36]

Without further insisting on these phenomena that are not studied enough and that can still offer the observer so many curious and interesting details, I shall merely point out here that it falls to physiology, assisted by an improved physics and chemistry, to enrich and to extend directly a branch of facts that intersects with the science of the phenomena of the mind, and can to a certain extent illuminate or complete its analysis.

---

[35] *Quod caeli mutatur in horas temperies, animi quoque simul et pectora mutant.* ["Just as the temperature of the air changes according to the hour, so do minds and feelings change." (Unknown source.)] (Note from the author.)

[36] The reader is familiar with the ideas of Reil, who attempted to explain the action of the nerves though a similar atmosphere that he attributes to each nervous organ or partial instrument of sensitivity. (Note from the author.)

§2 Of the affections of smell and taste

Each external sense being immediately subordinate, with respect to the order of immediate affections or impressions we are discussing, to the immediate contact of the object or fluid to which they naturally correspond, (philosophers) were able, from this point of view in truth quite partial, to assimilate, somewhat legitimately, all external senses with that of touch.

Indeed, this sort of passive touch, which must be clearly distinguished from active tact, is modified in a special way in each of the particular organs, and first becomes the particular seat of the affective part, which, although a mere element or sign of intellectual perception, can nonetheless constitute animal sensation as a whole.

It is thus that the sensations of smell and taste, which are wholly adapted to instinct, still preserve, even in man, the predominant affective character that they have at their source.

The olfactory or sapid molecules indeed act on their respective organs by a true immediate contact, and they seem to come and seek them out or to operate on them by virtue of a sort of instinctive sympathy or affinity of choice (*affinité de choix*).

Quite different from the senses of perception, activated on the one hand by the will, and on the other hand aroused by the fluids interposed between them and the objects perceived, smell and taste immediately receive the impression of the material corpuscles to which they correspond and that reach them in that state of extreme division, which is alone favourable to the combinations of a sort of wholly transcendent animal chemistry. It is also for this reason that the sensations of smell and taste in particular have been considered rightly as particular alterations of the general touch of the skin, to which the mucous membranes are analogous.[37] These three organs are indeed linked by the common relation between the sympathetic affections for which they are the respective seats.

---

[37] The mucous membranes corresponding to the senses of smell and taste, which are continuous with those of the respiratory and digestive tracts, essentially form the *organ*, or are the immediate and necessary seat of its function, which would cease if the membrane were removed or lost its sensitivity. The conjunctiva and the membrane of the ear canal, on the contrary, have no use in the respective phenomena of vision and hearing. These membranes are not the seats of the perceptions pertaining to these two senses; neither can they be classified as mucous membranes. Whence we may conclude that between the sensations of smell and taste and the purely internal affections, there is an analogy with respect to their organic conditions and their modes of receiving impressions, an analogy that explains their likeness of character and that shows us how these impressions, equally foreign to all perceptive forms, cannot be grouped under the class of perceptions to which the activity of the soul essentially and directly contributes.

We have already noted the intimate sympathy that links the sense of smell to the sixth sense, the extraordinary effect that the various impressions of this organ have upon the entire system and thereby upon the general sentiment of existence, now pleasant, now disagreeable. It is through this phenomenon that that remarkable sympathy operates which makes a mother attached to her young, and the young to their mother, and that makes it so that during mating season the two sexes seek one another out, recognize one another from afar, and precipitate towards one another; here we cannot doubt but that there is special feature that distinguishes animal emanations, either in the species or in the individual, a feature that animals, whose sense of smell is the most refined, never mistake. It even appears that that animal atmosphere that we were discussing above is variously modified according to the particular passions that the being from which it emanates experiences, and that it is instinct alone that teaches animals to differentiate these passions by their sense of smell, and to adapt their actions to it.

As for the sense of taste, we are not unfamiliar with the direct sympathies that link it to the functions of the internal organs or of the stomach in particular, all of whose vicissitudes and whims it follows. The internal impressions of this organ (*viscère*), which craves or rejects food according as it experiences a general affection of well-being or of discomfort, are always more or less mixed in with the sensations pertaining to the sense of taste, alter them, distort them, and contribute to giving them that character of indistinct impressions, inherent in the multiplicity of elements of which it is composed.

§3 Of the affections of sight

We have just considered the affective impressions from the point of view of external animal sensations relating to instinct, whose base, or at least whose predominant part, they constitute. If we now consider them from the point of view of sensations relating to perception or knowledge, of which they are an obscure and subordinate element, we find first, for the sense of sight, that corresponding to the immediate action of the luminous fluid on the retina is a particular affection that, remaining mixed up in the total phenomenon of objective representation, not distinguishing itself when this phenomenon takes place, not raising itself to the height of idea when it is alone and outside of objective representation, never itself produces an *image*.

Aside from the cases in which light beams act en masse upon the external organ and in which there is nothing more than a simple affection without any visual representation, there is little doubt but that there is also an impression relating particularly to each tone, to each shade of light, and it is for this very reason that this tint or that mixture of colours becomes more agreeable to us than any other, as a stimulant for the physical sensitivity of the eye, to that exact degree that constitutes the immediate pleasure associated with the use of this sense. I say immediate pleasure, because the direct visual affection I am speaking of here, pleasant or disagreeable in itself, has almost nothing in common with that pleasure of comparison and reflection which is afforded the trained eye by the extension and variety of perspectives, the vividness of sights, the harmonious proportions of figures, the concordant tones of colours. This sentiment of the beautiful, of the grand, for which sight is the primary organ, derives from another more elevated source and is only born of an intellectual effort that this is not the place to discuss. We shall merely observe as the principal mark of distinction that these superior sentiments derive from knowledge and are necessary effects of it, whereas the immediate affections long precede it and are independent from it, which suffices to justify a distinction that is established in Descartes' physiology.

The phenomena of direct vision, considered from the particular point of view that we are considering here, seem to exhibit a sort of vibratory property particularly characteristic of the immediate organ of sight; in virtue of this vibratility (*vibratilité*), impressions remain in the external sense with more or less force and duration, even after the external cause has stopped acting; it is this material shock that Buffon speaks of, etc.; spontaneously reproduced, these impressions can also combine together, follow one another in all different ways, doing so without any collaboration from perceptive activity and against the very efforts of the self, which vainly attempts to repudiate these adamant spectres.

Whence a faculty that I have characterized elsewhere under the heading passive immediate intuition, a faculty that is spontaneous in its exercise, independent of thought and of all reflexive operations, which, like all the determinations of instinct of which it is a part, subsists solely by virtue of the laws of the organism and of the type of cerebral elasticity that reproduces it. It is to such an *innate* intuition, as it were (for it precedes all experience), that we must ascribe those admirable phenomena pertaining to the instinct of certain animals that, after birth, reach immediatlely for the visible object adapted by nature to their nutritive needs. It is thus that there sometimes appear in the dark of night those spectres of the imagination that succeed one another before our eyes, successively take on a thousand bizarre forms, while the will is unable to turn away from them the organ of internal intuition from which they seem to arise. Those images that are now mobile, now faint, manic delirium, etc., are thus produced.

It is by giving full consideration to these direct sympathetic affections, of which the eye is a special sense, that one can evaluate the particular and too little observed nature that differentiates the immediate impressions made upon this organ by the light beams reflected by animate bodies, from those that are occasioned by other purely material objects: these initial impressions of light, modified by the animate organs that reflect them, especially those that emanate, as by scintillation, from those enlivened eyes in which sentiment and life shine, certainly produce rather particular immediate affections. How many unperceived impressions of this kind are communicated and exchanged immediately between various individuals who are unwittingly attracted or repulsed by a regard that penetrates them? It is by means of this living flame cast by the eye into the variable affections of the sensory soul that a passionate being energizes those who come near it and forces them, as it were, to harmonize with it (*se monter à son unisson*). I said the *sensory soul*: observe, indeed, that this is that purely affective part of man, whose special mirror is the eye; it is this affective part that paints itself whole in this mirror, and that can be read in it by a pure effect of sympathy; not so, or by similar means, do the phenomena of the mind or of the will penetrate and transmit themselves to the outside world.

§4 Of the affections of hearing

The sense of hearing, assisted by its supremely active tutor, speech and the voice, holds one of the highest ranks among those of intelligence. But we must still abstract from it, as it were, a very notable purely affective part that, confused in its ordinary state with the clear perception of successive and coordinated sounds, can nonetheless distinguish itself from these latter and emerge separate from them, in certain very particular modes of passive listening.

We cannot help, for example, but recognize the immediate effects of a material and truly imperceptible part of the sonorous or better soniferous (*sonifère*) impression that, starting from the primitively agitated external sense or even without the collaboration of this sense, stirs up all of internal sensitivity at its chief sources: thus, completely deaf have individuals been observed to experience particular affections in various regions of the body, especially in the epigastria, when one produces sounds of a certain timbre, and especially when they place their hand on the instrument from which these sounds emanate.[38] There is no doubt but that the very nerves of touch are the true conduits of the affective impressions, which are immediate

---

[38] A famous Parisian school teacher for deaf and mute children observed these results in his students, who were accustomed to describing their impressions as well as to expressing, with as much energy as truth, their sentiments or ideas. It was also discovered some time ago, in elephants from the Musuem of Natural History, that the tonalities of certain instruments can have an extraordinary effect upon the immediate affections that we are discussing, and through them upon certain passions that are linked to them, such as love, anger, fury, etc. (Note from the author.)

products of the shock or of a sort of sonorous undulation. In a state of perfect hearing, there is also a certain quality of sound, a certain timbre of voice or instrument, which arouses by itself, and independent of any effect related to the sense of auditory perception, supremely affective impressions, conducive now to awakening, now to calming various passions, at times to curing, at others to producing certain nervous illnesses. I myself have been witness to the extraordinary effects produced by the soft and melancholy sounds of a harmonica. I have seen people, too sensitive to withstand these sounds, shudder all over their body upon the first impression of them, be moved, shed tears and end up fainting.

Once again, similar affections, which are due to the immediate impression of sound, must be clearly distinguished and may even be separated from perception (*de la partie perceptive*) or from that rapid judgement that helps the ear perceive a harmonious pitch or melodious suite; even when these affections predominate, perception dims over (*s'obscurcit*); the more the sensory being is affected, the less the intelligent being evaluates and judges.

Note that the strictly affective part of auditory phenomena pertains to what one calls timbre in a sound and accent in a voice, and it is also for this reason that hearing is one of the chief organs of that sympathy which brings together and intimately bonds all beings endowed with the faculty to feel and to manifest what they feel by the various modifications of their voice, for each passion or emotion of sensory being (*l'être sensitif*).

Nature seems to have linked to each passion a particular accent that expresses it and made all those capable of understanding its sign sympathize with it. It is nature itself that inspires this profound cry of the soul, which all souls hear and to which they all reply in unison. Articulate speech, true intellectual expression is still far from the crib of infancy, and already a native instinct modifies the first wails to express appetites, needs, affections and incipient passions; already the mother, schooled by the same teacher, understands this kind of language; she replies in turn by other accented signs whose meaning sympathy explains and whose value it fixes.

This sympathetic power that accents and voices possess is also found in all the languages of primitive peoples, who have more sensations than ideas to communicate to one another. Such is also the extraordinary influence of those impassioned orators, who must learn to seize the inflections fit for moving the soul and to imitate or reproduce the sympathetic signs linked by nature to each of the passions he wishes to arouse. Such is that magic power not only of articulate speech as a symbol of intelligence, but of the accented voice as a talisman of sensitivity.

I cannot, without stepping outside the boundaries of my subject, which I have perhaps already exceeded, push any further the interesting overview of phenomena of this kind. It suffices for my purpose that those phenomena which I just laid out manifest that type of connection that quite certainly exists in this respect between the general facts of organized and feeling (*sentante*) nature, and those of a superior – intelligent and moral – nature. The various observations performed on the ill, the partial lesions of sensitivity, in certain external organs, its alterations in states of mania, delirium and vapor, especially in those very odd cases of paralysis in which external sensitivity is extinguished while perceptibility and motility subsist, all these facts and a multitude of others that strike the eye of the physiologist and of the experienced doctor, are as it were so many data that it is not a matter of *explaining*, but clarifying, verifying and tying together in a complete theory of the science of man. The contribution of physiology to this science emerges from all that we have just said: whence there will also follow a more precise application of that maxim of the father of medicine, which must be restricted within the limits that we attempted to establish previously: *quod de natura hominis manifestum quidpiam [cognoscere] non aliunde possibili fuit quam ex arte medica* (Hippocrates).[39]

Second article

Of internal affective impressions.

We place under this heading all those impressions received by the nerve endings of internal organs or produced in the very centre of these organs by certain intestinal causes that arouse them and immediately act upon them. These organs are made up of mucous membranes of the same nature as those that cover the internal of the *nostrils* and the surface of the *tongue*, which are the respective seats of the sensations of *odour* and *flavor* and whose external agents act on them immediately.

But it is remarkable that the impressions made upon such organs, thus disposed by bodies that immediately touch them, can only *affect* the sensory (*sensitif*) being, while there is nothing perceived by the *self*.[40]

---

[39] "[T]hat positive knowledge about human nature is not possible except by the medical art." Hippocrates, *De veteri medicina.*

[40] The functions of passive touch ought not be cited as an objection against me here, since it is not the object that first acts on the sensory organ and through it on the soul but, on the contrary, it is the soul or the hyper-organic motor force that first acts upon the sense and through it upon the object, which is only perceived or represented by its own force of resistance or antitypia, and not at all by its affective qualities. Take away these two forces, and the perceptions of touch (*toucher*) are reduced to the passive and immediate impressions of tact (*tact*), which affect without representing. (Note from the author.)

On the contrary, any perceived and represented object does not really act through itself on the sensory organ that represents it, but rather through an interposed medium or fluid, and the immediate impression of this fluid, which merely gives the soul the initial warning as it were of the presence of an external cause, or acts as a *sign*, as Reid says, is not perceived in itself, but always remains at the level of the most obscure *affections*.

But in comparing the organic conditions and circumstances that are respectively linked to each of the types of sensory and perceptive phenomena, we find that in the first case, the same membrane that is the immediate seat of the received impression is also that of the sensory function, which would no longer take place at all if the membrane were taken away, and would be different if the tissue or the structure of the same part were to change; in the second case, on the contrary, it is no longer the directly aroused or impressed membrane that is the seat of the perceptive function; this latter extends the impression further and no longer even has any relation to it. What relation, indeed, can one conceive between the faint impression of the luminous fluid on the retina, and the perception or idea of the external object, etc.? Thus the conjunctiva, though receiving an impression of light in a healthy eye, does not perceptibly contribute to visual perception, and if it becomes too involved in it, as happens in *ophthalmia*, or in a massive bombardment of light beams, there no longer is *perception*. The same effect occurs in the membrane that covers the auditory nerves and whose particular impressions have no essential and immediate relation to the clear perception of sounds.

Here we have a very marked difference in organic condition between the impressions that simply affect without representing, and those that represent, or serve to represent without affecting: a difference that, in concordance with the difference established by the testimony of intimate sense, helps us to establish the connections that exist between the two sciences and the ways in which they can help one another. We can infer from the important observation that we have just presented:

(1) that even supposing that physiology managed to explain affection by some interplay of organs, all these explicative theories would not even touch upon the phenomena of the mind's perception and the relation of externality, or causality on which it is founded;

(2) that there exists a real relationship between the organs of our passive external sensations, which are more suited to animal life and to instinctive needs than to knowledge; whence the character of exclusive or predominant sensitivity that is common to them

and that to a certain extent explains the sympathies of physical sensitivity we have spoken about;

(3) that in any given stimulation of internal organs, insofar as the part that receives the impression is at the same time the seat of sensory function, there can only be simple, passive and immediate affections in these organs, without any perception of the object or cause of immediate stimulation, which, not acting outside of the organ, cannot be perceived outside the self, and which has no *sense* of its own to represent it to the soul.

Thus, these multiple affections whose common derivative is physical life are not reflected in an internal sense. The kind of immediate touch that grasps them, or *becomes* them, is not consciousness; for it does not *know* itself, does not illuminate itself, and while these modifications incessantly vary, there is someone who *remains* and who *knows* it. The former is to the immediate affections of the *sensitive soul* what the latter is to the ideas or operations of the mind, to the products of its activity, and the difference that separates them and that precludes the thoughtful observer from confusing them, is that the latter has the ability to retire within itself (*se replier sur lui-même*) and to maintain itself present to a concentrated internal view; the other does not have any grip from which to grasp itself in any of its variable forms and disappears in the very instant that the *self* wishes to observe it more closely (*l'approfondir*), like Eurydice, whom a glance repels into the shadows.

If, then, we cannot follow them nor reach them directly by any appropriate sense, let us seek at least to link them to some signs that might help us to recognize them, by adopting that perspective from which the observer of the physical aspect of man meets up, collaborates and communicates with the immediate touch of the sensitive soul. Let us attempt to turn the discoveries of one to the advantage of the other.

To recognize these immediate internal affections, we would need, as it were, to catch their signs in the stages and circumstances of life in which they are dominant and isolated; in this state of native simplicity (*simplex in vitalitate*) in which the external senses are still silent and as it were *untainted by impressions* (*vièrge d'impressions*), where the power of effort and will that is constitutive of the *self*, the source of all the functions of an active and *super-animal* life, is merely *virtual*, still waiting to take action, or completely suspended; in those states in which the indelible imprint of an individual's organic temperament, to which his moral character is intimately linked, emerges in all its truth, without being modified, altered or disguised by so-called mental habits or the rule of an enlightened will; lastly in those cases in which the soul, deflected as it were by a sort of abnormal cause from the laws relating to its essence, no longer directs the immediate instrument of its operations, and lets it wander at the mercy of all the intestinal impulses. Such is the state that the fetus is in, or the newborn, or the individual during sleep, delirium or mania, which provide such extensive and instructive subjects of observation for the scrutinizer of the physical and moral in man.

Let us successively examine these various states, and let us seek out in them the signs as well as the effects of the internal affections pertaining to them.

§1 Immediate instinctual affections linked to the internal life of the fetus and of the nascent being

The determinations of *animal instinct*, revealed by unequivocal signs from the first moments of the individual's birth, are not formed in that very instant. We need to go further back to determine its origin and to recognize the first general features of this sensory (*sentante*) nature, subordinate throughout its development to the *law of continuity*, from which it never strays neither in the *living* nor in the dead.

Scarcely does the nascent being make its debut in external life, when it announces tastes and dislikes relating to the objects of this life. It executes various coordinated movements, suited to these same objects and tending towards the goal of preservation and nutrition. Now, if it is true that nature never makes any sudden leaps, shouldn't these appetites, these movements, refer back to a previous mode of existence in which they were prepared and preordained for the current end; but in what could this mode of *life* of the *fetus* have consisted before any external sense was turned on or activated by the objects pertaining to it, if not in the purely internal impressions of the organs that are generally recognized as being the only ones at work during gestation or the time at which the organic seed develops, is nourished and grows in the mother's womb.

The internal life of the fetus is not isolated and independent; like a piece of fruit having not yet reached full ripeness, it receives all the principles of its development from the animate tree that bears it; all the ingredients of life come to it only after passing through the internal organs of the sensitive being to whom its whole existence is linked.

Thus will the child be able to participate in all the organic phenomena that take place in the mother's womb and, as a result, in the immediate affections that are linked to them; but he will obviously participate only in these modes of specific impression; identity of organic functions, communality of internal immediate affections: such is the knot of sympathy that binds these two beings together, one of which, complete (*parfait*), is in possession of two lives, and the other, incomplete (*imparfait*), still enjoys but one.[41]

Organic sympathy finds its originating principle (*principe prochain*) in the tendency towards instinct, which seems to be a primordial law of organized nature: all the organs of the fetus that do not require the action of external objects in order to be activated will thus start by bringing themselves in tune with the mother's corresponding organs, and will repeat or imitate their functions. The internal life of the fetus will thus be complete before its relational life begins.

All the immediate impressions that hinge upon this initial life will be received and transmitted, either directly by its own organs, or sympathetically by the analogous ones of the mother, to the partial nerve centres, and will bring about the movements of instinct and that whole series of affective phenomena that can thereby imprint a sort of inalterable character on the physical temperament and as a result on the moral character. This is how far back one must go to find the source of various passions that escape the pure analysis of intellectual and moral phenomena, and of all the habits that may pertain to them.

It is through similar initial determinations of sensitivity, which are forged in the mother's own womb, and which quickly take on all the characteristics of energy, obstinacy and inflexibility typical of our oldest habits, that one can account, to a certain extent, not only for the appetites, penchants and inclinations of the nascent animal, but moreover for certain precocious passions, certain marked sympathies and antipathies towards certain things or persons, though one shall never be able to explain the obscure causes of this invincible attraction or repulsion.

Thus did Mary Stuart's unfortunate son, James VI, king of England and Scotland, having felt in his mother's womb the repercussions of the fear that had shaken the latter at the sight of the deadly sword about to stab her lover, David Rizzio, experience a shock or involuntary trembling his whole life on seeing an unsheathed sword, despite all the efforts he made to surmount this disposition of the organs, so much force does nature have, as the philosopher historian[42] who relates this fact observes, so unknown are the

---

[41] If it were well established that the traces of the mother's imagination can in certain cases leave a visible mark on some part of the child's body, we should then have to say that these imprints are transmitted by the action of the sensitive soul, and surely only a very high degree of emotion or affective stimulation, linked to the products of the mother's imagination, can bring about the transmission of these images through the affections with which they are associated. (Note from the author.)

[42] Voltaire, *General History*. (Note from the author.)

ways in which it operates. Thus, the most mild affections, the strongest and most constant penchants of human nature, especially those that hinge upon the preservation of the individual, the perpetuation of the race and the maintenance of the social state, such as the general sympathy that makes man tend towards man, the more specific sympathy that produces the attraction of the sexes, the need to propagate, as well as to commiserate, to love, to admire, etc., may pass invariably from mother to child, extend throughout all ages, all places, and thus mark the character of individuals, as well as the character common to the species, with a stamp that cannot be erased.

§2 Internal affections constitutive of the temperament and linked to the variable modes of the fundamental and immediate sentiment of internal life

That set of determinations that we may rightfully include under the heading *instinct* does not remain limited to the first stage of human life. The circle of phenomena over which that blind power continues to range, during the developmental progress of external life, far from narrowing, can on the contrary take on an even greater extension by meeting up at certain points with that of the passive habits that pertain to the functions of this new life. But beyond this circle in which instinct, the habits and all the modes of animal sensitivity are enveloped lies invariably the sphere of activity in which man, who has become *double* (*duplex in humanitate*), appears. Once again, we are not talking about a single order of facts, or of elements reducible to a single principle, to a single *feeling faculty* (*faculté sentante*). This inferior faculty does not transform itself[43] to produce the superior ones; rather there are really two orders of distinct and separate facts; so far as our minds are capable of rightly applying the principle of causality, or of recognizing and judging the difference of causes by the heterogeneity of effects, there are truly two principles, two forces that, without ever transforming into one another, act together, each in its domain, conspire and oppose one another, with each in turn having an unfair advantage . . . Who among us is not at every moment actor and witness to these intestinal battles?

There is not a single one of the internal parts of our body, said in his naive language a philosopher[44] who was an assiduous observer of such

---

[43] Condillac's doctrine. (Note from the author.)
[44] See the *Essays* of Michel de Montaigne. (Note from the author.)

phenomena, which does not often act against our will; they each have their own particular passions or affections that awaken them or put them to sleep without our leave.

Indeed, we clearly recognize the characteristics and *signs* of these affections peculiar to each part of the animate machine, or of those *partial passions*, as it were, in those sorts of appetites, of sudden stimulations, which start out in an organic centre, where they arose, such as in the sixth sense, the stomach, the heart, etc., extend out by a sort of *consensus*, take hold of all sensitivity, subjugate the imagination and end up absorbing any sentiment pertaining to the self, without whose knowledge all these brusque and automatic movements are executed and tend towards the object of passion with all the blindness, all the *fatum* of primitive instinct. It is here that we can speak of the triumph of a truly animal sensitivity.

It is from the habitual and more moderate cooperation of the immediate impressions of all these internal organs that affect one another by reciprocal sympathy that the general sentiment, or that sort of immediate vital sense, of which we have spoken derives, just as it is from the alternative predominance of each of these partial instruments[45] or from the variable manner in which their functions are carried out that the various modes of this sense derive, modes that are quite variable from individual to individual or in the same individual at different times.

The modes of this fleeting life thus flow like waves into the river that sweeps us away, and we find no place to throw down anchor. It is through them that we *become*, without any foreign cause and often without any possible return back to ourselves, alternatively sad and giddy, etc.

§3 Of the immediate internal affections that correspond to the states of sleep, dreaming, delirium, and mental alteration. The relationship that physiology can establish between these different types of phenomena, from which the philosophy of the human mind can also draw useful considerations

A judicious and profound analysis of the phenomena of the mind and of internal sense rightfully establishes, by purely psychological considerations,

---

[45] The reader is familiar with the ancient division of temperaments – sanguine, bilious, [melancholy, pituitous, or phlegmatic]; and one can see in the works of our most famous French physiologists, such as Cabanis, Bichat, Dumas, Richerand, how much this division

that the state of sleep consists in a temporary or periodic suspension of the exercise of the *will*, and of all the strictly *intellectual* phenomena that hinge essentially on this hyper-organic force. The exposition of Mr Dugald Stewart's doctrine on this subject conforms perfectly to my point of view. I shall limit myself here to deducing from it several important consequences supremely conducive to illuminating the subject of the question with which we are occupied.

(1) We know first of all, on the one hand, by the immediate testimony of intimate sense, that sleep differs from wakefulness only insofar as in the former state the *self*, which participates as a *witness* or as an *agent* in all the phenomena within its domain, is absent, and takes no active nor passive part in these phenomena during sleep. But on the other hand, it can be proved that the essential difference that exists between the two compared states hinges on the fact that the will or power of *effort* and of movement that is fully exerted in a waking state is suspended during sleep; whence it clearly follows that the apperception of the *self* is identical to that of the *effort* constitutive of wakefulness, just as the absence of this *self*, which characterizes sleep, is identical to the nullity of this effort, or to the suspension of the power that carries it out.

(2) This double identity, which I regard as a fundamental principle in psychology, emerges eminently from all the causes able to bring on sleep solely by suspending the will (or from the diversion or as it were the absorption of the *self*), as well as from all the singular circumstances and phenomena of passive sensitivity or imagination that are linked to this state in which individual personality is absent.

Among the circumstances relating to the state of sleep, those that strike us first are that persistence or even that excess of energy that various affections of sensitivity take on and the exclusive or predominate influence that they have upon the production or arousal of certain images that are associated with them by nature

---

is illuminated or clarified either by the predominance that various phenomena of this order demonstrate in certain internal organs, such as the heart, the chest, the liver, etc., or more generally by that of the two systems – sensory and motor. One can also see above all how important distinctions in the form of the moral character and the natural direction of the mind's ideas are linked by observation itself to these new doctrines on temperament; quite a fitting example to bring to light the kind of connection that exists between the class of facts with which the physiologist deals, and the corresponding particular class of internal phenomena that fall within the domain of psychology. (Note from the author.)

or by habit; moreover, the absolute independence that these affections and internal intuitions enjoy from any exercise of the *will*, from any presence of the *self*, and therefore from any intellectual phenomenon strictly speaking; in sum, the inverse relations that can be established by indubitable observations or *experiments* between these sensory or fantastic products of sleep and certain organic states of the viscera such as the stomach, the heart, the liver, etc.; it is thus possible to apply these phenomena directly to the physiological theories that align themselves in this regard with the facts of psychology itself.

(3) The phenomena of sleep observed in the way in which they follow upon one another and upon certain organic causes, indeed also serve to illuminate the joining or contact points between the two sciences, as well as to fix their limits.

But pressed for time, and myself startled at the extent of this treatise, I shall make haste to come to the most remarkable phenomena that accompany this state in which intellectual and moral life being suspended along with the *will*, which is their principle or *soul*, organic life as a whole, absolutely independent from this enlightened power, and an entire part of animal life that can also be exercised without its participation, reign supreme, and giving way to various phenomena that quite clearly cannot be attributed to them alone, thereby indicate the extent of their particular domain and circumscribe its limits. I am speaking of dreams and reveries (*des songes et des rêves*), the observation of which seems to me instructive for the metaphysician and the physiologist in that it can:

(1) bring the metaphysician and moralist to trace more exactly the limits separating the intellectual from the sensory in that spontaneous mode of exercise of the imagination that produces dreams, or even to unveil certain intimate secrets of thinking nature by the very aberrations of its principle; and

(2) call the physiologist's attention to singular and too little observed relations between the accidental lesions of certain internal organs and the nature of dreams, or what is the same, between certain immediate internal affections that prevail during a certain individual's sleep and the sort of spectres that then come and besiege his imagination.

And first, as to the causes that bring on sleep, it is not difficult to show that they act by making the influence of the internal organs predominate over that of the immediate instruments of the mind's operations or of the will's acts, the brain and the nerves, or by suspending the free exercise of the power of effort, and as a result, the apperception of the self.

If I were permitted to borrow the language of physiology, or to enter into the details of the delicate experiments and observations carried out or to be carried out on this quite peculiar branch of the phenomena of animalism, I would emphasize in accordance with great masters how the state of sleep is brought on by any cause that tends to concentrate the sensory and motor forces in particular internal organs, and thus to intercept or weaken the sympathy or reciprocal communication of all the parts of the system either between themselves, or with the general and common centre. I would speak of the effects of narcotics and liquors, which consist in first stimulating internal sensitivity, in letting the organs predominate, in thereby bringing about those flashes of spontaneous imagination that are so far removed from the calm, even and protracted light of intelligence, effects that are soon followed by a necessary collapse, in which the soul, already diverted from its laws, or stifled in its reign, seems to abandon the body, scarcely produces the degree of effort necessary to support it, and end us up handing it over to the laws of physics. I shall point out with respect to this successive invasion of the phenomena of sleep how delirium or mental alteration are, as it were, only a degree or circumstance of the same essential condition on which this state depends, namely the progressive suspension of the exercise of will and of effort, and as a direct result the obfuscation and total eclipse of the sentiment of the *self*, and of all that is strictly *intellectual*, etc.

If I were further permitted to give this subject the time and degree of development that it deserves, I would now lay the base of a new classification of dreams and reveries in which they would be ascribed to their organic causes or to the seats of these causes. I would show how the different parallel types of delirium, of vesania, or of alteration relating to the same cause can enter into equal or parallel classes.

I would distinguish, for instance:

(1) dreams or reveries that I would call *affective* or *organic* as having their seat in internal organs and as always being accompanied by more or less lively immediate affections;

(2) intuitive dreams or *visions*, which are in all probability due to a direct stimulation of the brain, are not accompanied by deep affections, and have a character of mobility and lightness that is peculiar to them;

(3) hybrid dreams in which there is a mixture of truly *intellectual* and sensory phenomena, the principle of thought or the *self* staying awake while the organs of external life are still asleep. Aren't these kinds of dreams that are typical of studious and meditative men similar to that sort of ecstatic delirium in which at times, on the point of death, when animal life seems all but extinguished, intellectual life takes on a heightened elevation and perhaps already participates in the form that it is about to assume? In this latter case, the dream's cause and seat appear to come from outside of internal organization.

I could also show how the confusion of these various causes, seats, or circumstances of dreams and of the types of mental alteration corresponding to them ended up leading astray two philosopher doctors whose salutary views were particularly focused on this last subject.[46]

However, it suffices here to point out a new salient proof of the services that the physiological or medical practice can render psychology, as well as those that the theory of the latter can render the practice of the former.

By dwelling a moment upon the character of *organic* dreams, which particularly interest us here, we observe that there could not be a more distinct relationship than that which on the one hand links the type of immediate affections that accompany a dream to the internal organs that are predominate and that are their seat, and on the other hand, the nature of these affections to the kind of spectre that besieges the imagination in various forms. It is thus that, falling asleep on an empty stomach, we dream of a table covered with meats we crave. If the stomach is too full, spectres appear that compress it and hinder any movement we wish to make to ward them off as in a nightmare. The sixth sense, aroused during a period of abstinence from amorous pleasure, brings about voluptuous dreams in which the imagination embraces a fantastic object and in this pleasant illusion fulfils nature's wish. The bilious plethora creates sombre spectres that arouse either fright or anger or hate and incite the individual to flee, or to brave chimerical perils; the sanguineous plethora presents the image of bloody combats, and we are all familiar with the case in which Galien

---

[46] Doctor Pinel, in his *Treatise on Mental Insanity*, ascribes everything to intellectual causes, and directs all his methods of treatment in this direction. Doctor Prost, on the contrary, sees in mental alterations mere organic causes, alterations or lesions of the abdominal viscera. Wouldn't it be possible to recognize by the very characteristics of the vesania whether their causes are purely organic, or moral first and intellectual by consequence? I do not doubt but that a series of observations carried out from the double physical and moral standpoint on this subject would succeed in illuminating the practice of art.

recognized the diagnosis of this plethora in the nature of a dream, and made the prognosis of a haemorrhage that was verified by the eventual outcome.

I abridge these examples to arrive at certain circumstances surrounding these phenomena that concern psychology more particularly, and that seem to me quite conducive to demonstrating still further the ties that unite it with physiological doctrines in the particular respect we are now considering.

Affective dreams have a certain character of depth, of persistence, whose effect not only manifests itself during sleep, but often extends further into the waking man's internal dispositions and frame of mind. How much more enamoured, for instance, in the happy cessation of expansive and tender sentiments, does one often feel for the object to which he owes the pleasures of a dream without even having any recollection of it? Conversely, can't a certain dreadful sentiment with which a bad dream filled our soul during the night bear an influence upon the secret dispositions of the day following it? How many good and bad actions might have their hidden source in the immediate affections that are the products of dreams already far removed from our remembrance?

What I believe I have confirmed by my own experience at least is that the sensory disposition that brought on the dream or that results from it long outlives the picture produced by the imagination (especially when this affection was profound) and can even contribute to resuscitating the latter by way of that sort of natural affinity that links certain affections of the sensitive soul to certain images of the *mind*. It is remarkable that in this reproduction of the spectres of sleep there is never perfect *remembrance*; the *self* cannot recognize itself in a mode in which it never really existed or that it was not able as it were to endow with the form of its personal identity. From another point of view, this reproduced dream does not affect us as if it were new; only the sensitive soul claims ownership of it by that sort of instinctive or sympathetic premonition similar to that which makes a mother recognize a child she has not seen since birth. In these instances the mind experiences a kind of unease, discomfort or uncertainty in linking to the familiar chain of existence an image that it cannot attribute to itself as past nor regard as altogether new and foreign.

I have also observed in myself another psychological effect that the immediate affections persisting after a dream have on this quite remarkable phenomenon of our moral existence that we call *belief*. Awakened, for instance, by a frightening dream, I found myself firmly believing in the actual existence of a spectre that had struck me and believing in it for as long as the passive affection of the immediate sentiment of fear lasted, so that if the same fearful disposition had persisted, nothing would have prevented me from believing that in some mysterious region there existed such and such a spectre, of such and such a colour, having such and such a form that my imagination retraced.[47]

This experience seems to me quite conducive to distinguishing three elements that are closely linked in one single product of passive imagination and that psychological analysis has not yet clearly distinguished, namely the image, the sentiment, or the immediate affection that is associated with it and that tints it as it were with its own colour, and lastly the *belief* that follows this affection and that adjusts itself to it. I thus believe we can conclude that there is a sort of faith or mechanical belief, the result of our animal or purely sensory nature, and quite different from that of intelligence, which reasons out its motives for believing, by disassociating affections and ideas so as to reduce these latter to their real and actual value.

I thus consider that a good analysis of dreams, considered from the double physiological-psychological standpoint, can be just as useful to the waking senses as the history of insanity, likewise considered from this double standpoint, can be useful to the wisest of men.

Second section

How certain functions or phenomena of the mind linked to spectres of the soul can influence the dispositions or functions pertaining to the body.

In the class of sensory phenomena that we have just examined, we felt warranted in expressly including those of a passive imagination subordinate in its exercise to the immediate affections of external or internal physical sensitivity. The products of this type of imagination have been insightfully analysed by several physiologists who dealt *ex professo* with the branch of facts we designate as moral or intellectual; it is indeed in this direction that they sought to determine the mutual relations between the physical or organic and what they call the *moral* in man – moral, which in the

---

[47] Th. Reid, in his work on the understanding, attacks the opinion of those who make *belief* in the reality of an object depend on the vivacity of the idea or image that represents it, etc. But it seems to me that he himself can be successfully challenged by experiments similar to those that I have just related, in which the kind and degree of the affective sentiment associated with an image indeed seems to be the fundamental principle of the belief in the reality of the object. It is true that we must clearly distinguish here the affection itself from the *image*, as well as this latter from belief; and this is what the philosophers of whom Reid speaks too often confused.

physiologists' sense can be further reduced to the functions or results of the functions of the various organs, internal as well as external.[48]

If we wished to limit ourselves here to this viewpoint after having shown in the previous section by a sufficiently large number of examples how the immediate affections of sensitivity could determine a certain mode in the production of images or spectres, and thus give way to what is called moral or intellectual phenomena, we would not need to insist further to prove by similar experiments or observations that these same phenomena, taking the initiative through some given cause, can in turn determine a series of corresponding sensitive functions and thus proportionately influence the functions of the internal organs that are the seats of the latter.

As a result of this same viewpoint, we should have already established not only the reciprocal connections, but also the kind of identity that exists between the two sciences, considered from the common point of view of their organic functions or their most immediate results.

Indeed, we have previously seen how internal affectability, aroused first, activates the imagination, or brings with it certain spectres analogous in kind to our dominant impressions, without stepping outside the same confine of facts, but merely turning them around. It will now be easy to show through various examples how the imagination can be spontaneously activated by a series of dispositions of the central organ that is its seat, that is, of the brain and of the nervous system of animal life, without any direct or indirect influence of the self or of internal sensitivity, and how the production of these spontaneous images, which no longer have the same character of depth, of persistence, of affective energy, nor therefore of reality, can arouse this dulled sensitivity at its main sources, bring it into harmony with them, and produce (*déterminer*) predominant images that transmit their direction to it after receiving its own.

---

[48] See the work of M. Cabanis entitled *The Relationship between the Physical and Moral in Man*, a work inspired by the spirit of physiological science and very rich in facts, especially of that kind that are only perceptible to the internal tact that we are discussing, but that, by singularly restricting, from too systematic a point of view, the meaning of the term *moral*, completely leaves out the whole intellectual and truly *moral* part of the phenomena of man double in humanity (*duplex in humanitate*). This great work seems to me supremely conducive to showing on the one hand the abuse and the danger of physiological doctrines in the explanation or deduction of the phenomena of internal sense, and on the other the type of truly useful applications one can make of these doctrines to a particular class of sensory phenomena that occupy a necessary place in the philosophy of the human mind. (Note from the author.)

The affections of sorrow, joy and timidity, or of courage, hope and fear can thus arise now from certain causes that can only act on the imagination, now (or more often, as we have seen) from those immediate affections all relating to causes that act directly on internal sensitivity and thus give the objects of the imagination itself the form and colour peculiar to them.

Thus, in erotic dreams, for example, as well as in the reveries of the same sort that the waking man may have, it is now the predisposed internal organ that awakens the imagination, now the imagination, arousing itself with certain spectres that it produces and caresses, which awakens the sense that on its own is dozing and inert. There are easy-to-recognize characteristics that distinguish these two modes of arousal, one sensory and the other imaginary, one of which corresponds to fickle, superficial and shifting tastes and appetites, whereas the other constitutes the animal passions, which are vigorous, deep and stirring like the *fatum*.

Thus again, with respect to the different types of mental alteration, the observer, borrowing – it is true – the data of a reflective sense, or the enlightenment of psychological analysis, can distinguish the distinctive colour of the spectres pursuing the madman, or the kind of *affections* that accompany them, and even the absence of these latter, if the cause of alteration is inherent to certain primitively injured or altered viscera.

Now, if this cause carries the object into the heart of imagination itself, whose functions it immediately subverts, it is evident that in this case the treatment must be administered according to a psychological or moral plan, and in the other case, according to purely organic or physical views. To choose among the objects most conducive to awakening ideas or sentiments contrary to those that pursue the madman, to shield from his view all the objects that are linked to his predominant delirium, to create a strong diversion for all the habits of his imagination, etc., such is the substance of this moral treatment, whose details psychology can do so much to illuminate, and whose means to justify.

By generalizing here the results of the preceding analyses and applying them to all the facts of the same kind, in which imagination and internal immediate affectability are present, follow upon another, and predominate over one another successively, after having likewise distinguished all the hybrid modes that are included under the too vague and too general heading *passions of the soul* as sensory passions and imaginative passions, we would still find ourselves induced to form an altogether separate class of intellectual passions in which there reigns a moral sensitivity that is to the ideas of the mind what physical sensitivity is to the spectres or spontaneous products of the imagination.

It would follow from this division, as we have already sufficiently shown in all that precedes, that the role that *passive imagination* plays in a given series of affective phenomena does not characterize the intellectual or moral aspects of a *passion*, and that it is not in this direction that we may claim to adapt physiological doctrines or experiments to an order of facts that is in fact quite removed from them by nature. On the contrary, all the signs of this *fatum* peculiar to the organism in the forced production of certain images, the character now of mobility, now of obstinate persistence, the power that these spectres possess to subjugate thought, to enchain the will, to obfuscate the light of consciousness; such indeed is the nature of the physical passions that, of whatever nature their means, their products or their results may be, constitute, at the very heart of thought, a sort of spiritual reflex (*automatisme*), to which the laws of physiology may to a certain extent be rightfully applied.

But here it is expressly a matter of the intellectual passions or the relations that the phenomena pertaining to the mind may have with the affections of the sensitive soul, and as a result with certain functions of the organs immediately linked to these affections. This is a sort of *transcendental* physiology whose subject seems indeed to defy those who, wishing to analyse the relationship between the physical and moral in man, were not able to see this *moral* dimension except in further physical effects.

The brevity of time and the length of this treatise allow me only to present a few abridged observations on this last subject. The *imagination* or the faculty of internal intuition, forms as it were the link between the two natures, or if you prefer, between the two sorts of elements that constitute double man (*duplex in humanitate*). But while on the one hand imagination communicates with the internal organism that arouses it with its immediate impressions and that it affects with its spectres, on the other it corresponds with the hyper-organic force, which dictates its laws to it, when the reverse is not true. Imagination, thus regulated by the will, acts upon the sensitive soul, and produces that superior order of affections we call *moral sentiments*.

The order of subordination that I have just indicated seems to result from a simple fact of intimate sense or from a very consistent observation, although so often unknown or concealed: namely that moral sentiment only emerges following an intellectual effort or certain perceptions or comparisons of the mind (such is the sentiment of the *beautiful*, of admiration, of surprise, etc.), whereas immediate affection, as its name indicates, precedes all perception, and often produces its entire effect in the organism before there is even any apprehension of the mind.

Perhaps the will has absolutely no dominion over its *affections*, nor even any *direct* influence on its moral sentiments,[49] but it does have an influence on the ideas or images of the mind, especially insofar as they are linked to conventional signs (*signes institués*); these images can in turn awaken the affections or sentiments to which they are associated by nature or by habit.

Whence the possibility of arousing certain affections in the sensitive soul, and as a result certain revolutions in the organs of internal life, with a certain *intellectual* regimen, a certain direction impressed upon the will or the understanding, as well as of influencing these other faculties to a certain extent with a certain regimen, either physical or moral. To gain serenity and be content with ourselves and with our acts – that is all . . .

The circumstances of this double regimen

Let us indicate the principle circumstances of this double regimen and the observations that, in this superior order of relations, are the foundation for the harmony between the two *sciences* or between the two parts of the complete science of man, and for the type of services that they can mutually render one another.

(1) Each of us can observe in himself that that the direct perceptions of the senses, the images of intuition, as well as the most elaborate ideas of intelligence, received, produced and contemplated in turn with variable internal affective dispositions, for instance, with an immediate sentiment of well-being or of discomfort, of extreme force or of weakness, of self-confidence or of discouragement, of activity or of indolence, in sum of organic equilibrium or of organic turmoil – that the perceptions, I say, or intellectual ideas corresponding to each of these affective states, seem to adapt to the tenor of internal sensitivity and to taint itself as it were with its distinctive colours; this, in passing, is a notable circumstance that gives our moral and psychological ideas in particular such a variable form in certain individuals, or in the same individual at different times, and that as a result prevents certain truths of *consciousness* or of intimate sense from equally penetrating into all minds, from there enjoying an equal clarity even when

---

[49] It does not fall to this power to awaken or imitate any of those impressions that form the basis of our existence, which is immediately happy or unhappy. These likeable or pleasant affections, which depend upon an even higher moral nature, are equally outside the limits of our power; much worse, they would lose all the natural sway that they have to move us and would even cease to exist, in the instant in which the will sought to dictate laws to them and to reproduce or to imitate their supreme charm. (Note from the author.)

expressed unequivocally (*sous les expressions même univoques*); this, in a word, is what so often renders these truths incommunicable by the signs of language, and will always preclude them, whatever Locke and Condillac may have said, from being *proved* like mathematical truths, which are the most separated from any affective mixture.

But, since, firstly, the modes of internal sensitivity have such a marked influence on the way in which each individual feels about his own ideas, or since his intellectual progress truly depends on this very disposition, or on the degree of confidence he attaches to the products of his understanding, on the force with which he adheres to them, on the sentiment of internal calm or serenity with which he contemplates them; and since, secondly, there is an art, although little known, little practised, and hardly susceptible to being reduced to fixed rules, a wholly physiological art, that of directly influencing the general tenor of internal sensitivity, either by the regular combination of appropriate dietetic means or a certain use of *things* that medicine describes as *unnatural*, or by the use of certain substances recognized for their stimulating, calming or mollifying effects; by directing more in-depth analyses and more varied observations in this direction, physiology could thus to a certain extent perfect its means by immediately modifying internal sensitivity, individual temperament and as a result the dispositions of the moral character, and lastly, in a more mediate way, the faculties of the mind, whose *inaction* or mobility, whose pleasant or arduous exercise, are linked to these dispositions. If ever we had a good theoretical and practical treatise on the great art of *good living*, of right acting and right thinking,[50] surely this book, the most useful of any that could written, would be the work of a physiologist *ex professo* who would unite the spirit of his science with the most extensive psychological and moral knowledge.[51]

(2) But it must be recognized that in the order of phenomena that we are considering here, the predominant influence seems indeed to come from psychology; or in other words, there seems to be still more ways to act upon

---

[50] Mr Cabanis, at the time of his death, so ill-fated for the progress of the science of man, pondered the foundations of that important work that he wished to entitle *Art of Living*, and that was to be followed by a more extensive investigation to which this latter was merely the introduction and whose title was to be *Perfecting the Human Species*. (Note from the author.)

[51] "For the mind depends so much on the temperament and disposition of the bodily organs that, if it is possible to find a means of rendering men wiser and cleverer than they have hitherto been, I believe that it is in medicine that it must be sought." Descartes, *Discourse on the Method*, VI. The philosophers of antiquity, the Pythagoreans especially, had recognized this truth and the physical regimen was of first importance in their precepts and principles of wisdom.

the immediate affections of sensitivity, on the organic dispositions of the body, with a certain regimen of the mind, than to influence the phenomena of the mind with a certain order of modifications impressed upon the body; and we can establish the truth of this result in advance from all that was already said about the relative independence of the principle that wills, acts and thinks in man, and about its superiority, and about the sort of uniqueness (*l'espèce de mise-à-part*) of any fact pertaining to intimate sense or the self, considered with respect to that which is organic or purely passive in animals.

If, for instance, as we cannot doubt from experience, a given mode of exercising thought turns out to be facilitated by certain sensory dispositions that relate to the machine, there is no doubt but that a vigorous and strong will often fights against the organic obstacles in the way of its goal, and manages to triumph over them or even to change these dispositions altogether, to induce (*déterminer*) an altogether different series of organic movements and thus to break the chains of the *fatum* (*quod fati foedera rumpat*).

The author of this treatise, of a weak and sickly constitution, bears within him the living example of this dominion or *mediate* influence that the will can exercise upon the organic and affective dispositions of the body, by a direct effort that it exercises upon the operations of the mind, or on the ideas, which it tends to reduce to a certain regular pattern (*type*). How many times has he observed in himself how an intellectual effort undertaken by fighting against the most marked organic inertia or against an affective state of turmoil, of unease, of suffering, produced, after an obstinate and protracted effort, a state of activity, of serenity, of internal calm and equilibrium?

How much does he experience each day how the very functions of the most crude organism bends and adapts itself to the exercise of thought, by adhering to the same intervals of indolence and activity: for example, digestion, the organic secretions or excretions are or are not carried out, according as one does or does not work at his habitual hours, etc.?

These observations and a host of others that each of us could carry out on ourselves, if we were less distracted by the external world (*du dehors*), more accustomed to seize and to conserve an empire of will (*un empire de vouloir*) that our immediate affections tend incessantly to usurp, but that can extend over these affections themselves, to an unlimited point, which no man has perhaps yet conceived nor tried to attain. All these facts, I say, of internal experience, prove rather clearly the infinitely precious aide that even practical physiology or medicine stands to gain from a more exact knowledge of the active faculties of man and of the moral or intellectual regimen that is to be prescribed to them in order to change the modifications of a depraved sensitivity, to remedy various organic disorders or, what is still better, to prevent them, stop them from arising or from becoming ingrained, by certain diversions of the ideas or by the opposing effort of a vigorous will.

The reader is familiar with the method of scolding iron that Boerhaave so propitiously used, in the hospital of *Haarlem*, to stop the convulsive trembling of several children whom a particular sympathetic affection incited to imitate one another; there is no doubt but that similar diversions, and especially the acquired habit of a greater dominion over oneself, would succeed in cutting out from the root nearly all the causes of nervous illnesses and even of several other organic alterations.

(3) It is another fact of internal observation that the health of the soul influences that of the *body* at least as much as the latter does the former; the imperfect harmony that the will produces and conserves between the ideas of the mind and the moral sentiments can quite certainly bring about or to a certain extent maintain that other harmony between the functions of the organs or the immediate affections of sensitivity that constitutes the healthy state and the well-being of the machine.

These two kinds of health sometimes coincide wonderfully in certain privileged beings in whom the physical and the moral, each well regulated in its respective order, support one another and better themselves through one another. But the example of such a harmony must be rare, and it is precisely with the objective of making it more common that the two sciences we are discussing can, perhaps successfully, unite all their theoretical insights and all the data of a double observation, *internal* and *external*.

When the physical is not properly adjusted, the soul is necessarily affected by this disorder in a sombre and painful way. If the self then allows itself to be absorbed, as it were, by these painful affections, the disorder increases and redoubles by this very same cause; but it is possible and it happens in certain cases that the self morally suffers or takes pleasure while the sensory principle is affected in a contrary way, or even that a given moral sentiment is founded upon an opposite affection.

We thus sometimes take pleasure in our sad affections, in our sorrows, in our woes; we ourselves experience a certain melancholy enjoyment, by participating as sympathizing witnesses in these movements of our internal *sensitivity*; or a truly intellectual and moral contentment in bearing witness to a superior force within us that does not allow itself to be overcome. Conversely, it can happen that our intellectual being is internally afflicted by a sort of uncontrolled joy, which our sensitive being experiences, and which our good sense condemns and represses.

In the rear of the theatre of consciousness there then occurs an effect similar to that which we experience during dramatic performances. This interesting observation could not escape the attention of a philosopher so supremely reflective as Descartes. 'When we read of strange adventures,' he says in his *Treatise on the Passions* [§ 135],

> in a book or see them acted out on the stage, this sometimes rouses sadness in us, sometimes joy, or love, or hatred, and generally any of the passions, depending on what kinds objects are presented to our imagination. But we also get pleasure from feeling these passions aroused in us, and this pleasure is an intellectual joy that can originate in sadness as much in any of the other passions.

Here indeed is the intellectual component of *passion*. How could we confuse it with the *sensory* component; how could we fail to distinguish immediate affection from *reflective* and truly *moral* sentiment?

Now, in the ordinary modes of our *sensitive* and moral life, these affections and sentiments can be in harmony and reinforce one another – which preserves the health of the soul and of the body – whence internal anguish is born, a state of turmoil and of disorder, *moral* as well as *physical*.

It seems certain to me, for instance, that in the abominable passion of crime, the intimate sentiments and the cry of the soul that the villain seeks in vain to muffle, constitutes a state of perpetual torment at the very heart of a brutal and savage joy. The ineffable pleasures of charity, on the contrary, increase in duration and intensity by the active participation of the soul, which experiences the pleasant affection of satisfied moral instinct, and *consents* to it, in all the range of meanings that this word can take on, and redoubles it by sharing it . . . Thus the usual state of a charitable soul is the most agreeable that it is man's lot to experience in his current mode of existence. It is the most perfect type of health the soul can have, as well as an efficient means to achieve the *health of the body*.

What shall we say of those purely intellectual enjoyments, so agreeable, so elevated, which derive from the very exercise of the most noble faculties of the mind and of the soul, to the contemplation or discovery of that eternal and immutable truth towards which a superior nature gravitates?

Do you feel all that is ineffable and almost divine in that intellectual or moral enjoyment of the true and the beautiful, whose image fills the soul with an enthusiasm such as that which inspires the poet with those strokes of the sublime or reveals to the geometer that admirable chain of relations that ties together rotating spheres and all the parts of this immense universe?

Do you believe that raptures such as those of a Pythagoras, or of a Archimedes, on first catching sight of a truth so ardently sought after, are not quite conducive to establishing, between the life of the soul and that of the body, that precious solidarity that conveys to one the energy and the sort of immortality belonging to the other?

It is perhaps for this reason that one finds among the most distinguished scholars such a great many examples of *longevity*, and of exemption from certain infirmities that attack those men whose animal life is worn out more quickly by the very inertia or indolence of their intellectual and moral life.

(4) However, it is in the coming together of the *two lives* and in their equal participation that one finds the enjoyments that are more natural and more accessible to the common man, dominated by so many kinds of imperious needs. But in this very mixture of the impressions of the organism and the sentiments of the soul and the ideas of the mind, we shall still have many occasions to note to what extent the activity or the energy of one can influence the happy and regular succession of the other; and especially to what extent the hybrid enjoyments, in which the intellectual element predominates, are more lively and pure! It is thus that when, at the dinner table, or after a meal, we give ourselves up to the charms of an animated and instructive conversation, to the pleasures of poetry, music and all that which can impart a certain degree of animation to the mind, the organic functions are carried out with more ease, and even the pleasures related to the satisfaction of our needs becomes more agreeable!

How much we would have to say about the hybrid pleasure of love, in which the phenomena of both lives accompany one another, succeed one another, or predominate over one another in an alternative order of influence that so often blends the physical and the moral aspects of passion; in which the senses borrow from the imagination that charm, that irresistible allure imparted to the loved object, and in which purely sensual pleasure plays so subordinate a role ...

How unequivocally a thousand detailed facts prove to the observer of phenomena relating to the sick and to the healthy man the particular influence upon the accidental circumstances of a given illness that is exercised by the ideas and sentiments with which the individual is struck, the confidence he has in the person caring for him, the hope of being cured that he holds out for certain remedies, or, on the contrary, unfavourable bias, mistrust, fear ...

But I forget that I am not here giving a complete course on moral therapy, and it suffices to show by several incontestable examples that the science of moral and intellectual man could illuminate the practical science of physical man, just as the latter could provide the former with useful applied data (*données d'application*). This is what I believe I have shown in this last section, from which one may deduce as a general result that those who disdainfully reject *psychological considerations in investigations whose object is the body*, or who restrict their use to their application to certain illnesses, are just as unjustified in their refusal as are those who believe they could *explain* the phenomena of the mind and of internal sense by physical doctrines or experiments.

6 Maine de Biran and the Mind–Body Problem: An Introduction and Commentary on *The Relationship between the Physical and the Moral in Man*

Pierre Montebello, University of Toulouse II, le Mirail

Maine de Biran (1766–1824) is considered the inventor of the philosophy of consciousness, and at times he is celebrated for developing a philosophy of the *lived* body. But his signature discovery does not lie in the feeling of free activity coinciding with personal existence and self-consciousness, nor even in the feeling of a subjective body, lived as one's own; it is rather the idea that our consciousness derives from a relationship of effort between voluntary force and body. This relationship includes the body, by essence. The body is there; it exists; it is part of consciousness. One cannot be conscious without a body, nor can one think without a body. But consciousness is characterized by a duality – voluntary force and body. Thus, the body does not belong to consciousness as a particular mode of thought, but as the other pole to the voluntary (hyper-organic) force that we exercise over our bodies. Thought and consciousness are born of this *polarity of forces* (resistance and will). This explains why our own psychological reality is never given in the form of an absolute. The absolute designates that which can be grasped in and of itself, in its substantial, objective, exterior unity, without any fissures, whereas the free, conscious, existing subject only perceives itself within a relationship of effort that constitutes it – a relationship that is at the heart of psychology.

In a sense, Biran never ceased opposing consciousness's *'life of relation'*[1] to the *metaphysical absolutes* that pose a subsistent reality, complete in itself, such as the soul or body. Biran wrote to Destutt de Tracy that one must consider 'the self in the unitary will, always the same, which is not in an absolute manner abstracted from all conditions, but only in relation to the whole of all the parts that obey it, in an *essentially relative effort* whose object, resistant but obedient, and whose subject (which only exists as conscious force in resisting its action) are *inseparable and are only constituted with respect to each other'*.[2] In other words, what is called consciousness, or existence, or thought, or individual liberty (all equivalent concepts), is given to us in a dual, heterogeneous, strained experience that at the same time is simple, unique, and incapable of being split into parts. Such is the 'primitive fact' that imposes itself upon us;[3] such also is the transcendental horizon of all philosophical consciousness and, for that matter, of all perception, all representation and all knowledge.

Although Maine de Biran's thought had a prestigious influence on the philosophers of his time and those of the late nineteenth century (in particular, Cousin, Renouvier, Ravaission, Tarde and Bergson), it faded little by little from memory before finding a renewed interest today. His philosophy has even been described recently as the precursor to Husserl's phenomenology (though Biran's philosophy differs in that it gives to the body a role that Husserl does not). In reality, if Biran's philosophy remains of interest to us, it is because we have not yet escaped from the question that it poses. Through his philosophy, Biran sought to explore an unexplored domain, a *terra incognita*: psychology – but without leaving the body. Biran's philosophy sought to give the status of explicit philosophical question to personal existence (or consciousness or apperception), which cannot be reduced to anatomy or psychology,

---

[1] Maine de Biran, *The Relationship between the Physical and Moral in Man*, p. 101.

[2] Maine de Biran, *Correspondance avec Destutt de tracy*, Edition Pierre Tisserand, Paris: Librairie Félix Alcan, 1930, p. 256.

[3] Maine de Biran, *The Relationship between the Physical and Moral in Man*, p. 69.

and whose phenomena are never truly grasped in and of themselves. The exploration of the phenomenon of consciousness requires a radically different method, an internal observation, a study of the acts of consciousness and of the way in which they envelop the body. No physico-physiological analysis is capable of reducing this singular mode of being and its unique apperceptive and phenomenal order. It is the feeling of this irreducibility that defines Biran's philosophy. While the clean divide between neurology and psychology does not exclude empirical correlations, physiological observation and psychological observation do not have the same foundation, are not talking about the same thing, and do not describe the same causal chain. The masterful work, *The Relationship between the Physical and Moral in Man*, is a testament to Biran's modernity concerning the mind–body problem.

Because it does not have an objectivist perspective, Biran's philosophy is without doubt the first philosophy really to take into account the role of the body in the genesis of the intellectual and passive faculties. The body apprehended here is not the body of the anatomist (a spatial and objective body), nor that of the metaphysician (absolute substance); it is first and foremost that immediate and lived body through which sensations are situated and perceptions are constructed. This lived body, which is one with our existence, is connected to our voluntary power, and can only be known subjectively, is clearly distinct from the body of the anatomist, whose representation is objective and anonymous, and from the absolutist body of the metaphysician, which is pure exteriority-to-self of extensive substance. But this initial understanding of a subjective body could not become a philosophical problem so long as the very definition of consciousness as immaterial 'thinking substance' was taken for a definitive truth. Biran will destroy this construct of dualism by pushing the entire psycho-physical question towards that point of action within us: effort. If the feeling of personal existence coincides with effort, it implies the immediate apperception of an action exercised upon the body by the will (there is no need to understand how the body works; it is lived from within by being subjected to our motor power, contrary to the desiring body which is permeated by affects and passions). The lived body resides in a causal relationship between will and the physical body, without which there are neither sensations, nor perceptions, nor even apperceptions. This new idea of what must indeed be called the *corps propre* will have notorious success in psychology.

But what exactly does the term 'effort' indicate? What is the significance of effort as a relationship between a non-organic force and the body? First, it signifies that consciousness is not pure thinking presence-to-self, but an *activity*, which is not pure physiological presence-to-self, but tension and attention, and even intention. Effort is proof that consciousness is not a substantial reality; it is the uninterrupted activity that implicates the body in the genesis of sensory, perceptive, and reflective series. If effort is primary, one cannot construct a theory of the faculties without taking it into account. Our psychological activity implies a differentiated relationship with the body through which affects, sensations, intuitions, perceptions and reflections are distinguished. However, underlining the preeminent role of the body in the relationship to hyper-organic power in no way involves reducing the intellectual faculties to an objective and neutral body. Such an approach would destroy the body's internal and intimate connection to the will and, with it, the psychological sphere.

Biran's philosophy is an urgent reminder that ultimately no one has been able to trace the genesis of our psychological activity from the primitive will/body duality that is constitutive of the phenomenon of consciousness, nor sought to probe the modalities of its exercise, nor even attempted to define the main functions of consciousness. What is feeling, perceiving, remembering, imagining, reflecting? Must we adopt the attitude of many modern philosophers of mind who claim to rid us of these questions? Is it possible, in constituting a philosophy of mind, to do without reflecting on the unique acts of thought in relation to the subjective body? These are questions that surpass historical doctrines; they involve tacit philosophical assumptions that will long structure the modern discourse on the relationship between mind and body.

Let us note a strange reversal of our era, perhaps a sign: after a long eclipse, the problem of mind has resurfaced, as John Searle noted disappointedly in his book *The Rediscovery of the Mind*, one chapter of which bears the telling title: 'What's Wrong With the Philosophy of Mind'[4] In this book, Searle simply rediscovers Biranian arguments. He critiques the materialism that prevails in the science of mind, the bad reductionism, the lack of a *subjective ontology*. What's wrong with the philosophy of mind is exactly what Biran denounced a long time ago, namely the tendency to objectivize the mind, which over the centuries has taken the form of cybernetism, emergentism, functionalism, etc. Many have accepted the idea that physical reality is the only reality that exists is physical reality, and that there is no point retaining the concept of psychological experience. At bottom, Searle laments that modern science let itself fall into this trap, that it tacitly accepted that mental phenomena are reducible to causal physical

---

[4] John R. Searle, *The Rediscovery of the Mind*, Cambridge, MA: MIT Press, 1992.

structures, computational states, behavioural dispositions in which none of the properties of consciousness can be found.

Searle's attitude stems from a desire to rethink the relationship between mind and body. Searle re-examines the tenants of 'biological naturalism', which still dominates today and which holds that '[m]ental phenomena are caused by neurophysiological processes in the brain and are themselves features of the brain'.[5] This framework is simple enough, but what is not simple are the postulates on which it rests. The problem is not merely that we do not know what to do with irreducible consciousness, non-'phenomenic apperception', as Biran would call it, nor that we cannot escape from interminable discussions about the 'mental', 'phenomenal' or 'immaterial', nor that an *objective* methodology appears inappropriate as soon as the psyche is at issue. The problem is also, according to Searle, why this methodology has dominated the mind–body problem.

Searle adopts Biran's position almost verbatim in asserting that Descartes, in substantivizing thought, paved the way for the objective analysis of subjectivity. In the chapter of *The Rediscovery of the Mind* entitled 'What's Wrong With the Philosophy of Mind', Searle undertakes to account for the materialist tradition that is 'massive, complex, ubiquitous and yet elusive'.[6] According to Searle, the materialist tradition is founded on several axioms that rest upon an undemonstrated metaphysical postulate: the belief that reality is physical. Even if this belief goes against our deepest intuitions, materialist solutions are inspired by the obvious fear of Cartesian dualism: that one cannot imagine a substance that is not *res extensa*. And believing in mentalism is believing that consciousness is not physical.

Searle attacks materialist discourse by developing a four-part argument:

(1) The mental is tied to consciousness.

(2) Reality is in part subjective: mental states have an irreducibly subjective ontology that is in the first person and non-neutral. Searle laments:

> It would be difficult to exaggerate the disastrous effects that the failure to come to terms with the subjectivity of consciousness has had on the philosophical and psychological work of the past half century. In ways that are not at all obvious on the surface, much of the bankruptcy of most work in the philosophy of

---

[5] Ibid., p. 1.
[6] Ibid., p. 9.

mind and a great deal of the sterility of academic psychology over the past fifty years, over the whole of my intellectual lifetime, have come from a persistent failure to recognize and come to terms with the fact that the ontology of the mental is an irreducibly first-person ontology.[7]

(3) 'Because it is a mistake to suppose that the ontology of the mental is objective, it is a mistake to suppose that the methodology of a science of the mind must concern itself only with objectively observable behavior.'[8] Searle thus rediscovers the very Biranian idea of a first-person science. This idea forms the basis of Biran's constant critique of Condillac. Thought cannot be observed from the exterior. Thought is essentially activity, and the position of the spectator presupposes an inevitable passivity. Subjectivity cannot be understood in the third person.

(4) 'The Cartesian conception of the physical, the conception of the physical reality as *res extensa*, is simply not adequate to describe the facts that correspond to statements about physical reality.'[9] Conceiving the real in micro-physical terms, or believing that everything is made up of particles, is the inevitable paradigm of modernity. But it is also a simplistic belief system that does not resolve anything since it does not give precision to reality's differentiated modes of existence. By accepting as given the Cartesian definitions, dualism, like materialism, exhibits a certain incoherence. Searle remarks that 'materialism is ... the finest flower of dualism'.[10] Biran has said the same thing a hundred times. Indeed, once two substances are posited, the belief that physical reality excludes the mental leads inevitably to materialism. 'The mistake is to suppose that these two theses are inconsistent.'[11] The reality is that one leads to the other; the mind ends up having the same experimental status as the body. How else can one understand the relationship between two realities that have nothing in common? But, more broadly, how can one escape from a dualism that leads so inevitably to the monism of matter? Finally, how does one deal with all these

---

[7] Ibid., p. 95.
[8] Ibid., p. 20.
[9] Ibid., p. 25.
[10] Ibid., p. 25.
[11] Ibid., p. 28.

intermediary processes: grammar, coding, programming, unconscious, etc.?

What must be underscored above all is that, for Searle, 'the fact that a feature is mental does not imply that it is not physical; the fact that a feature is physical does not imply that it is not mental'.[12] This position undermines the foundations of scientific materialism and calls into question the postulates that have been commonly accepted over the last half-century. Physicalism deals with the mind on a physical level and claims to identify mental states and brain states. If consciousness is a mere cerebral process, mental states can be reduced to processes of cerebral physiology – or alternatively to functions. Nonetheless, contrary to the various forms of functionalism that attempt to break the mind down into a series of simple mental processes that can be compared to the basic operations of a computer, few experiments shed light on the brutal affirmations of an identity between the mental and physical. Functionalism is more fertile because it draws upon artificial intelligence to arrive at … an impasse. According to functionalism, '[a]ny system whatever, no matter what it is made of, could have mental states provided only that it had the right causal relations between its inputs, its inner functioning, and its outputs.'[13] Thus, the brain is no longer the only object possibly endowed with mental states. Such an analysis coincides with behaviourism by excluding all subjective and affective references. As Searle notes, this full-blooded materialism, in the Cartesian manner, holds that the brain is not really important to the mind! But all these materialisms are not the same. Identity materialism is not that same as functionalist materialism, which rejects the strong type-type version of identity (since the functions can also be produced by a computer), and is not the same as emergent materialism, which attempts to surpass identity itself by affirming that mental states are caused by the interaction of subsystems of the brain and emerge from cellular components. How is this emergence accomplished? What does it consist of? The transition problem remains.

For Searle, the 'irreducibility' of consciousness is nothing mysterious; it derives from our existence, from the subjective experience we have of it, from undeniable structural qualities: fine sensory modalities, unity of states of consciousness, intentionality, subjective feelings …[14] This is not to say

---

[12] Ibid., p. 15.
[13] Ibid., pp. 41–42.
[14] Ibid., p. 118ff.

that these mental states are not *supervenient* with respect to neuro-physiological events (emergentism), or that they lack a real causality. Contemporary discussion of these issues has often been very confused, and disconnected from reality. Sometimes it is argued that the irreducibility of consciousness proves that dualism is correct; other times, it is argued that this irreducibility mars the scientific process by creating an exception in nature. But although it is likely that 'macro mental phenomena are all caused by lower-level micro phenomena',[15] this does not prevent these macrophenomena from possessing a reality, an ontological sphere of their own. We can understand this fact by transcending the tendency to objectify (and to fall into spontaneous dualism) whereby we consider as of lesser being, or as nothingness, anything that does not belong to the microphenomenal level, or anything that cannot be reduced to it. There is a 'causal efficacy' to the macrophenomenal level that cannot be denied. That new forms of top-down causality arise from the relationship between micro and macro does not diminish the real causal features of macro-physical forms. In other words, if consciousness is a characteristic property that emerges from neural systems, it cannot be reduced to the mere *physical structure* of neurons, but involves the *causal interaction* between these neurons or parts of the brain. This also means that consciousness has a real causality that can only be explained by the *causal behavior* of neurons.[16] Searle distances himself from reductionism as much as from radical emergentism, which holds that 'consciousness could *cause* things that could not be explained by the *causal behavior* of the neurons'.[17] Finally, he denies any intermediary, any common background between the two levels of brain and conscience:

> There are brute, blind neurophysiological processes and there is consciousness, but there is nothing else. If we are looking for phenomena that are intrinsically intentional in principle to consciousness, there is nothing there: no rule following, no mental information processing, no unconscious interferences, no mental models, no language of thought, no 2 ½-D images, no three-dimensional descriptions, no language of thoughts, and no universal grammar.[18]

---

[15] Ibid., p. 125.
[16] Ibid., p. 112.
[17] Ibid., p. 112.
[18] Ibid., p. 228.

That clarifies things; psychology must account for the phenomenon of mind in and of itself.

Without realizing it, Searle basically reinvents Maine de Biran. *The Relationship between the Physical and Moral in Man* articulates many of the Searlean arguments that I just laid out. The motto with which Biran began *Relationship* speaks for itself: 'O Psychology, preserve thyself from physics.' By violating this precept, the emerging science of man attempts to objectify thought, to read thought through the movement of brain fibres. The project of a science of man is haunted by the dream that the inner workings of thought can be completely unveiled, and by the belief that we can put thought 'into images'.

Very generally, if thought is broadly understood as an activity, it cannot be described as a thing. An activity is not a structure of any kind. We can certainly establish a relationship between structure and activity, between conditions and conditioning, but we also must understand when conditions no longer explain things – and are incapable of doing so – because the acts specific to thought can only be examined by considering a higher apperceptive order. Biran does not stop repeating this position.

To put thought into images (modern imaging technology aids this metaphysical project without ever questioning it) is not really to explain thought, to say what constitutes acts of thought, or differences between affects, sensations, perceptions, memories and thoughts:

> Can all modes, ideas or acts that enter the mind also be subjected to an external perspective and grasped in the material traces of received impressions? Are these impressions themselves not in some cases the product of acts that are perceived before them or without them? Are there not thoughts, inner wants, which can in no way be read from the outside, or be represented by any kind of *image*? To conceive of them, would one not need to identify with the active and knowingly productive force of such acts; with the *ego* itself that is felt or perceived in its operations, but not seen as *object*, nor imagined as phenomenon?[19]

What is troubling in the desire to put thought into images is the way in which it defaces our singular activity and utterly nullifies the differentiation process by which we distinguish between feeling, perceiving, remembering, imagining, etc. Thought reduced to images is thoughtless thought, akin to

---

[19] Maine de Biran, *Mémoire sur la décomposition de la pensée, Œuvres complètes*, V. III, Paris: Vrin, 1988, p. 326.

the lifeless life of the mechanistic Cartesian paradigm. Knowing what thinking means cannot consist in reducing every thought process to its underlying hardware; it requires us to examine multiple features of experienced consciousness. When we attempt to translate psychological life into what Biran calls 'the movement of the fibres', we lose the personal individuality and the movement of consciousness. Just as the body is not equivalent to life, psychological life cannot simply be equated to animal life, for '*internal fact* cannot be conceived or felt outside of the individual's sense of its *cause or productive force*'.[20] Biran often quoted the formula of Boerhaave: man is simple in vitality, double in humanity. *Homo duplex* means that human physiology is complicated by an additional causal, psychological order.

Thus, Biran's critique of the phrenology of Dr Gall proclaims the divorce between two emerging sciences: neurology and psychology. Gall's phrenology may seem laughable when it attempts to explain coquetry in women or thieves' propensity to steal by means of physiological flaws. Gall's project is nevertheless the first robust attempt to connect the manifestation of mind with organic structure, the intellectual faculties with cerebral organs: 'The various properties of the soul and spirit each have various organs, and the manifestation of these properties depends on their organization.'[21] Biran immediately understands that such a theory brings the relationship between physical and psychic into a new episteme, into a metaphysics of manifestation that subordinates thought to the image and the visible. The entire science of man takes this very path. Does this science seek a clear correspondence between the intellectual faculties and the brain? In this context, one often speaks of dispositions of the mind (in the double meaning of a *topos* and a *habitus*, a brain mapping and a mental development). For the phrenologist, a disposition of the mind reflects not only an ability but an arrangement of the skull's surface. The mind itself forms a bodily protuberance, sticks out, offers itself to sight, becomes legible in the silent arrangement of cranial convolutions. The mind leaves the inner sphere, abandons its immateriality, becomes an image for the viewer, a boney text for science. The paradigm of the complete determination of man – a paradigm that is so prevalent even today – is based on the implicit metaphysical principle that the mind can be exhibited in spatial and material form: 'This doctor must have told himself at the outset: I must throw all of interior man into a kind of relief, so that one may know him by

---

[20] Maine de Biran, *Mémoire sur la décomposition de la pensée*, p. 331.

[21] Gall, *Sur l'origine des qualités morales et des facultés intellectuelles de l'homme et sur les conditions de leur manifestation*, Paris: T I, Librairie J.B. Baillière, 1825, p. 433.

inspecting and touching the bumps of his skull.'[22] The secret hope of this enterprise is clear, its unspoken dream is transparent: to make thought visible, legible. Thus, the physicalist paradigm is accompanied by a fantasy that also permeated Cartesianism (embodied in Descartes's mistake regarding the thinking *substance*, which paved the way for a *physical* characterization of this impersonal substance): the fantasy of a radical unveiling of thought. To go behind the curtain and see thought, see the movement of neurons perfectly isomorphic to our actions. Is this not the dream of neuroscience? To read man as one reads a letter, to map out man – neurologically and genetically.

The extreme violence of this new paradigm consists in separating the individual from herself, turning her mind into unravelled physicality, and assigning to science a power that deprives the individual of its own truth, for this truth is only revealed after death. The subject is expelled from her own existence, from her own dimension of being. The truth of the individual is subjected to anatomical inspection and only emerges in the cold anonymity of death. To put thought into images is to objectify the subject, physiologize psychology; it means perpetual confusion between physical and psychic, imagination (which sees only extended things) and apperception (existence):

> The sense of sight is dominant in human organization, to it we reduce all; it communicates its own forms to the entire system of our signs and our ideas, and one need not look further for the cause of our penchant to move always toward the outside, of our general disgust of interior observation, of the challenges that are unique to this study, whether we are simply collecting phenomena, or especially when we are expressing them, and to transmit them by appropriate signs. *It is by reducing to the sense of sight the principles of language and psychology that we managed to exclude the facts of reflection or inner perception, and thus put the whole intellectual system into representations, all of thought into images.*[23]

Biran is not questioning the procedure of science. He does not dispute the need to correlate heterogeneous phenomena to clarify what belongs to physiology and what belongs to psychology. So long as anatomophysiology

---

[22] Maine de Biran, *Discours à la société médicale de Bergerac, Œuvres complètes*, V. V, Paris: Vrin, 1984, p. 68.

[23] Maine de Biran, *Essai sur les fondements de la psychologie et sur ses rapports avec l'étude de la nature*, Edition Pierre Tisserand, Paris: Librairie Félix Alcan, 1932, p. 367.

seeks to establish vital conditions, it is within its rights. But it cannot claim to reduce apperceptive and reflexive phenomena to these conditions. Its analysis must stop at the organic without claiming to determine from the outside the forms that the intellectual faculties take on for inner sense; these are two different orders: 'This relationship of coexistence between the facts of two natures excludes any parity, any analogy, any immediate and necessary relationship of cause and effect, or between the acting force and its product.'[24] By relying on the joint observations of the physiologist, who observes vital functions, and the physiologist, who observes intellectual faculties, the psychologist can teach us how psychological facts are linked to the organic conditions without which they could not manifest themselves or take place. But she can tell us nothing more; she can give us no insight into the nature of the organic causes that purportedly produce thought. On this issue, one may formulate all sorts of hypotheses, but 'in each case', says Biran, 'you will only imagine or form a *representation* of types or modes of movement which have no relationship with the self's sensation or perception, nor with any of the phenomena of internal sense'.[25] The conditional organic relationship is not a causal relationship capable of taking us from the organic to the psychological. The relationship between condition and conditioned is a relationship of existence: if the condition does not exist, the conditioned does not exist. The anatomophysiology goes further: it claims to assign a causal link; it holds that the condition *produces* the conditioned.

But it's not so simple. For example, regarding the question: 'What is the faculty of understanding which is particularly impaired as a result of organ damage . . . imagination, memory, attention, thinking, etc.', physiology leaves its domain and must borrow from psychology.[26] What force guides and psychologically actualizes vital conditions? Can we identify it by its mere structure? Gall himself was aware of the problem: 'I do not mean that our faculties are a *product* of organization; that would be to confound conditions with efficient causes. I limit myself to what we can submit to observation.'[27] However, by assuming an analogy between faculties and organs, Gall already has gone too far according to Biran; he thereby destroys the empirical method on which he claims to rely, goes beyond experience.

---

[24] Maine de Biran, *Discours à la société médicale de Bergerac*, p. 39.

[25] Maine de Biran, *The Relationship between the Physical and Moral in Man*, pp. 57, 60, 78, 90, 128.

[26] Maine de Biran, *Dernière philosophie, Existence et anthropologie, Œuvres complètes*, V. X-2 Paris: Vrin, 1989, p. 41.

[27] Gall, *Sur l'origine des qualités morales et des facultés intellectuelles de l'homme et sur les conditions de leur manifestation*, Paris: T I, Librairie J.B. Baillière, 1825, p. 189.

Empirical observation can show us how often or how consistently these heterogeneous phenomena correlate to each other. But the phrenologist goes far beyond this method when he claims to locate the productive centre of thought in organic conditions, or when he claims to be able to situate within organic structure the psychological faculties themselves. In so doing, he continues to confuse organic conditions and psychological causality. And if he reflects on this relationship that he established surreptitiously, he is forced to admit that, to locate a psychological faculty, he must first have the inner sense of this faculty; he must first have some apperception of it. What does Gall mean by the term 'faculty'? On what psychological experience does he base its value?

Gall does not at all realize that his starting point for dividing up the brain mass into parts is precisely these 'actually distinct' faculties that derive from inner sense and that are the subject of psychology. The idea that the faculties are naturally divided is based on the inner feeling that we have of their distinction. And in fact, Biran wonders whether we can even establish the meaning of these faculties on any other basis than the value that they have psychologically for the subject, the inner sense of their distinction. Gall did not end his inquiry there because he did not see the problem. He did not dwell for a moment on the feeling of an internal psychological distinction of intellectual faculties, because he was so preoccupied with discovering an assignable link between brain organization and mental faculties. 'Who will deny,' he writes, 'that the inclinations and faculties are the domain of the physiologist?'[28] Gall nominally distinguishes faculties without knowing how they are formed, nor what operations of thought they echo, nor how they are differentiated by inner sense. Without worrying in the least about psychological analysis, he gives a conventional value to each faculty, then assigns *ex abrupto* a given faculty to a given cerebral zone or protuberance. Gall fixes the value of these faculties without any psychology. Gall's analysis is so permeated with the morals of the time, those of a certain era, that Biran asks ironically if brain forms vary in nature according to the type of society and the degree of civilization in which they emerge.

A physiological division tells us nothing about the meaning to be given to the corresponding psychological faculties; this calls for an entirely different investigation. Biran attempted to defend the point of view of psychological understanding against the emerging hegemony of physiological explanation. He emphasized the need to consider a dimension

---

[28] Gall, *Sur l'origine des qualités morales et des facultés intellectuelles de l'homme et sur les conditions de leur manifestation*, p. 10.

of being in his own originality, that of the psyche. The psyche is indeed constituted in direct relation to the body, but can never be reduced to the body of the anatomist: 'Whatever we do,' Biran writes, 'there will always be absolute heterogeneity or complete lack of analogy between the two orders of facts.'[29] 'Miniature neurology', as Bonnet called it, was driven by the hope of a full determination of the brain that would amount to a complete reading of man, a complete prediction of his actions. But this desire to reconstruct the life of the psychological faculties by the summation of infinitely small components is a chimera. The subject lies neither in this spatial dispersion nor in its functional dissemination. However you look at it, the psychological sense of our own activity is never elucidated by anatomophysiological analysis, which can only provide the ever more complicated conditions of this activity.

Biran's interest in the relationship of thought to the body led him to raise a second, equally modern problem. He saw that consciousness is always traversed by something that it does not create but that is imposed upon it. He thus developed a deep theory of the impersonality of emotional life, which immerses us in the unconscious order of spontaneous sequences of images, movements, passions, affects. From this point of view again, nothing is 'more informative for the reasonable man than the history of madness.'[30] Biran's *Journal* is a wonderful testament to the impotence of thought when impersonal life rises up within consciousness like a dark and tormented background. This vital impersonal background threatens at every moment to engulf awareness and to collapse the exercise of active faculties. The threat is serious – serious enough to poison an existence and be the object of a journal. In this sense, Biran's *Journal* is not an autobiography. It does not tell the story of a life; its only topic is the impotence that threatens thought. 'There is no balance in my being. I think of nothing, I am nothing.' 'Empty thoughts and meditations.' 'I have no ideas or views of any kind; I lack energy: my moral being is destroyed.' 'Inability to think.' 'I have no more thoughts.' The *Journal* is the testimony of a growing inability to 'exist', to bring oneself into being. It is the sign of a life that escapes, that escapes from the subject to the point that we can probably say this text foreshadows the relationship between romanticism and melancholy.

Biran finds here a whole plane beneath consciousness that extends, as it were *existentially*, his studies of dreams, delusions, magnetism, and somnambulism. What is at issue in Biran's *Journal* is quite simply the discovery of an affective unconscious. Biran has even been compared to

---

[29] Maine de Biran, *The Relationship between the Physical and Moral in Man*, pp. 71, 92, 93.
[30] Maine de Biran, *Discours à la société médicale de Bergerac*, p. 105.

Freud in this regard. Indeed, Biran painted an unsettling picture – based on the simple observation of himself – of the spontaneous associations of affects, images and movements that arise from the concentration of sensory or motor forces in the internal organs or brain, and that inhibit thought:

> The current mode of exercise of conscious force itself depends on the condition and specific arrangements of the body on which the force is deployed, and thus all the changes that we experience in the state of our faculties, in the sad or pleasant feeling of existence, in the disorder or order and harmony that we feel in ourselves and that we enjoy outside ourselves, depend upon certain organic conditions, which it is not in our power to change and over which we have even less power in that they are the very sources of our power and of our will.[31]

An individual's temperament depends primarily on affective life, which for each of us takes on the allure of *destiny* (Freud also speaks of a *destiny of the drives*). Affective life is characterized by spontaneity, by the eclipse of the self and the will. And thus a very unpredictable, insistent, fluid life, consisting of bizarre, strange associations, starts to cross consciousness without being in any way constituted by consciousness – a life that 'works in us without us'. This life consists in the persistence of affective traces and spontaneous resonances of affects, persistence of images linked to affects and spontaneous association of images (in irregular, bizarre combinations, aggregated without connection or order), persistence of motor determinations (responses to excitative stimuli), and spontaneous production of movements. Spontaneous reactions are felt at all levels of affective life, in all phenomena that are associated with it. Pure affects, image-affects and movement-affects are the fabric of a sensory life that exists beneath consciousness, the marker of an 'absolute nullity of consciousness'. Affect is the positive mode of existence radically cut off from the ego. The *Journal* says that we find this mode 'whenever the intellectual nature is weakened or degraded, thought is dormant, the will is limp, the self is absorbed in sensory impressions, the moral person no longer exists; in sum, whenever our nature, mixed, double in humanity, becomes simple in vitality'.[32]

These spontaneous associations of affects, images and movements form an underground stream into which our general sense of existence is tossed;

---

[31] Maine de Biran, *Journal*, III, Neuchâtel: Editons de la Baconnière, 1957, pp. 317–318.
[32] Maine de Biran, *Journal*, III p. 286.

they give us this 'vague feeling of a kind of inner life that we might call impersonal as there is not yet a person or ego able to see and know'.[33] It is not a psychic unconscious that Biran discovers, but a somatic unconscious that permeates consciousness and alters its concatenations, often precluding them from even occurring – which explains Biran's melancholy. This affective life is the ultimate domain of the unknowable. It is what the individual feels without thought, what he cannot communicate to himself and others, an unfathomable background, an invincible otherness within oneself: from affective life 'comes the inability which we all experience to know thoroughly what one of our fellows is as living and feeling and *to show what he is in himself*'.[34] Affective disorders are not likely to be illuminated by an act of consciousness. They flee as soon as consciousness is exercised. They cannot be memorialized as they are not linked to acts of consciousness. Hence the impression of a fleeting, mobile, elusive life, which runs through us and opens within us its unpredictable successions, which can border on delirium. For Biran, the concept of destiny has no other source. He expresses this rising of life, this emergence of the moving background, this choppiness of the surface caused by the movement of the depths – in short, a life that one cannot connect to our voluntary acts: 'The power of destiny, which was one of the most powerful theatrical forces, is perhaps but an expression of this fact of internal sense that shows us, in the depths of our being, a kind of organic necessity opposed to moral freedom.'[35] Our first destiny is this unconscious life to which 'we are forbidden to return'; it is that 'part of our being to which we are most totally blind'.[36] Biran's philosophy of the body captures these dual modes of the body, which depend on whether or not it enters within our voluntary power: as anonymous power of life and as personal power to exist, as unconscious affective life and as personal conscious life, as involuntary activity and as voluntary effort. Conscious life does not free us from the power of rich emotional life. Indeed, it tends to channel it, to connect it with voluntary acts, but what the *Journal* teaches us is that nothing can ever fully emancipate the subject from the threat of a momentary or radical dispossession.

Our baseline feeling of existence is thus the expression of the general communication of sensations, sometimes pleasant, sometimes painful – 'of

---

[33] Maine de Biran, *Journal*, III, p. 288.

[34] Maine de Biran, *Discours à la société médicale de Bergerac*, p. 29.

[35] Maine de Biran, *Journal*, III, p. 291.

[36] Maine de Biran, *Journal*, III, p. 291.

the infinite multitude of simultaneous impressions' that flow from internal nerve centres. This makes up the baseline tone of our existence, the gaiety or the unspeakable sadness that invades us, or inundates us, without our control. These 'various modifications of the general feeling of existence' form the background of our lives, and are a sign of our deep character. 'There is no mirror' for this part of ourselves, no face for this part of our face, no shape to this obscure and fluid life. Our ego is irreparably fractured by the moving background of affective life that overflows in us – a strange affective life that 'does not have the capacity to grasp itself in any of its variable forms and disappears in the very instant that the *self* wishes to observe it more closely (*l'approfondir*), like Eurydice, whom a glance repels into the shadows'.[37] Maine de Biran's *Journal* is the story of this foreignness to self and the melancholic echo it causes: never being able to fully belong to oneself.

Once thought is linked to the body, new questions arise: What becomes of thought if it is no longer closed upon itself, if it is not a substance that always thinks, if it does not stand in opposition to the body as that which is absolutely heterogeneous to it? What does it mean to think day by day, yet not at all times, to think with your body, not against your body, to think when effort alone – never substantiality – reveals us to ourselves? What does it mean if forming a plane of bodily resistance is necessary for thought to guide itself and think properly? This body that thought must create by habit, this plane of bodily resistance that it must erect within itself to lean upon, this consistency that requires all the operations of thought, hides a more mobile, fluid, fleeting body, the incessant flow of affects, movements, spontaneous pulses of the nervous machine, bizarre associations of all kinds that threaten at every moment to take us in an unpredictable direction, that reminds us every day how difficult thought is, always threatened from within by the powerlessness of thought, by imbecility and idiocy. Has there ever been a more beautiful testament to the impotence of thinking than this *Journal* of Biran, this profound meditation on the relationship between bodily forces and forms of thinking. 'It is these conditions that we experience too often,' writes Biran, 'where, absolutely incapable of thinking . . ., I rebel against my ineptitude, I try to pull myself out of it by applying myself to various things, I move from one object to another; but all my efforts only render my inanity more perceptible.' The *Journal* is not a diary; Biran describes it 'as being totally devoid of adventure'. The only adventure is that of the flashes and eclipses of thought; the only theme is that thought

---

[37] Maine de Biran, *The Relationship between the Physical and Moral in Man*, p. 117.

contains within it the very possibility of unthought in the form of agitations, delusions, nervous states – of these thousand affective movements of internal sensitivity that form a fluid body unfit for the consistency of effort. Biranianism is a unique experience of the disaster of thought that is the exact inverse of its freedom.

7 A Universal and Absolute Spiritualism, Maine de Biran's Leibniz

Jeremy Dunham, University of Sheffield

In France during the nineteenth century, the production of new editions, interpretations and expositions of early modern philosophical texts was a flourishing activity. However, it is important to recognize when examining the scholarly works of this period that such interpretation and exposition was almost never produced without an agenda. A favourable interpretation of one of the giants of early modern philosophy that shows them to be the natural 'father' of one's own philosophical perspective could act as a significant legitimation of this view and, consequently, could become a weapon in philosophical combat. In this chapter, I argue that Maine de Biran's interpretation of Leibniz, and in particular his 1819 *Exposition de la doctrine philosophique de Leibniz*, should be partially understood in this spirit. I show that the importance of Biran's *selective* Leibnizianism is clear already in the 1811 Copenhagen treatise; however, it gains added significance in the 1819 text since he, I argue, uses his selective interpretation as a defence of his own position and critiques the remaining aspects of Leibniz's philosophy to demonstrate the weaknesses of another philosophical position developed by one of Biran's contemporaries: the 'young professor' Victor Cousin. Furthermore, even after Biran's death in 1824, this strategic encounter with Leibniz turned out to be crucial for the development of nineteenth-century French thought. Not only did Biran present an alternative spiritualism to Cousin's eclecticism (which was to become the orthodox philosophy of the state); he also correctly identified its major faults, and left the seeds for its eventual overthrow. Understood as such, therefore, we can recognize the vital historical role played by Biran's short *Exposition de la philosophie de Leibniz*. It was in part responsible for a significant change of direction in French philosophy and its influence can be recognized in a lineage that passes through Félix Ravaisson, Pierre Leroux, Émile Boutroux, Henri Bergson, to Gilles Deleuze.

The question driving this chapter is: why did Maine de Biran believe it to be productive to engage selectively with Leibnizianism? I argue that there are three main reasons, and this chapter is structured so that each reason is addressed in turn roughly following the chronological development of Biran's thought. In §1, I show that by separating the a priori from the a posteriori aspects of Leibniz's philosophical method, Biran believed he could more distinctly bring to light a key part of Leibniz's metaphysics of experience. Contrary to previous commentators on Biranian Leibnizianism, I argue that Biran's project is not opposed to Leibniz's conception of force and experience, but fundamentally in line with it. Nonetheless, I do not suggest that Biran's project is reducible to Leibniz's, and in §2 I show how Biran used this engagement with Leibnizian philosophy to develop his own. I focus on (i) his defence of force contra Hume and (ii) his theory of the virtual, and I argue that these promising developments of Leibniz's metaphysics, although not without problems, are crucial for understanding both the fertility of Leibniz's system and the influence of spiritualism in French philosophy more generally. The final reason Biran engages with Leibnizianism is that he could use the argument for the necessity of the selection to present a clandestine critique of Victor Cousin's eclecticism. As I show in §2, Biran believed that his philosophy was a spiritualist development of the best parts of Leibnizianism; and, I argue in §3, he was able to use the opportunity of the 1819 *Exposition* to show the superiority of his spiritualism to Cousin's alternative by concurrently insinuating that the latter's was in line with Leibnizianism's worst parts. In the battle for the true heart of Leibniz's philosophy, Biran believed his own spiritualism to be the real descendant of the monadology properly understood.

1. Maine de Biran's selective Leibnizianism

Biran's 1811 Copenhagen Treatise opens with an epigraph from Leibniz's 1707 letter to Michael Gottlieb Hansch on Platonic philosophy

(D.II.222–25).[1] Both the choice of text and the way the quote has been cut are important. The choice of this reasonably esoteric text shows us that Biran must have already been deeply engaged in his study of Leibniz's work. Nonetheless, the most interesting point for understanding Biran's appropriation of Leibnizian philosophy is the cut. Here is the sentence in full, with the part used for the epigraph in bold:

> For we have now seen, from the pre-established harmony, that God has ordered all things so wonderfully that **corporeal machines serve minds and what is providence in a mind is fate in a body**.
>
> E.446: L.593

The relevance of the cut is that Biran believes that Leibniz's philosophy is crucial for presenting us with a way to reconsider the mind's 'providence' in relation to organic corporal machines. Nonetheless, Leibniz undermines this insight's full potential by overshadowing it with his rationalist theory of pre-established harmony (PEH). However, if we cut this latter part from his system, we are left with a philosophy of experience that is a stark improvement on either the Descartes-Malebranche-Spinoza rationalist school or the Locke-Hume-Condillac sensualist school. I call Biranian Leibnizianism 'selective Leibnizianism' because I disagree with the previous commentators on this work[2] who agree that the Leibniz whom Biran creates through this move is more Biranian than Leibnizian and the conception of force that results is distinctly opposed to Leibniz's own. On the contrary, I argue in this section that Biran was a remarkably insightful reader of Leibniz's philosophy, and a close reading of texts that were available to him, as well as of texts that were not, show that Biranian Leibnizianism is still recognizably Leibnizian. As I show in §2, it is an *ampliative* rather than a *distortive* Leibnizianism, even if, as I argue in §3, Biran's choice to write an exposition of Leibniz's philosophy was made with a significant strategic agenda.

---

[1] A key to the in-text references in this chapter can be found at the end of the chapter.

[2] Ernst Naville (1859) 'Introduction générale aux oeuvres inédites de Maine de Biran'. In: Ernst Naville (ed.) *Œuvres Inédites de Maine de Biran*. Paris: Dezorby, E. Magdeleine; Ernst Robef (1925) *Leibniz et Maine de Biran*. Paris: Jouve et Cie, Éditeurs; Naert, É. (1983) 'Maine de Biran lecteur de Leibniz'. *Revue de Métaphysique et de Morale*. 88(4): 499–513; Patrice Vermeren (1987) 'Les aventures de la force active en France: Leibniz et Maine de Biran sur la route philosophique menant à l'éclectisme de Victor Cousin. *Exercices de la patience*: 147–168; and, Patrice Vermeren (1995) *Victor Cousin: Le jeu de la philosophie et de l'état*. Paris: L'Harmattan.

Although Leibniz's philosophy was always a presence in Biran's writing, its importance considerably increased towards the end of the first decade of the nineteenth century. At the century's commencement, Leibniz is the audacious genius who attempted but failed to execute the impossible project of the universal characteristic (OMDB.I.297; II.290–291); yet by 1811 (as I suggest the epigraph is supposed to signify) he has become Biran's important influence: thinking *with* Leibniz became one of Biran's most important strategies for the development of his own thought. This is also exemplified by the fact that one of the mere two texts that Biran published after the 1802 *Influence de l'habitude* and before his death in 1824 was an exposition of Leibniz's philosophy. His change of attitude was principally encouraged by an engagement with two books: Joseph Marie Degérando's (1804) *Histoire comparée des systèmes de philosophe* and Madame de Staël's (1810) *De l'Allemagne*. The first caused a global change in Biran's attitude to philosophy's history. As Henri Gouhier[3] shows, before reading Degérando's text, Biran believed it was not possible to develop both the 'intense erudition' necessary for historical scholarship and the judgement and reflection necessary for progress in 'psychology'. However, the former's book proved that the two could be 'very happily reconciled . . . and even lend mutual aid to each other.'[4] Degérando showed Biran that the history of philosophy need not simply be thinking *about* a past great philosopher; thinking *with* a past great philosopher could be to do philosophy, and even significantly improve one's philosophizing. Nonetheless, it would be Staël's work (and conversation[5]) that would suggest to Biran the great profit that could be gained from thinking specifically with Leibniz and present in embryo the view of his work Biran would develop in his philosophy – especially in the 1819 *Exposition*.

Staël's engaging three-volume work on Germany was of the utmost importance for the reception of German philosophy in France during the first half of the nineteenth century.[6] *De l'Allemagne* was pioneering because it clearly identified both the problems with eighteenth-century French philosophy and the direction it should take in the nineteenth century. For Staël, the sensualism or Lockean empiricism that took hold of French and English philosophy throughout the eighteenth century was the 'principal cause of immorality'. Locke and Condillac's replacement of conscience and liberty with interest and determinism made philosophy the enemy of

---

[3] Henri Gouhier (1948) *Les Conversions de Maine de Biran*. Paris. J. Vrin, pp. 251–252.

[4] Gouhier, *Les Conversions de Maine de Biran*, p. 252.

[5] 'Conversation with this famous woman is always brilliant and animated' (JI.I.224–225).

[6] See Vermeren, *Victor Cousin*, pp. 35–39, to which the discussion of Staël owes much.

humanity and alienated it from the profoundest 'beliefs of the heart' (see MDS.III.29–30). Nonetheless, since Leibniz, Staël claims, the greatest German minds have taken a more productive route, one in tune with the spirit of humanity. They have shown there is an inextricable link between metaphysics and morality. This, she believes, is a profound discovery since it shows why philosophy must be studied by all educated minds. The difference between a philosophy of mind which defends the doctrine of the passive *tabula rasa* and one which defends the existence of the *causa sui* active mind which can draw truth from its own resources carries with it the greatest of consequences. It is the latter on which liberty and morality depend. The father of this 'true philosophy' is, according to Staël, Leibniz. He is both Germany's

> Bacon and Descartes. We find in this excellent genius all the qualities which the German philosophers in general glory to aim at: immense erudition, good faith, enthusiasm hidden under strict form and method ... everything in Leibniz displayed those virtues which are allied to sublimity of thought, and which deserve at once our admiration and our respect.
>
> MDS.III.58–59

After stressing her admiration, she proceeds to split Leibniz's work into two halves, a division Biran will follow. First, she claims that Leibniz's wild a priori reasonings are indefensible. He 'pushed his abstractions too far' (MDS.III.63), and the result – PEH and the theory of monads qua the universe's 'simple elements' – were gratuitous over-speculations. Nonetheless, when Leibniz resisted the temptation to be led astray by abstraction, and stuck to concrete reflection on the soul's inner workings, the results were among the most insightful in philosophy's history. His greatest achievement was to add the sublime restriction 'except the intellect itself' to the empiricist claim that there is nothing in the intellect that was not first in the senses (NE.111). This restriction is the result, and signifies his defence, of the activity of the soul, his experimental reflection on inner sense, his affirmation of moral liberty, and his maintenance of the 'moral being in its independence and rights' (MDS.III.69). This is the everlasting foundation on which the great German speculative systems were built.

Importantly, Staël insists that France's turn to the Locke-Hume-Condillac school has been an unfortunate detour. Had France continued to follow its seventeenth-century great minds, such as Descartes and Malebranche, it would now share the same philosophical opinions as those promoted in Germany. France's philosophical progress in the nineteenth century could be significantly boosted by a return to the systems of its early modern genii. Leibniz then should become a crucial figure for French philosophers wishing to reinstate the conversation with those intellects *outre-Rhin*, since 'in the progress of philosophy', she claims, 'Leibniz is the natural successor of Descartes and Malebranche, and Kant of Leibniz' (MDS.III.38). Nonetheless, despite emphasizing the era-changing importance of Kant's work, she is lukewarm regarding the necessity of studying it with the requisite rigour to master it. She even says that '[n]o one in France would give himself the trouble of studying works so thickly set with difficulties as those of Kant' (MDS.III.96). Her judgement that Leibniz provided modern philosophy's everlasting foundation while Kant was barely worth studying in original was probably a major contributing factor for why France's philosophy for the first three quarters of the nineteenth century is better understood as 'post-Leibnizian' than 'post-Kantian'.[7]

Biran follows Staël's evaluation of the most important aspect of Leibniz's metaphysics, since he too regards it is a system capable of providing a proper analysis of the inner workings of the soul. Furthermore, for Biran, it offers a metaphysics of personality, a way to do justice to individuality without it either being swallowed up in the all-encompassing power of the God of the occasionalists, or becoming, with the empiricists, the mere passive effect of impressions. Leibniz's metaphysics presents us with a 'universal and absolute spiritualism' (OMB.XI–I.151), a doctrine capable of conquering the inherent passivity in both the aforementioned positions, leaving us with a truly free moral subject. Again, metaphysics and morals are inextricably linked[8]. Following Staël further, Biran divides Leibniz's work into two parts: the first rationalistic, the second experiential. However, he advances on Staël by demonstrating that these two parts are fundamentally incompatible. First, we have the Leibniz of forces and free individuals, but second, we have Leibniz's rationalist God, or absolute, that, in common with the Gods of all of the Cartesian metaphysical systems, threatens to subsume the freedom of the individual under its all-encompassing power and leads to pantheism. In this section, I explain Biran's understanding of the experiential part, but I leave his argument for its incompatibility with the a priori part until §3.

---

[7] See Jeremy Dunham, 'From Habit to Monads: Félix Ravaisson's Theory of Substance. *British Journal for the History of Philosophy*, 2015–23(6): 1089–1105.

[8] 'Madame de Staël appeared to have been well aware of the intimate links which unite metaphysics and morality in a common principle' (JI.I.84).

Metaphysics begins, for Biran, with Descartes (OMB.VI.17–18). His philosophy marked its genuine commencement for three related reasons. First, he established the dividing line between the functions of the body and those of the mind while he, second, inaugurated the proper introspective method or 'way of reflection' to study the latter. Finally – and for Biran consequently – he made the testimony of inner sense the generative principle of all knowledge. Nonetheless, Biran argued that the Cartesian metaphysical system suffers from a serious flaw. The fundamental system is prone to slip towards pantheism. As soon as the idea of a 'passive' substance is introduced, the Cartesian metaphysics begins to collapse into a form of monism; both *res extensa* and *res cogitans* are swallowed up by the infinite substance – God. According to Biran's interpretation of Descartes's metaphysics, no power belongs to 'extended substance' through which it could cause itself to act. The only qualities that belong to its essence are extension, flexibility and changeability (AT.VII.31: CSM.II.20). As extension has no power of its own, whenever it feels as though we are resisting the power of a material object, we are actually resisting God. Unfortunately, extension is not the only passive substance in Descartes's system. For he argues that the distinction between creation and preservation is only 'conceptual' and the same force needed to initially create the world, i.e. the infinite force of God, is required at every moment to preserve it: duration is constant recreation (AT.VII.48–49: CSM.II.33). Thus, whenever it feels as though I voluntarily will an action, it is not the I that wills, but God. I have the desire (itself caused by God), but I am not responsible for the causal action (cf. G.IV.515: AG.165–166). The dynamic play of the mind and universe results from God's power alone. Biran argues that the pantheist consequence of this hypothesis is the same for all of the Cartesian systems. His logic is simple:

(1) God is the sole cause, and every other existing being is merely an effect of God's power.

(2) It is 'logically certain that all effects are eminently or formally enclosed in their cause' (OMB.XI–I.142).

(3) Every created being is enclosed in God and there is no real distinction between God and nature (by (1) and (2)).

Spinoza's route is different, but the destination is the same. For the Spinozist argues that if the distinction between extension and thought depends on a difference of *attribute* or *fundamental mode* alone, there is no reason why these attributes or modes should not belong to one ultimate substance. This logically follows from Descartes's definition of substance as a 'thing which

exists in such a way as to depend on no other thing for its existence'
(AT.VIIIA.24: CSM.II.210) and his belief that 'extension' and 'thought'
exist 'only with the help of God's concurrence'. Biran concludes that only
mysticism separates occasionalism and Spinozism, 'logic unites them'
(OMB.XI–I.142).

Leibniz's great merit is that he escaped the errors of pantheism by
developing a metaphysics of forces and refused to allow 'force' to be
subsumed under the power of the infinite being:

> To what did Leibniz grasp onto to keep himself from this dangerous
> precipice, which, since the origin of philosophy, has led the boldest and
> most profound speculators towards the empty concept of the *great
> whole*, *nothingness* deified, the devouring abyss that comes to absorb all
> individual existence? We must say it, the author of the system of monads
> was saved from this disastrous aberration only by the nature or the
> proper character of the principle on which he based his system; a
> principle truly one and individual – the primitive fact of the existence of
> the *I*, before having acquired a unique and absolute notion. A system
> that multiplied or divided the living forces in accordance with the
> intelligible elements or atoms of nature, would, it seems, prevent or
> dissipate forever those sad and disastrous illusions of Spinozism, too
> favoured by Descartes's principle.
>
> OMB.XI–I.140

While all Cartesian-created substances are, on the final analysis, passive,
Leibniz presents a metaphysics where all created substances are ultimately
active: *'Toute substance est force en soi, et toute force ou être simple est
substance.'* For Leibniz, rather than substance being a placeholder for forces
in which they inhere, force *constitutes* substance. While Descartes
'constructed thought with elements borrowed from a passive nature', Leibniz
'constructed nature with elements taken from the activity of the I'
(OMDB.VIII.223). Biran places a great deal of importance on a 1694 text
called 'On the Corrections of Metaphysics and the Concept of Substance'
(G.IV.468–470: L.432–434), and on one short passage in which he claims to
find Leibniz's whole system condensed. The passage follows (I have divided
it into five parts for analytical reasons):

> [A] from the concept of substance I offer ... follow ... primary truths
> even about God and minds and the nature of bodies – truths ... of the
> greatest utility for the future in the other sciences ... [B] the concept of
> *forces* or *powers*, which the Germans call *Kraft* and the French *la force*,

and for whose explanation I have set up a distinct science of *dynamics*, brings the strongest light to bear upon our understanding of the true concept of *substance*. [C] Active force differs from the mere power familiar to the Schools, for the active power or faculty of the schools is nothing but a close possibility of acting, which needs an external excitation or a stimulus, as it were, to be transferred into action. Active force, in contrast, contains a certain act or entelechy and is thus midway between the faculty of acting and the act itself and involves a conatus. It is thus carried into action by itself and needs no help but only the removal of an impediment. [D] This can be illustrated by the example of a heavy hanging body which strains at the rope which holds it or by a bent bow. For though gravity and elasticity can and ought to be explained mechanically by the motion of the ether, the ultimate reason for motion in matter is nevertheless the force impressed upon it in creation, which inheres in every body but is variously limited and restrained in nature through the impact of bodies upon each other. [E] I say that this power of acting inheres in all substance and that some action always arises from it, so that corporal substance itself does not, any more than spiritual substance, ever cease to act.

G.IV.469–470: L.433; cf. UL.VI.530: WFNS.35 &
G.IV.472: WFNS.22

This passage is so valuable for Biran for two reasons. First, the novel conception of force in [C] presents an alternative to the Cartesian theory of passive substance and thus blocks one route to pantheism; and, second, he believes it shows that the notion of force, which replaces substance, is gained from analogical reflection on the active nature of the primitive fact of our self-consciousness, and we can methodologically work from first-person introspection to metaphysical truths concerning souls, bodies and God. Most commentators have argued that by reading Leibniz this way, Biran has actually *reversed* Leibniz's method. Euthyme Robef argued that Leibniz introduced active force into philosophy to make it 'fully rational following the purely a priori type of objective truth'. Leibniz's concept of force is obtained from external origins and is 'objective, abstract, formal, and universal' and 'not at all subjective, inner, reflexive'.[9] Robef concludes that we could even say that Biran's and Leibniz's doctrines of active force diverge so profoundly that they are in fact opposed to each other. Rather

[9] Robef, *Leibniz et Maine de Biran*, pp. 22–23; cf. Navile, O.C.I.cv; Naert 'Maine de Biran', p. 511; Vermeren; *Victor Cousin*, pp. 55–56.

than 'spiritualize' nature, Leibniz 'materializes the mind': 'The reflexive notions of radical energy, active force, or tendency participate more in pure automatism and the passivity of matter, than in the final efficacy and freedom of the mind.'[10] From the passage above, we can see that this claim is not without some prima facie plausibility. In [B] Leibniz relates 'force' to his science of dynamics, and the examples he uses in [D] to illustrate active force as described in [C] are drawn from external sense perception, not from ideas of reflection. Nonetheless, I suggest that if we play close attention to [E], the real role of [D] is illuminated. In [E], Leibniz takes it for granted that spiritual substances never cease to act. He believes we cannot doubt this, because we have constant access to its proof: internal reflection. What needs to be shown is that this is true also of corporeal substances and this is what he attempts to show with the examples in [D], i.e. we are justified in going by *analogy* from all spiritual to all corporeal substances. Leibniz says elsewhere, 'nature, as is her custom, gives us several visible examples to help us work out what she keeps hidden' (G.III.340: WFNS.204). [A] bolsters this point by implicitly suggesting the 'principle of uniformity' (PU), which states that (when Leibniz makes it explicit) 'all the time and everywhere everything's the same as here' (G.III.343: WFNS.220–221). We can go by analogy to discover truths not only about the nature of created substances, but even about the ultimate substance: God.

As Paul Lodge has shown,[11] an interesting aspect of Leibniz's argumentation for this new conception of substance is emphasized in his correspondence with the Cartesian Burchard De Volder. In at least eleven letters, De Volder pushed Leibniz for an a priori proof to demonstrate that the essence of substance is active force. However, contrary to Robef's claim that Leibniz's concept of active force purely follows 'the a priori type of objective truth', Leibniz never attempted to and instead insisted that 'the fact is demonstrated a posteriori'. He tells him, 'I do not see how you could have doubts about the internal tendency to change in things since we are taught that there are changes in things by our experience of the phenomena, as well as from the inside, where the operations of the mind themselves exhibit changes' (LDV.279; cf. 157, 277, and 307). That

---

[10] Robef, *Leibniz et Maine de Biran*, p. 100.

[11] Paul Lodge, 'Leibniz on Created Substance and Occasionalism', in: Paul Lodge, and Tom Stoneham, T. (eds.) *Locke and Leibniz on Substance*. Routledge, 2014, pp. 186–202. I am grateful to Lodge for allowing me to see this work before publication and for a helpful discussion concerning Leibniz's work. The following quotes from the *Leibniz-De Volder Correspondence* and *Of Nature Itself* are from Lodge's article.

Leibniz considers this so obvious lends credit to my claim about the role of [D] and [E] above. Leibniz can then reason from our experience of internal activity to the nature of all substances via the application of the PU. Biran would have been aware that Leibniz uses such a method from works such as *On Nature Itself*. Leibniz there writes:

> if we attribute an inherent force to our mind, a force for producing immanent actions, or … a force for acting immanently, then … it is reasonable to suppose that the same force would be found in other souls or forms, or … in the nature of substances – unless someone were to think that, in the natural world accessible to us, our minds alone are active, or that all power for acting immanently, and … all power for acting vitally is joined to an intellect, assertions that are neither confirmed by any rational arguments, nor can they be defended except by distorting the truth.

G.IV.510: AG.161

What is especially interesting about Leibniz's two-step argument from experience is that he uses it in two ways relevant for Biran's purposes: First, in texts such as *Of Nature Itself* and the *Conversation between Theodore and Ariste* (see G.IV.589: AG.265), he uses it to argue against passive substance and occasionalism. Crucially, for Biran, the argument is used to allow ontological space for the willing subject. However, second, as Pauline Phemister[12] has shown, Leibniz uses it in relation to English empiricist philosophers such as Locke. This use is vital because Biran's work was an attempt to reform empiricism.[13] Biran's central methodological claim is that the true metaphysics or science of principles must start from introspection, i.e. the examination of *sens intime*. He writes that

> internal observation is nothing other than the present application of this sense to that which is in us, or which properly belongs to us, and whatever idealism may say, it is by focusing upon its testimony, and not by raising ourselves up to the *heavens* or by descending into the abyss,

---

[12] Pauline Phemister, "'All the time and everywhere everything's the same as here": The Principle of Uniformity in the Correspondence Between Leibniz and Lady Masham', in: Lodge, P. (ed.) *Leibniz and His Correspondents*. Cambridge: Cambridge University Press, 2004, pp. 193–213. I am very grateful to Pauline Phemister for many very helpful discussions during the writing of this article.

[13] See P.P. Hallie, *Maine de Biran: Reformer of Empiricism*. London: Harvard University Press, 1959.

on the wings of the senses or of imagination, that we may contemplate our thought and know our nature.

OMB.VI.5

The fundamental mistake of the empiricists has been, he argues, to leave the analysis of inner sense incomplete and to confuse it with the outer senses. His work is intended to be a development of an empiricism of inner sense which would entail the discovery of primitive facts that are not obtained by any process of deduction, but immediately experienced whenever we are conscious. As Phemister explains, Leibniz's use of the PU can also be seen as a reformation of Lockean empiricism. It will therefore be of profit to this discussion to summarize some of Phemister's main points regarding Leibniz's reformation of the Lockean PU, to show how Biran adopted and amplified this reformation.

Like both Leibniz and Biran, Locke's empiricism relies on a PU and he 'assumes that our sensory experience provides the standard upon which our understanding of the indivisible microscopic and the macroscopic aspects of the universe should be modelled'.[14] For Locke, this principle is applied solely to primary qualities. We can divide a grain of wheat however many times we like; the remaining parts will always possess such qualities. For Locke, as for Leibniz and Biran, *analogy* plays a vital role in his philosophical method: 'We can,' he writes, 'go no farther than particular Experience informs us of matter of fact, and by Analogy to guess what Effects the like Bodies are, upon other tryals, like to produce' (EHU.4.3.29; cf. NE.473). However, when Leibniz appropriates Locke's PU, he relies, as Phemister shows, on a fundamentally different conception of experience 'that demands a far wider application'.[15] When Locke uses the word 'experience', he uses it as a noun – it is that by which we receive ideas, but it is the ideas themselves rather than experience as such that interest him. In contrast, Leibniz uses it as a verb in the active voice. As Phemister shows, 'Leibniz's focus is . . . on the nature of experience itself. And this experiential state is one in which sensation and reflection are combined so that, through self-awareness he can understand himself as a thinking and perceiving being who is embodied and has sense-experiences of a world outside.'[16] This is a radical move, one which, in fact, is not given its full due if merely referred to as a reformation of empiricism. It is rather a true 'philosophy of

---

[14] Phemister, 'All the time and everywhere everything's the same as here', p. 201.

[15] Ibid., p. 204.

[16] Ibid., p. 207.

experience' which attempts to go beyond rationalism and empiricism to do justice to both the evidence of our external senses as well as the inner activity of our minds. Such reflection reveals to us our nature as spontaneous and active beings embodied in a material world governed by mechanical laws. This is the essential connection by which we are shown, returning to the epigraph, 'that corporeal machines serve minds and what is providence in a mind is fate in a body' (E.446: L.593). Most importantly, we can see from this discussion that rather than provide a philosophy in the final analysis opposed to Biran's, Leibniz's project from the perspective of the philosophy of experience is almost exactly Biran's project.

Patrice Vermeren has written that 'the reading Biran proposes of Leibniz's philosophy aims not at the simple reproduction of the doctrine, but constitutes an *enjeu décsif* for the elaboration of his thought in the agnostic field which opposes, under the Restauration, the sensualist heritage of the eighteenth century to the renascent French spiritualism'.[17] I do not want to suggest, as Cousin did, that Biran found all his ideas in Leibniz's writings (FP.III.77), nor do I wish to deny that Biran's reading is more than a simple reproduction. What I do claim is that the aspects of Leibniz's philosophy that Biran emphasizes are real elements and not distortions – real elements that Biran amplifies in novel and interesting ways. Therefore, he shows the fertility of *thinking with* this side of Leibniz's thought. To show the importance of these ampliative aspects of Biran's work, in §2 I discuss two crucial developments that reveal the distinctive character of Biranianism: (1) his defence of 'active force' contra Hume; and (2) his theory of the virtual. These two developments map respectively onto the order of progression of Leibniz's two-step methodology from the philosophy of experience.

2. Maine de Biran's ampliative Leibnizianism

2.1 Leibniz contra Hume

Leibniz's theory of force and his reconceptualization of experience as a verb in the active voice are vital for Biran because he regards active force as the consciousness of *effort voulu*. The experience of force or *willed effort* reveals our very sense of self to ourselves. As Ravaisson wrote, for Biran, 'to be, to

---

[17] Vermeren, *Victor Cousin*, p. 45.

act, to will' are just different terms to refer to 'one and the same thing' (RR.16). By beginning our deductions from the concrete *fact* of this force, Biran believes that we have a proper foundation for metaphysics, freed from the abstractions of the empiricist and idealist schools. However, unlike Leibniz, Biran lived in a post-Humean context and the idea that we could obtain a meaningful concept of 'force' or 'necessary connexion' from introspection had received a powerful and by now widely known attack from the Scottish empiricist. Biran engages with Hume's arguments in his incomplete *Fondements de la psychologie* (circa 1813) and considers Hume's work as merely an important stepping-stone on the route to the true conception of force found via inner sense. Biran's arguments are careful and challenging, and he showed in a more striking way than any of his contemporaries that the question 'Is a Leibnizian spiritualist metaphysics possible after Hume?' could be answered in the affirmative.

In §VII of Hume's *Enquiry*, he famously argues that there are three possible sources for the idea of force or necessary connection: external objects; reflection on the operation of our minds; and divine power. In the first two cases, Hume shows, we only ever experience distinct events, but, try as we might, we would never perceive the necessary connection between any two events. The third, divine power, is dismissed as a theoretical 'fairy land'. Hume provides a 'sceptical solution' to this problem: the idea of necessary connection is derived from the 'customary transition of the imagination from one object to its usual attendant ... the connexion ... which we feel in the mind' (HE.75). This is a *meaningful* idea, because it is derived from an impression – the customary transition from one mental event to another – but ultimately an *imperfect* idea, because it is not derived from 'forces' or 'necessary connections' themselves. Such forces, Hume believes, will remain forever hidden from view and a *scientia* capable of discovering the true essence of power or force is impossible.

Biran considered it Hume's achievement to have shown that we cannot discover force in external objects, but finds Hume's argument to be misguided when he attempts to extend it to the evidence of *sens intime*. Hume, like Locke and Condillac, failed to distinguish adequately between what Locke referred to as ideas of 'sensation' (understood by Biran as 'ideas obtained from the external senses') and ideas of 'reflection' (understood by Biran as 'ideas obtained from inner sense'). Locke introduced 'ideas of reflection', Biran argues, failed to adequately distinguish these ideas from ideas of sensation and thus left us with an imperfect analysis. However, once this distinction is clarified, we can understand that it is only through the feeling of the I, the primitive fact of consciousness identified with *effort*, that we can 'recognize the real character of the principle of all metaphysics'

(OMB.VII.159). Biran agrees with Hume that we could only discover the influence of the will on the body through experience, but argues that we must recognize a fundamental distinction between an act of will and a mere sense impression. This distinction is a 'true antithesis': the antithesis between activity and passivity, which he regards as equivalent to the antithesis between freedom and necessity (OMB.VII.162). Hume's error is to conceive the subject as merely *subjected* and to subsume the active will under impressions. Consequently, Hume has closed himself off from any possible recognition of the fact under investigation. I shall now turn to how Biran applies this to Hume's arguments.

Perhaps the most crucial element of Hume's argument for Biran is the claim that if we were able to perceive a causal connection or power, we would be able to 'foresee' the effect in the energy of its cause. Biran responds that it is not a question of 'foreseeing', but rather *feeling* (*bien sentir*). He claims that 'at the moment when the will, the motive force, goes to exercise itself, when an effort is determined, and indeed the first willed effort (*effort voulu*), it is necessary that the *energy* of the cause carries with it a sort of *presentiment* or vision (*prévoyance*) of success; otherwise there would only be simple desire and no willing' (OMB.VII.162). To clarify Biran here and to understand what he means by this *presentiment* or *prévoyance* of success, we must advance in two stages: we need (1) to introduce the distinction between what he calls *desire* and *will*; and (2) further explain his concept of *effort voulu*. First, Biran argues that desire and will are two distinct but often-confused faculties. To clarify this distinction he puts forward an imagined hypothesis: his version of Condillac's statue. Biran's statue enjoys only the sense of smell and the ability either to inhale or not in accordance with its will. Placing odorous flowers next to the statue would not suffice for the statue to smell the scent of the flowers. The statue must inhale to smell anything; if it is not inhaling, the scent of the flower will not be sensed. Imagine the flowers are next to the statue's nose and whenever the statue inhales, it smells the pleasant scent of the *jasminium polyanthum*. As this smell is 'constantly conjoined' with the statue's active willing, the statue will believe it is the scent's cause. An outside observer would not see this connection. She would believe the statue was only passively receiving the flowers' scent. In truth, the statue is neither merely passive nor fully active. It is active insofar as it inhales, passive insofar as it receives the odour. However, as the statue has never experienced the two separately, it cannot make this distinction. Now let us imagine that the flowers have been removed from the statue's olfactory organ and that it chooses again to inhale, wishing to smell the jasmine. This time the smell will be absent and after attempting and failing to smell it a few times, it will realize it was not the scent's true cause after all. The scent of jasmine has become the *object of desire*, rather than the *effect of willing*. Our desires more often than not precede our willings, but they are distinct from them and are not their sufficient conditions.

To understand the second step of Biran's argument and to clarify what he means by *effort voulu*, we must now consider Hume's argument that if there were a necessary connection between the 'movement' of the arm and the conscious 'willing-to-move' the arm, it would be impossible to have the latter without the former. A true cause necessitates its effect. However, in the case of the man with paralysis of the arm, Hume argues, we have precisely this occurrence. The man wills the arm's movement, yet the arm does not move. Biran's response again depends on the distinction between desire and will (see GH.239). Through the inner sense the 'willing the movement of the arm', on the one hand, and the 'movement of the arm', on the other, are not experienced at distinct moments of time, but felt simultaneously. If the willing did not carry with it the feeling of success, there would be no feeling of *effort voulu*; rather, there would be only desire. This illuminates Biran's claim that there is a 'feeling of success' which accompanies the willing, rather than a 'foreseeing'. To expect a 'foreseeing' is to confuse desire with *effort voulu*. If we were to take the case of an amputee who has had their arm removed, there would be two possibilities. First, if the amputee attempted to move their arm, forgetting the operation had taken place, and moved only the residual limb, there would still be *effort voulu*. It would be a mistake in memory, not a mistake in feeling.[18] Second, if there were no effect at all, no movement, not even in the residual limb, there would be no *effort voulu*, but desire alone. This concurs with Biran's claim that the individual who has never once voluntarily moved any of their limbs could never have experienced *effort voulu*. Experience is necessarily embodied. In sum, Biran claims that Hume is wrong to conclude that we do not have an experience of power or necessary connection because he has mistaken desire for will. Unless there is some relation between a willing and the feeling of an effect – even if this is the movement of a residual limb rather than the intended arm – there is no willing, only desire: willing *is* necessarily connected to its effect, desire is not. The essential point is that examples where *desires* do not lead necessarily to effects cannot be used as exceptions to the necessary connection between *willings* and their effects.

For Biran, *willing* – the primitive fact of consciousness in which the true concept of force is discovered – reveals to us a 'hyper-organic force' that is

---

[18] See Hallie, *Maine de Biran*, p. 89.

ontologically inseparable from 'organic resistance'. Although 'hyper-organic force' is distinct from the body, it is only realized in relation to it. Unless there is organic resistance, there is no hyper-organic force. In addition, it is only through this relationship that our feeling of personal existence emerges. This feeling raises human consciousness above the mere sensitive being of animals. It is responsible for *apperception* as opposed to mere *perception*. Biran is clear that he understands apperception in Leibniz's sense, *perception cum reflexione conjuncta* (OMB.VI.104), yet where Leibniz saw a difference in degree, Biran sees a difference in kind; the force responsible for apperception is not the same kind of force as the kind responsible for sensibility. This distinction amounts to a real distinction between physiology and psychology. Animal experience reduced to material actions and reactions dependent on the external senses alone would amount to little more than a 'vague and confused feeling of existence'. This is the empire of destiny in which no being can rise above the 'blind determinations of instinct' (OI.I.225). Biran calls the force essential for human apperception 'hyper-organic' to distinguish it from the organic forces of the physiological world. It is a *sui generis* force dependent on nothing exterior to itself for its activation and is the source of our free will and inner sense of identity. Even though this force has an ontological reality distinct from organic forces, it is impossible to experience it except in relation to organic force; the two forces together form for us an essential and indivisible correlation (OMB.VII.125). Nonetheless, as highlighted by the epigraph, cited at the beginning of this chapter, hyper-organic force takes a superior and providential role.

Returning to Hume's *Enquiry*, anyone who knows this work well will wonder how Biran responds to Hume's argument that if we really were able to observe a connection between our volitions and corporeal movements, we would be intimately aware of the movements of the nerves and muscles responsible for the chain of events that leads from the volition to the arm's movements. Again, Biran believes that this line of attack follows from the misconceived assimilation of inner to outer. It is true that we do not observe this connection, but this is because it involves two heterogeneous kinds of knowledge. The fact that we cannot represent these effects of external movement does not, he argues, prevent us from assuredly experiencing the feeling of our 'primordial power' or what he calls the 'empire of the will over its organs'. He asks:

What species of analogy is there between the representative knowledge of position, of the interplay and the functions of our organs, such as an anatomist or physiologist can know them, and the inner feeling which corresponds to these functions, and also the internal knowledge of the parts localized in the continuous resistance of which we spoke previously? How could one not see the opposition that occurs between these two kinds of knowledge, an opposition such that at the very moment when the will moves an organ, if the instruments of motility could represent themselves instead of being felt, or be inwardly apperceived, the will could never arise?

OI.I.262

If we were able to observe all of the internal actions and reactions inside the retina, we could not experience the colours. This is why the 'hidden springs and principles' are withdrawn from view of external senses. However, this does not mean we have no feeling of power or causal force, but rather that we can only know this force through *sens intime*. The real reason for Hume's ignorance, Biran believed, is that it is exactly the development of habit to which Hume attributed the origin of the *idea* of cause that conceals the feeling of effort from many of our actions. To the extent that our actions are undertaken more easily, less consciously, and more through the influence of habit, the determinations of inner sense fade and the impressions of external senses dominate. However, we should not be misled by habit. Real reflection on the feeling of *sens intime* proves Hume indisputably wrong. For Biran, Hume's real success was (even though he was misled through his confusion of inner and outer sense on the one hand, and will and desire on the other) his careful demonstration of the impossibility of deriving the idea of force from outer sense, which showed conclusively that it must be located in the operations of inner sense. For this, 'Hume deserves our gratitude' (OMB.VII.167).

To clarify further what he means by *effort voulu*, Biran compares his theory to Johann Jakob Engel's. Engel argued that we discover force through the exercise of muscular sensation when attempting to resist an exterior force. If I attempt to lift a heavy box, I grasp the idea of force from attempting to overcome its weight. For Engel, Hume's error was to attempt to obtain the idea of force from the wrong senses (sight, sound, touch, etc.), force appears to muscular sensation alone. The problem with his argument is that Hume has already addressed it (HE.67 n.1). He argues that although we experience some feeling of resistance, it is too obscure and we consequently attribute it to too many objects 'where we never can suppose this resistance of existence of force to take place', such as in inanimate matter or even the supreme being. Biran was frequently misrepresented for simply attempting to defend force as Engel did (see Cousin, EE.65–66, and Renouvier, ECG.156). But this ignores the extra distinction Biran makes, not just between a foreign body and my body, but also between my body and hyper-organic force. In the experience of lifting a box, there are two essential distinctions: first, the distinction between my hyper-organic force which initiates the action and my body which resists my initiation according to its inertia, but nevertheless obeys my commands; and, second, the distinction between my body and the resistance of the box as a foreign body. Consequently, Biran argues that while Engel takes a step in the right direction, by attributing this feeling of 'effort' to *sens intime*, he fails to go far enough. Engel derives the experience of effort from the *mediate* feeling of muscular sensation resisting an exterior object. If the sensation were only experienced mediately, Hume would be right that we cannot accurately attribute this sensation to a particular source. However, we do not experience a *mediate* feeling of effort, but rather an *immediate* one and it is only by recognizing this vital fact that we can overcome Hume's problem:

> The true origin (I do not say essence) of the idea that we attach to the word *force*, consists in the immediate power of the will to grasp and determine the inertial or resistant force proper to the muscular organs, and thereby to enter into a conflict of actions. In the sense of M. Engel, it follows from the complication or from the conflict of our force with the alien exterior force, either that the latter is overcome, or that ours is momentarily suspended or as if paralysed by the object. In my sense, the muscular inertia is always surmounted, and the hyper-organic force, far from being relaxed [*détendue*] or as if paralysed by this resistance, believes [*croit*] in energy and activity, to the degree that this resistance increases.

OMB.VII.169–170

The key distinction is that the muscular sensation is still *presented to us*, in the same way as the impressions of our external senses; thus, Engel's theory does not emphasize the essential activity that cannot be dissociated from the feeling of effort. To understand this feeling, we need only reflect on our active exercise of willing (OMB.VII.118–119). A person born paralysed, who has never moved any of their organs willingly, could not understand this feeling of effort, just as a person born blind could never understand the feeling of sight. Biran extends this thesis further and argues that the paralysed person mentioned above would not even experience self-consciousness, as self-consciousness and the activity of willing are identical (ibid.); even our passive sensory impressions are only knowable in contrast to our essential activity, just as we could not know shadows without light. At this point the importance of Leibniz's metaphysics of forces becomes clear. First, like Leibniz's force which is 'half-way between a faculty and an action, and contains in itself a certain effort, or *conatus*' (UL.VI.526: WFNS.32–33), Biran's *effort voulu* requires no impetus from outside, it contains its action within itself; 'we apperceive and reproduce it at every instant' (OMB.VII.121). The action is both indivisible and instantaneous. This is in contrast to our sensible impressions for which we are not responsible. Second, for Biran, we complete Locke's incomplete analysis of the distinction between ideas of sensation and reflection, when we understand it as a distinction Hallie sums up as between 'presentation to' and 'living through'.[19] Ideas of sensation are *presented to* us, while we *live through* ideas of reflection. The first are received passively, the latter are the result of our agency: Locke's analysis of inner sense is therefore reconceived according to Leibniz's theory of force. Again, recall the previous discussion of experience as understood as a noun on the one hand, and as an active verb on the other. The distinction between Engel's and Biran's theories is that while Engel was unable to move past understanding experience as *presented to*, Biran's analysis of hyper-organic force completes the theory of inner sense and moves us to experience as *living through*. This analysis has deep metaphysical consequences because it means that instead of having to think causation in terms of customary transitions from one event to the next, we can obtain a true understanding of agent causation based on our internal activity. Biran's next step, following Leibniz's two-step methodology, is to show we can apply this new understanding of causation to our understanding of nature.

2.2 The virtual

Once we realize that we must discover the 'science of principles' by reasoning from the introspective view and not the God's-eye view, Biran insists that the true importance of Leibniz's system is unveiled: 'The fixed point being given, thought takes to the air, and, on the wings of Leibniz, swiftly flies from pole to pole, or ascends, with the calmness of reflection, through each link in this great chain of being, of which the system of monads offers so great and so magnificent a representation' (OMB.XI–I.149). Biran asks us to consider Descartes's famous 'piece of wax' argument. Descartes asks: 'What remains of the wax when all the sensible qualities

---

[19] Hallie, *Maine de Biran*, p. 34.

have been changed or removed?' His answer is 'pure extension' alone (AT.VII.31: CSM.II.20). This extension involves no power of its own, and to activate its 'potential' (flexibility and changeability), it must receive excitation from outside: from God's force. Descartes's theory of extension is, Biran argues, really a scholastic theory of 'bare faculties'. Consequently, it is Leibniz who provides the true answer to the question 'what remains of the wax after every secondary quality has been removed?' The 'direct and true response' is that *force* remains. Force is the proper ground of our being, which exists either as *actualized*, in particular determinate qualities, or *virtually*. When there is no self-consciousness, i.e. *effort voulu*, we do not become *nothing*, or a naked faculty waiting for excitation from outside, our being remains virtual; there is always a *tendency* to action. Biran believes that this distinction found in Leibniz helps to clarify the question of innate ideas obscured by Descartes and Locke. Our innate ideas and modes are virtual forces which ground our proper being. They are tendencies to action which subsist even when not actualized in consciousness or *effort voulu*. This theory of virtuality is crucial to Biran's theory of the self. This is because he is highly critical of the Cartesian inference from the existence of thought to the claim that there must be some sort of passive receptacle – substance – in which all of these individual thoughts are united. Yet Biran is no bundle theorist; there is a unity to the self, but the unity comes from these virtual tendencies: tendencies which are not passive or bare possibilities, but rather 'half way between power and act'. As he explains in his 1817 *Anthropologie*:

> In us, and only in ourselves, the cause, the productive force of the movements or free acts executed by the organs, is immediately manifested, both as phenomenon or fact of inner sense in willed and felt effort, and as [a] notion or conception of the active being in its essence, or of *virtual absolute force* which exists before the manifestation, and which remains the same after, even though its exercise is suspended. The phenomenon and the reality, being and appearance coincide therefore in the consciousness of the *I*, identical with the immediate feeling of force, or cause, which operates by the will.

OI.III.412

Leibniz argued that our knowledge of necessary and eternal truths, gained through our reflective acts, causes us to rise above simple animals and brings us closer to God. Biran argues that Leibniz was correct in inferring that it is from our reflective acts that we gain knowledge of necessary truths, and these truths raise us above simple animals; however, he was wrong to infer knowledge of abstract ideas.[20] Biran believes that we do not gain such abstract knowledge, but rather *concrete* knowledge of the virtualities, tendencies or forms of the human mind, which are concrete conditions of the possibility of knowledge. The 'conditions' that Biran discovers through his introspective reflective analysis, such as *substance, cause, unity* and *identity*, are what he calls simple reflective ideas and sound prima facie like Kantian categories. In the process of forming 'general abstract ideas', one experiences a number of similar external objects, for example, books, and one removes everything unique to the individual books, leaving only the general characteristic or idea of 'book'. However, by doing so, Biran argues, we have eliminated the reality of any individual book. The idea has become a mere logical concept and does not reflect the reality of any individual thing. Unlike general abstract ideas, which refer to characteristics common to many particulars, the simple reflective ideas are always individual and simple. Like Kant, Biran believes these concepts are not abstracted from sensible things, but are rather heterogeneous to external sensibility. These simple concepts are discovered once we abstract from all sensible perception:

> The *I* which exists or apperceives itself internally, as *one*, as *simple*, as *identical*, is not itself abstracted from those sensations such as may be of the common or of the general in themselves, except insofar as it abstracts

---

[20] Biran is wrong to claim that Leibniz defended bare abstract ideas. In the *New Essays* Leibniz says the 'thorniest brambles' of the Scholastics 'disappear in a flash if one is willing to banish abstract entities' (NE 217–218). Biran comes close to Leibniz's theory; he argues that the 'forms' of the mind that exist as virtual tendencies underlying our conscious thoughts are what provide the unity of our personal identity. However, Biran limits these forms to his own 'categories': substance, cause, unity, and identity. He fails to recognize that for Leibniz all our forms or ideas have this kind of pre-existent reality as virtualities. Whether or not we are able to clearly and distinctly express these ideas, they always play an essential and constitutive role in our thought. Using a nice example Leibniz says 'we use these maxims without having them explicitly in mind. It is rather like the way in which one has implicitly in mind the suppressed premises in enthymemes, which are omitted in our thinking of the argument as well as in our outward expression of it' (NE.76). Biran comes close to recognizing the full novelty of Leibniz's own theory of ideas (which makes a distinction between bare abstract ideas and efficacious Platonic ideas, i.e. ideas qua forces), but then ends up criticizing Leibniz for a mistake he does not make. This is surprising since Biran will later put the distinction between Descartes and Leibniz clearly as a distinction between Aristotelianism and Platonism: 'Descartes's system is linked to Aristotelianism by the nature of its . . . purely modifiable passive substance, endowed with receptivity, and . . . Leibniz's system is linked to Platonism by the principle of force' (OP.III.153–154).

itself by the act of internal apperception, which distinguishes and separates up to a certain point the individual or the *one* from the collective and from the multiple; the active force or the cause, from the effect produced; the action from passion; in a word the subject which makes the effort, from the term which resists and which undergoes diverse modifications. The *I* is therefore truly *abstrahens* in its reflective action, and not *abstractus*.[21]

OMB.VII.200

Biran's categories are the inseparable characteristics of *effort voulu* discoverable from reflection. Our primitive metaphysical ideas, such as cause, substance and unity, have meaning only insofar as they are derived from this introspective analysis.

With the theory of virtual force in place, Biran claims that '[t]he *reformed* metaphysics no longer allows two great classes of being, entirely separated from each other and excluding all intermediaries, but one and the same chain embracing and bonding all of the beings of creation' (OMB.XI–I.151). He agrees with Descartes that there must be a distinction between the organic and the 'hyper-organic', but he does not believe that this distinction must lead us to a separation between two heterogeneous substances. Virtual force is the metaphysical ground of nature; it is what remains when the sensible qualities of the wax change. We can, Biran argues, perform a kind of 'natural induction' from our experience of causal activity, to true causal action all throughout nature. We know from Biran's *Journal Intime* that his friends Ampère and Cousin had insisted to him that such natural induction was problematic and Ampère convinced him that there is 'between the individual feeling of the causality of the *I*, and the belief or necessary universal notion of cause, an abyss that cannot be crossed by recourse to analysis alone, or by analogy or induction'. Nonetheless, Biran stuck to his defence of the PU and maintained that

it is natural that we should perceive, or that we should conceive things which do not depend on the *I*, in the manner in which we exist, and under the form or idea which constitutes our individual existence. We exist as an *I*, or as an individual person only insofar as we are causes; it is therefore natural that we could conceive of nothing, or realize it outside of ourselves except in the same way: 'I would like to know,' said Leibniz,

---

[21] The distinction comes from Kant's 1770 *Inaugural Dissertation*, the only one of Kant's works Biran read.

'how we could conceive of the idea of *being* if we did not, as beings ourselves, find being within us' [NE.86]. I extend this principle and I ask how we could not conceive that there are causes, or a single cause alone throughout, when we exist only as causes.

JI.I.226–27; cf. NE.473

Biran cannot admit the principle of causality as a necessary truth throughout nature, but as this shows, he accepts that. Even with this admitted, he believes we nevertheless cannot consider causality in any other way than by analogy with our *effort voulu*. It remains the safest ground for our reflections on the metaphysics of nature.

I shall conclude this section by emphasizing two main problems involved in Biran's developments of Leibniz's metaphysics. First, by postulating a difference not in degree but in kind between the *sui generis* nature of his hyper-organic force and the lesser organic forces, Biran introduces a lacuna in nature between physiology and psychology that is almost as severe as Descartes's. Yet this does not concern him. Partly, this is because he claims to have replaced Descartes' heterogeneous substances with a metaphysics of forces. However, even so, Biran still argues for a troubling heterogeneity within these forces, between the *sui generis* hyper-organic forces, on the one hand, and the organic forces determined by the laws of dynamics, on the other. The postulation of one ontological type outside of space and the constraints of the physical, and another within, reproduces the interaction problem in its entirety and Biran has no recourse to PEH to escape it. This primitive duality is made evident by the primitive fact of consciousness and cannot be rejected, but also cannot be explained. However, a second, perhaps more serious, problem stems from the fact that he starts his natural induction from the reflective experience of spontaneous and active embodied beings endowed with inner sense and infers from this the existence of forces throughout nature. Nonetheless, there is a stark difference in kind between the hyper-organic force of human beings and the organic and mechanical forces in the rest of nature. It seems that for Biran all the time and everywhere, things are not the same as they are here. Consistently followed, Biran's use of the PU should have led to panpsychism and this was recognized and implemented by later Biran-influenced spiritualists such as Ravaisson and Boutroux. For this reason, highlighting Biran's fecund metaphysical suggestions is more interesting than criticizing his systematic inconsistencies. He was, first and foremost, a psychologist and his metaphysical speculations of cause, substance and existence only began to be of explicit concern to him in the last two decades of his life. His was not a final polished systematic theory and most of our sources he had not intended to publish. What is most important is the influence his essays on these ideas had for later generations and, therefore, the resources they provided for those philosophers more explicitly concerned with such fundamental issues in metaphysics and epistemology.

3. Maine de Biran's Leibniz and Victor Cousin

Vermeren argued that we can only understand the nineteenth-century readings of Leibniz and Biran in the context of the 'struggle for the conquest and maintenance of the philosophical hegemony of university spiritualism in the emerging modern constitutional state'.[22] In this final section, I argue that the 1819 *Exposition* played a foundational role in the creation of this situation. This is because the article's most cutting critical argument was in truth aimed not at Leibniz's philosophy (and, as Biran must have known, it would have not successfully hit its target if it were), but rather at the young professor Cousin. The professor who would, after Biran's death, gain an all-encompassing control over the direction of France's philosophical education and be instrumental in the creation of a national philosophy: eclectic spiritualism. The critiques in the *Exposition* showed that the system Cousin was developing is fundamentally flawed.

The story of Cousin's life is an extraordinary journey from rags to riches. Although born into abject poverty in 1792, by 1830 he had become a philosopher king who would determine the hegemony of his spiritualist philosophy. As Jules Simon wrote: 'The 1830 Revolution, which made Louis-Philippe king of France, made Cousin king of philosophers. But Louis-Philippe was only a constitutional king, Cousin was an absolute king.'[23] Simon also tells us that Cousin considered France's philosophy instructors his 'philosophical regiment' and that 'he had every hold over this regiment' (1888: 98; cf. 116).[24] However, when Biran wrote the 1819 *Exposition*, Cousin did not enjoy such absolute power; he was, in Biran's mind, a talented young professor with the potential to guide French philosophy from sensualism to spiritualism. Despite being too 'hot-headed',

---

[22] Vermeren, 'Les aventures de la force active en France', p. 167.

[23] *La philosophie et l'enseignement official de la philosophie*, archives privés, fonds Jules Simon 87 AP 16. Cited in Vermeren, *Victor Cousin*, p. 176.

[24] Jules Simon, (1888) Victor Cousin. Translated by M.B. Anderson and E.P. Anderson. Chicago: McClurg and Company, p. 98; cf. p. 116.

he was France's greatest hope for fulfilling the hopes expressed by Staël (JI.II.303). We know from Biran's *Journal* that from around 1816 Biran and Cousin met frequently, that Cousin was a member of Biran's 'metaphysical society', that Biran attended some of Cousin's lectures, and that they discussed their philosophical systems, their metaphysics, substance and the absolute in great detail.[25] Therefore, Cousin's philosophy was well known to Biran. But why would Biran publish a critique of Cousin's philosophy under the pretence of a critique of Leibniz? My hypothesis is based on three main claims: (1) Cousin's character prevented Biran from wanting to name the true aim of this critique; (2) Biran was enough of a scholar to recognize that the critique did not affect Leibniz; and (3) Biran knew and cared enough about Cousin's philosophy to recognize that his argument fundamentally undermines it. Although this does not amount to conclusive proof, nonetheless, even if I am wrong about the intention of the author, we can be certain that Cousin and many of his contemporaries read it as such, and this is why the text plays such an important role in the struggle for the hegemony of Cousin's spiritualism in the nineteenth century.[26]

Starting with (1), although Cousin was not then a philosopher king, he had never been able to take criticism. As Simon tells us, 'even in boyhood, Cousin had the habit and instinct of superiority; if a dispute arose, instead of arguing, he inveighed, wounded, crushed. This was a life-long characteristic.'[27] Biran clearly recognized this (see JI.II.303). Biran was also nervous about publishing his work, so published very little. Therefore, it is reasonable to believe he would not have wanted to suffer a public philosophical 'crushing' from Cousin. Consequently, (1) seems a fair assumption. To defend (2) and (3), we must turn to the critique itself.

Biran states that there is a major problem with Leibniz's system because he argues for its truth from two separate and incompatible points of view. Biran 'selects' a part of Leibniz's philosophy, but this selection is necessary given the overall inconsistency of the system. On the one hand, Leibniz starts from the 'introspective' method and argues deductively from

---

[25] See JI.I.126–127, 128–129, 131, 224. 228, 230, 235, 245, 247; JI.II.10, 23, 37, 120, 177, 185–186, 303.

[26] This reason is why Leibniz's philosophy was on the 'first level' in the French intellectual climate from at least 1810, and not only from the 1850s as Moreau (2014) has attempted to show. See Pierre-François Moreau. '"In Naturalismo" Leibniz, Spinoza et les spiritualistes français', in: R.Andrault, M. Laerke, R. Andrault, (eds.) *Spinoza/Leibniz. Rencontres, controverses, réceptions*. Paris: Presses universitaires de Paris Sorbonne, 2014.

[27] Simon, *Victor Cousin*, p. 110.

indubitable facts of inner sense; but, on the other, he argues from the 'God's-eye view'. From the first perspective, Biran claims, Leibniz provides us with a real foundation for metaphysics; however, from the second, he fares no better than the other rationalists whose systems collapse into pantheism. Leibniz's early meditations on the universal calculus caused him, Biran says, to search for the fundamental elements of reality through a process of analysis that would lead him to *final abstracts*. Through logic we are taken from the concrete to the abstract, and the abstract ideas of God's understanding are found to be the source of all reality. When Leibniz derives his fundamental metaphysics using his faith in logic alone, he ends up in the same place as Spinoza, and his monads become nothing more than the passive effects of God's ideas. Biran argues that the central problem is that these two perspectives contradict one another. The 'psychological' perspective emphasizes the importance of force, freedom and individuality, and the 'God's-eye view' eliminates all three.

Biran's methodology is founded on what we might call the 'Principle of the Primacy of Introspective Constraint' (PIC). This asserts that there are fundamental introspective truths that cannot be denied without consequently denying existence. Any hypothesis that undermines these indubitable truths must therefore be rejected. Descartes claimed that '[t]he *freedom of the will is self-evident* ... so evident that it must be counted among the first and most common notions that are innate in us' (AT.VIIIA.19: CSM.I.205–206). Biran agrees with this wholeheartedly, but, unlike Descartes, he is unwilling to let freedom be watered down by a compatibilist theory that would lead to the conclusion that God is the only true cause. We have an exclusive disjunction: either the individual is free and responsible for her actions, or God is the only true cause. Biran's adherence to the PIC means that the latter disjunct is prohibited. Since Leibniz's 'God's-eye view' and the metaphysics of PEH would undermine the former disjunct, they must be abandoned. However, Biran sees this rejection of PEH not as altering Leibniz's doctrine 'at its essence', but rather as re-affirming it and establishing its full importance freed from rationalist dogmas.

According to Biran, the 'absurd' nature of the a priori reasoning that led Descartes, Spinoza, Malebranche and even Leibniz to determinism is shown by the fact that we begin reasoning from the free individual and then end up at a rationalist system that denies the existence of the free individual from which it began. Nonetheless, as it stands this is a weak argument. There is nothing wrong in principle with starting from a proposition we believe to be certain and then via a process of reasoning coming to find that this proposition is false or that it needs to be revised with regard to a fuller understanding. This is the Socratic method. It only becomes a problem if the conclusion can only be true if the original proposition is understood as necessarily true. Now we can turn to my defence of (2): Leibniz need not be worried by this problem and Biran would have known it. This is because Leibniz does not accept the PIC. In the *Theodicy*, a text which Biran owned and read, Leibniz agrees with Biran that Descartes's attempt to combine the inner experience of free will with God's providence left his philosophy with an inexorable problem (T§292). Indeed, this is one of the 'two famous labyrinths': the one that 'perplexes almost all the human race' (G.VII.29: T.53). However, Leibniz did not agree that introspection provides us with proof of the existence of freedom (even if he did believe that it provides us with evidence of internal activity and spontaneity). He cites Pierre Bayle's discussion of the weathervane and agrees that if an external force unfailingly moved us whenever we desired to move, we would believe ourselves to be the source of this action. The weathervane that always desired to move in the direction it was coincidently blown, would be, for Bayle and Leibniz, 'persuaded that it moved of itself to fulfil the desires which it conceived' (T§299). Leibniz claims that Bayle's arguments are 'excellent' (T§300). However, he believes they have no effect against the fact of freedom when it comes to the system of PEH, because the arguments for it are a priori and not from introspection. Given that Leibniz rejects introspective analysis in this case, his theory would not collapse under the weight of the PIC. Contrary to Biran and (as we shall see) Cousin, Leibniz argues that it is only from the rationalist proof of PEH and the independence of monads that we can defend free will, since only then can we regard individual beings as free from outside influence and therefore acting in complete accordance with their will (T§300; cf. G.III.471).

Turning to (3), we can now discuss why it affects Cousin in a way it does not Leibniz. Cousin agreed with Biran that psychology was the foundation of philosophy (FP.Ia.XII). He believed that faulty psychological analyses have been the cause of the major philosophical errors of eighteenth-century philosophy and these errors led to disastrous consequences. Sensualism led to scepticism by explicitly relativizing all knowledge to the individual. However, Kantian criticism led to a 'new and original' scepticism by relativizing reason to the phenomena of individuals.[28] Together, these

---

[28] For Cousin, Fichte shows the necessary consequences of Kant's philosophy. The I that posits itself, the world, and God 'is the final degree of all subjectivity, the extreme and necessary term of Kant's system, and, at the same time, its refutation' (FP.Ib.10). Clearly Cousin, despite what he claimed, did not have a good understanding of classical German philosophy.

philosophies were responsible for an 'age of criticism and destructions' that 'let loose tempests'. The aim of the nineteenth century, he insisted, should be 'intelligent restorations' (TBG.31). Such restorations would bring together the ideals of the French revolution – freedom and equality – with principles essential for the stability of the nation, such as immutable principles of truth, beauty and goodness. Cousin's recommendation was that philosophy should progress according to a principle of eclecticism 'which judging with equity, and even with benevolence, all schools, borrows from them what they possess of the true, and neglects what in them is false' (TBG.33), a statement which sounds as sensible as it is trite until we add that careful psychological analysis must act as said judge.

Summarizing his 1817 and 1818 lectures, the lectures Biran would have attended and discussed with Cousin prior to the writing of the 1819 *Exposition*,[29] Cousin tells us that their main aim was to establish the truth of both 'voluntary' and 'rational' facts in addition to the already well-established 'sensual' facts (FP.ia.xiii–xiv). A complete psychological analysis will show the necessity of all three classes and that not one can be reduced to another. An example of a 'rational fact', he claims, is that every effect must have a cause. Despite the ingenuity of Hume's arguments, Cousin thought it impossible, if we are honest to ourselves, to deny our belief in this principle. Honest reflection on our consciousness brings the principle with it, and shows that it is both universal and necessary, since an uncaused experience is unfathomable. As further reflection shows that our experience is not principally caused by our volition, we must admit the existence of an external cause. Concurrently, we move from ontology to psychology and this is the reason why psychology is philosophy's essential foundation. The most important claim for Cousin is that the principal light for our phenomena comes from reason. No knowledge would be possible without it and 'reason perceives itself, and the sensibility that envelops it, and the will that it compels without constraining' (FP.ia.xvii–xviii). Furthermore, as Cousin argues that reflection on our reason shows us that these 'rational facts' are universal and necessary, we are led to infer the existence of a foundation for them that is also universal and necessary. This foundation cannot be our finite and contingent minds. As the universal and necessary principle is absolute, it leads us to an impersonal, absolute, universal and necessary cause. 'The laws of intelligence,' Cousin tells us, 'constitute a separate world, which governs the visible world, presides over its movements, sustains and preserves it, but does not depend on it' (FP.ia.xxiii). This, he

---

[29] Biran wrote this text between 10 April and 1 July 1819 (see JI.II.229–231).

claims, is the theory of the realm of ideas, introduced by Plato, but crowned and completed by Leibniz's theory of God or the Absolute (TBG.79, 89).[30] For Cousin, God is

> at once true and real, substance and cause, always substance and always cause, being substance only insofar as he is cause, and cause only insofar as he is substance, that is to say, being absolute cause, one and many, eternity and time, space and number, essence and life, indivisibility and totality, principle, end and centre, at the summit of Being and at its lowest degree, infinite and finite together, finally triple, in a word, that is to say, at the same time God, nature, and humanity. In effect, if God is not every thing, he is nothing.

FP.Ia.XL

We can begin to see why Biran's argument in the 1819 *Exposition* affects Cousin in a way that it did not Leibniz. As I showed in §1, Biran argued that all Cartesian systems are led to pantheism by means of the following argument:

(1) God is the sole cause, and every other existing being is merely an effect of God's power.

(2) It is 'logically certain that all effects are eminently or formally enclosed in their cause' (OMB.XI–I.142).

(3) Every created being is enclosed in God and there is no real distinction between God and nature (by (1) and (2)).

It is difficult to see how Cousin could escape the consequences of this argument. Unsurprisingly, therefore, he would be continually pestered by accusations of pantheism (see FP.Ib.18–23 and Vermeren 1995: 223–244). However, Biran did more than simply demonstrate that the eclectic system is pantheistic; he showed it is inconsistent. This is because it asserts the existence not only of 'rational facts', which lead to the existence of an all-encompassing absolute, but also of 'volitional facts', facts that reveal our freedom and personality. For Cousin, unlike Leibniz, these volitional facts

---

[30] As Manns and Madden show, when Cousin uses the term 'Absolute', he conceptualizes it in a way that is much closer to Leibniz's 'Absolute' than Schelling's or Hegel's. Indeed, Cousin frequently references Leibniz's use of the term in *The True, the Beautiful, and the Good*. (See NE.157, 158, D.II.17, 24, & T§189). See James W. Manns, and Edward, H. Madden, 'Victor Cousin: Commonsense and the Absolute'. *The Review of Metaphysics*. 43/3 (1990): 569–589.

are principal facts of conscious experience (FP.ia.xxv; cf. TBG.114). Our first 'immediate internal perception' presents us as free personalities and by reflecting on this free experience, we are led to rational facts; nonetheless, Cousin's further reflection on these facts leads him to a theory of the absolute that undermines the possibility of the evidence presented in the first immediate internal impression: volitional facts. The criticism is fatal for Cousin's project because the evidence for the truth of free will is on the same level as the evidence for the truth of 'universal and necessary' principles, such as 'every effect has a cause'. If his argument turns out in the end to undermine the evidence for freedom, it follows that the evidence of the universal and necessary truths is similarly undermined. Yet these were the premises on which the proof of the infinite being depends: the argument's conclusion entails the falsehood of the premises. In addition, Cousin would not accept either the truth of 'individual freedom' or 'God as absolute' alone; both are necessary. Biran's argument against the possibility of this reconciliation – at least upon the arguments that Cousin has provided – proves fatal for the latter's whole project. This then is my reason for (3) and completes my defence of the claim that the argument was always intended for Cousin.

Although together, (1), (2) and (3) provide a strong case for my hypothesis, one need not be convinced to see that Cousin understood it as an attack on his work, or at least as a serious threat to his philosophy's prominence. He was concerned with the establishment of his eclectic philosophical system as France's official philosophy, and did not want Biran's spiritualism to emerge as an alternative. Nonetheless, he could only repress Biranianism for a definite period of time. It was a ticking time bomb that would eventually explode and leave his eclecticism in tatters. Cousin's method of repression began when he inherited Biran's Œuvre after his death. Despite the riches known to be contained within these manuscripts, he delayed publication for ten years, and then published at first only one volume – a volume he claimed (falsely) to contain Biran's thought in its entirety (FP.III.63). Vermeren (1987: 159) offers two reasons for this delay. First, Cousin wanted to retain the glory of being the philosopher who overturned eighteenth-century sensualism; and, second, he feared that Biran's spiritualism would contest the hegemony of his own. As we have seen above, Cousin was right to be afraid and the *Exposition* required special treatment in his introduction to Biran's *Œuvres posthumes*. Cousin's treatment proceeds in three steps. First, he shows Biran was wrong to claim that Leibniz's philosophy is fundamentally inconsistent. He insists that when Biran presents an absolute and universal spiritualism, freed from the universal and necessary principles of reason that support both his and Leibniz's spiritualisms, it is an incomplete philosophy. It is the commencement of a system, but not a system properly speaking. Second, Cousin argues that his philosophy is more Leibnizian than Biran's. This is because Leibnizian apperception leads not only to the consciousness of the I qua force, but also to the awareness of the not-I. Then the awareness of the rational facts that are also part of the not-I, via Cousin's method, leads us to the cause of causes. Here we reach not only 'the foundation of the monadology, but the monadology in its entirety, and perhaps also pre-established harmony' – with Cousin's important proviso added – 'well-understood' (FP.III.80). Bringing the first two steps together, Cousin argues that PEH does not deny the action of monads or lead to pantheism; quite to the contrary, it contends that the I and the not-I act together and modify each other according to their own actions governed by laws. Every being acts on every other being within limits. This well-governed universal concordance is all PEH is supposed to suggest (FP.III.81). The scene is then set for Cousin's attempt to reclaim Leibniz properly for his eclectic school:

> [I]t is necessary for my eclecticism to recognize and savour the eclectic direction found throughout all of Leibniz's works. To the degree that I advance, or believe to advance in philosophy, it seems to me that I see more clearly into the thought of this great man and all my progress consists in better understanding him. Maine de Biran, at the point when he stopped, grasped well from the whole system of Leibniz only the part that clarified in his eyes his own theory.
>
> FP.III.83

With this reappropriation in place, he moves on to his third and final step, attempting to reverse Biran's critique and show that it is actually Biran's philosophy and not his own that leads to pantheism.[31] Cousin's argument is typically unpromising. He claims Biran has dangerously 'over-animated' nature. If we start from our free internal causality and argue that we can infer the existence of analogous active substances throughout nature, our unique causality ends up being no different in kind than the activity of any corporeal substance, and ultimately human liberty is reduced to the destiny of nature (PS.181). As all causality is reduced to the same level, it is Biran's system, not Cousin's, that brings with it the true threat of pantheism.

---

[31] See Antoine-Mahut on 'La cousinianisation du biranisme'. In: Delphine Antoine-Mahut. *Le cartésianisme selon l'expérience. La métaphysique à l'épreuve des sciences de la vie au XIXe siècle.* Paris: J Vrin, 2015.

Nevertheless, Cousin's attempt to become the true Leibnizian failed. This was probably due partly to the unconvincing nature of his arguments, but also because Leibniz was appropriated by Cousin's fiercest critics. Pierre Leroux,[32] Charles Renouvier and Félix Ravaisson all used distinctly Biran-influenced readings of Leibniz to attack the philosopher king. Finally, Cousin changed his strategy and turned to Descartes, who became the great founder of spiritualist philosophy, and Cousin significantly reduced Leibniz's role in his historical story. By turning to Descartes, he could retain the importance of the psychology of reflection, but also gain the benefits of a safe political philosophy, which he believed lent support to the constitutional monarchy, while concurrently providing France with a national hero.[33] At the start of his career, he built his reputation on his supposed knowledge of the philosophies of Germany, but by the end he was at pains to distance himself from the accusations of presenting a naturalized German pantheism. Appropriating Descartes turned out to be the most effective strategy to do so. The battle turned from one over the true heart of Leibniz's philosophy to one between Leibnizian and Cartesian spiritualisms.

Simon recounts a conversation with Cousin from around 1848 that would turn out to be prophetic. Simon had just come from a discussion with Cousin's critic Leroux, who had told him that 'the whole structure will fall with Cousin. When Cousin disappears, your whole gang of professors and your whole school will disappear with him.' Simon says that he was 'boiling over with rage after this conversation ... I repeated the story to Cousin as he was breakfasting on bread and honey. "Leroux is right," he calmly replied, eating away at the slice he had spread.'[34] As Cousin almost predicted, the text that put the final nail in his philosophical coffin was published the same year the final nail was put in his real coffin – 1867. In 1840, Ravaisson published a savage critique of Cousin's philosophy that had, due to Cousin's all-encompassing influence at the time, cost him his university career. Ravaisson's return to philosophy came in 1863. He was asked by Victor Duruy, the minister of public instruction, to be the chair of the committee in charge of setting the *agrégation*. When the government decided that a series of reports on the progress of the sciences and the arts should be written, Duruy again chose Ravaisson for the philosophy report – a decision which had an enormous impact. His *Rapport*

---

[32] See Lucie Rey. *Les enjeux de l'histoire de la philosophie en France au* XIX*e siècle.* Paris: L'Harmattan, 2012, pp. 410–421.
[33] See, C.P. Ziljstra. *The Rebirth of Descartes: The Nineteenth-Century Reinstatement of Cartesian Metaphysics in France and Germany.* PhD thesis. University of Groningen, 2005.
[34] Simon, *Victor Cousin*, pp. 136–137.

sur la philosophie en France au XIX*ème siècle* provided a summary of the development of French philosophy throughout the century, but at the same time served as a manifesto for a Biran-inspired Leibnizian spiritualism in sharp opposition to Cousin's eclecticism and Comte's positivism. Published in 1867, the year Cousin died, Ravaisson's *Rapport* gave French philosophy a whole new lease of life. It gave rise to a veritable sea change in philosophy because it became essential reading for the hundreds of students studying for the *agrégation* for several generations. In terms of understanding the renaissance of Leibnizian ideas towards the end of the nineteenth century, it is difficult to overestimate the importance of this work. Bergson explains this well:

> No analysis can give an idea of these admirable pages. Twenty generations have learned them by heart. They have counted for a great deal in the influence exercised by the *Rapport* on philosophy as studied in the universities, an influence whose precise limits cannot be determined, nor whose depth be plumbed, nor whose nature be exactly described, any more than one can convey the inexpressible colouring which a great enthusiasm of early youth sometimes diffuses over the whole life of man ... The *Rapport* ... [gave] rise to a change of orientation in philosophy in the university [and] Ravaisson's influence succeeded the influence of Cousin.[35]

4. Conclusion

Interpreting and thinking with Leibniz played a central role in the development and battles that characterized nineteenth-century philosophy in France. Understanding this strategic role for Leibniz's metaphysics in this period is crucial for grasping why many philosophers provided their particular interpretations of his thought. Nonetheless, as I have shown in this chapter, this does not mean that they did not gain important insights into the sage of Hannover's philosophy. In fact, Biran developed strikingly original arguments that breathed new life into Leibniz's work and showed the great potential of his spiritualist experiential metaphysics, so that, through Ravaisson, it would become deeply embedded in French thought in such a way that the limits of this influence could never be precisely

---

[35] Henri Bergson (1946) 'The Life and Works of Ravaisson'. In: *The Creative Mind*, edited by M. L. Andison. New York: Philosophical Library, pp. 261–300.

determined. Boutroux, Renouvier and Émile Boirac, among others, would all further explore the great potential of experiential Leibnizian spiritualism throughout the nineteenth century and provide ingenious insights of their own. However, the first to expose this great potential was Maine de Biran.

Bibliography

Abbreviations

AG   Leibniz, G.W. *Leibniz: Philosophical Essays.* Translated by R. Ariew, & D. Garber. Indianapolis: Hackett, 1989.

AT   Descartes, R. *Oeuvres de Descartes.* Edited by C. Adam & P. Tannery. Paris: J. Vrin, 1974–1989.

CSM   Descartes, R. *The Philosophical Writings of Descartes.* 3 Vols. Translated by Cottingham, J., Stoothoff, D. & Murdoch, D. Cambridge: Cambridge University Press, 1984–1991.

D   Leibniz, G.W. *Leibniz: Opera Omnia.* Edited by L. Dutens. Geneva: De Tournes, 1768.

E   Leibniz, G.W. *God. Guild. Leibntinii Opera quae existant Latina, Gallica, Germanica Omnia.* Edited by J.E. Erdmann. Berlin: Eichler, 1839–1840.

ECG   Renouvier, C.B. *Essai de critique générale. Deuxième Essai: Traité de psychologie rationnelle d'après les principes du criticisme.* 3 Vols. Paris: Librairie Armand Colin, 1912.

EHU   Locke, J. *An Essay Concerning Human Understanding.* Edited by P.H. Nidditch. Oxford: Oxford University Press, [1690] 1975.

FP   Cousin, V. *Fragmens philosophiques.* Paris: Ladrange, Ia tome I 1826 edition; Ib tome I 1838 edition; III tome III 1840 edition.

G   Leibniz, G.W. *Die Philosophischen Scrhiften von Leibniz.* 7 vols. Edited by C.I. Gerhardt. Berlin: Weidmann, 1875–1890.

GH   Gouhier, H. *Maine de Biran: Oeuvres Choisies.* Paris: Aubier Montaigne-Bibliothèque Philosophique, 1942.

HE   Hume, D. *Enquiries Concerning Human Understanding and Concerning the Principles of Morals.* Third Edition. Ed. P.H. Nidditch. Oxford: Oxford University Press, [1777] 1975.

JI   Maine de Biran. *Journal Intime.* 3 Vols. Edited by H. Gouhier. Neuchatel: Éditions de la Baconnière, 1954.

L   Leibniz, G.W. *Gottfried Wilhelm Leibniz: Philosophical Papers and Letters.* Translated by L. Loemker. London: Kluwer, 1989.

LDV   Leibniz, G.W. *The Leibniz-De Volder Correspondence.* Translated by P. Lodge. New Haven: Yale University Press, 2014.

MDS   Staël-Holstein, A.L.G. *Germany*. Translator Unknown. London: John Murray, [1810] 1814.

NE   Leibniz, G.W. *New Essays on Human Understanding*. Cambridge: Cambridge University Press, 1996.

OI   Maine de Biran. *Œuvres Inédites de Maine de Biran*. Edited by E. Naville. Paris: Dezorby, E. Magdeleine, 1859.

OMB   Maine de Biran. *Œuvres de Maine de Biran*. 20 Vols. Edited by F. Azouvi *et al.* Paris: Vrin, 1984–2001.

OMDB   Maine de Biran *Œuvres de Maine de Biran*. Edited by P. Tisserand. Paris: Félix Alcan.

OP   Maine de Biran. *Œuvre Philosophiques de Maine De Biran*. Edited by V. Cousin. 4 Vols. Paris: Librairie de Ladrange, 1841.

RR   Ravaisson, F. *Rapport sur La Philosophie en France au XIXeme Siècle*. Paris: Librairie Hachette, 1895.

T   Leibniz, G.W. *The Theodicy*. Translated by E.M. Huggard. Open Court: Chicago, 1985.

TBG   Cousin, V. *Lectures on the True, the Beautiful, and the Good*. New York: D. Appleton, 1854.

UL   Urbain, C. & Levesque, E. *Correspondance de Bossuet*. 15 vols. Paris: Librairie Hachette, 1912.

WFNS   Woolhouse, R.S., & Francks, R. *Leibniz's 'New System'*. Oxford: Oxford University Press, 1997.

8 Listen, Hear, Understand: Maine de Biran's Phenomenological Breakthrough

Pierre Kerszberg, University of Toulouse[1]

The kinship between Maine de Biran's philosophy and contemporary phenomenology is confirmed by the latter's most eminent representatives. Merleau-Ponty hails Maine de Biran's philosophy as an anticipation of phenomenology because it is indifferent to the distinction between interiority and exteriority;[2] Michel Henry goes so far as to say that Biran's whole philosophy is nothing but a broad phenomenological reduction;[3] and Marc Richir took inspiration from Biran's philosophy to develop his conception of language and emotion.[4] Thus, when Maine de Biran

---

[1] The following abbreviations are used in this article: *The Relationship between the Physical and Moral in Man* ('RPM'); *Mémoire sur la décomposition de la pensée*, *Œuvres* III. Paris: Vrin, 1998 ('MDP').

[2] Maurice Merleau-Ponty, *The Incarnate Subject: Malebranche, Biran, and Bergson on the Union of Body and Soul*, New York: Humanity Books, 2001, pp. 72, 84. [Maurice Merleau-Ponty, *L'Union de l'âme et du corps chez Malebranche, Biran et Bergson*, J. Deprun (ed.), Paris: Vrin, 1978, pp. 61, 76.]

[3] Michel Henry, *Philosophy and Phenomenology of the Body*, Dordrecht: Springer, 1975, p. 18. [Michel Henry, *Philosophie et phénoménologie du corps*, Paris: PUF, 1965, p. 25.]

[4] Marc Richir, *Phénoménologie en esquisses*, Grenoble: J. Millon, 2000, pp. 350–351, 419–420.

undertook to answer the question posed by the Academy of Copenhagen on the 'utility of physical doctrines and experiments to explain the phenomena of mind and inner sense', it is not surprising that he sided with those who deny the utility of the physical in explaining the mental. What is surprising, however, is the radicality of his position. The Academy's question was addressed to those who *still* deny this utility, and Biran agrees with them to the extent that they deny it *now*. Nonetheless, the question left open the possibility of a future physicalist explanation of consciousness, or in any case the utility of this type of explanation in understanding the mind or soul, even if such doctrines were not presently established. Biran's answer categorically precludes such an explanation from ever contributing to its purported goal. This subtle distinction allows Biran to strip physicalist doctrines of their cloak of utility. Indeed, the refutation of a physicalist explanation of consciousness proves more useful than anything that is understood as useful in any possible physicalist explanation (RPM 92). Such a refutation is at the service of the 'very nature of things', which by principle demands the *absolute* heterogeneity of the two orders of phenomena: the physical and the mental. All the explanatory models invented until now yield to these same facts and the laws that purportedly govern them provided that this heterogeneity is accepted. But what justifies Biran's principled stance if not the refutation of a certain type of explanation, namely a *causal* explanation? For us, there is no other light, writes Biran, than that which emerges from contrasts (MDP 403); such is the method to which he adamantly adheres. Physicalism's defect lies not in its concern for the facts and the laws that subsume these facts, but rather in its exclusive commitment to a causal explanation. If the principle of heterogeneity were posed arbitrarily to challenge this exclusivity, it would be still at the mercy of an always better causal explanation because such an explanation would always be possible in principle. Thus, what justifies heterogeneity's superior value as a principle compared to that of causal explanation?

This very 'nature of things' that the principle of heterogeneity invokes is traditionally the subject of metaphysics. Does the principle of heterogeneity thus involve a break with the exact sciences of nature, in which nature is no longer that of the ipseity of things but the simple observation that things 'are' and that they fit within a framework of laws that describe their relations to one other? Not at all. From the precepts of Bacon's experimental method, for example, Biran retains the false teachings of abstract reason. Metaphysics still deals with *facts* but with *internal* facts of consciousness that are equally positive as the external facts of nature described by physics; only the *meaning* of this positivity differs. How does one discover facts and laws that belong to an order of being where causal explanations are not possible? The way in which facts and laws are discovered in the physical sciences serves as a helpful contrast to the discovery of meaning in the sciences of the mind.

As long as the human mind is beholden to causal explanations, it is induced to establish general laws for phenomena with a haste that makes it dispense with patient observation and verification (RPM 7). Indeed, it is hard to imagine how it could be otherwise. Without this characteristic precipitation of imagination that outpaces the testimony of the senses, an exact science of physical nature would indeed not be possible or even conceivable as a project. Husserl's phenomenology takes precisely this view. The mathematical science of nature is based on laws that are viewed as empirical generalizations of facts grouped together by their similarities. These facts are not, strictly speaking, simple natural facts; they are produced by experimentation, which brings out analogies. In this sense, experimentation can be seen as a free imaginative variation on the part of the physicist, similar to an eidetic; indeed, the whole science of physics can be seen as a sort of eidetic of nature. Under this view, once it is expressed in mathematical language, the connection between facts produces the *eidos* of phenomena. But if this view were correct, physics would be no more than a descriptive science like mineralogy or botany. Its mathematical language makes it something entirely different. In addition to 'describing', it 'explains', but its explanations do not escape ambiguity because they are not based on descriptions of fact.[5] According to Husserl, experimentation in physics is a 'strange' eidetic variation because it operates through an *eidos* that the physicist possesses in advance, rather than discovering it patiently by induction. But patience is the path to clarification – clarification of an essence first perceived only faintly.

For a psychological science that must align itself with the phenomena of internal sense, however, patience is what allows it to become a science. Biran says exactly this when he flatly rejects all attempts to explain these phenomena by organic considerations, from which they are distinct if not separate. The question is *to what extent* the observable features of the organic body are linked to affects or passions of the soul: that is, 'in what specific species of phenomena' (RPM 89) we are likely to observe the double experience of the simultaneous facts of mind and body. Although the organic in itself cannot explain the soul, there will always remain signs

---

[5] E. Husserl, *Ideas Pertaining to a Pure Phenomenology and to a Phenomenological Philosophy: Third Book: Phenomenology and the Foundation of the Sciences*, Dordrecht: Springer, 1980, §11, pp. 73–74.

of the soul in the organic, and it is incumbent on the mind to *seek out*, through these signs, the phenomena that define it. These phenomena are not simply given but rather are identified through a classification process that defines them as such: 'the mind first seeks to link the signs that express its various faculties to so many truly distinct phenomena of its intimate sense' (RPM 83). The psychological science that Biran advocates is thus comparable to a mineralogy or botany of the mind: it is not duped by imagination, which presupposes causes before discovering them (when in fact it invents them). What does this patient science gain in exchange? Aren't the distinct phenomena it establishes dependent on a system of classification and division selected in advance?

The first distinct phenomenon that is perceived and can be identified as such in this eidetic of the mind is indeed the ego itself, or self-perception. I am constantly buffeted by various floating impressions that beset me on all sides in a permanent instability, and yet I observe within myself a remarkable psychological fact that gives consistency and persistence to the self: voluntary effort, which reveals the indissoluble link between will and consciousness. Escaping both the realm of the body as well as the images of the mind, voluntary effort is a hyper-organic force to which only inner experience is witness. Effort sneaks in all passive determinations of organic life, including the discovery that voluntary initiative may sustain itself without relying on sense data. Effort thus ends up *living* its own essence in self-reflection, and reflection in this sense is the tool of this very special eidetic of the mind where no essence rises to the level of *knowledge*. If knowledge of the mind were possible (RPM 54–55), it would build on the almost mechanical effect that objects have on our neurological processes. We would expect that these processes – which can in principle be identified one at a time – would in turn produce ideas and operations of the mind. The latter would thus be reduced to passive changes in perception. Inversely, however, hyper-organic force can produce an *initial action* that unfolds and develops into results that are *immediate* in that they skip over the theoretically traceable chain of causes and effects. These phenomena are reflected in the subject from which they emanate, and 'we absolutely lack any *differential* expression to represent at the *limit* this infinitesimal *fluxion* from one mode to the other' (MDP 119). Science – inspired by the experimental method and its search for causal series – transforms the human being into a purely passive receptacle (RPM 81). By contrast, reflection tends to give us the 'first idea'[6] of our voluntary activity: the idea

[6] Maine de Biran, *Essai sur les fondements de la psychologie et sur ses rapports avec l'étude de la nature*, *Œuvres*, VII, Paris: Vrin, p. 368.

that cannot be represented and yet serves as the foundation for all future representations because it is not self-sufficient and it cannot pose itself. How does the first unrepresentable idea come to motivate (rather than cause) representation? Representation arises from a very special desire, namely the desire that turns back on itself to trace the origin of felt effort. In order to achieve this, we must place ourselves in a perspective external to the self, so that the only thing that really subsists is an image or an abstract notion of the felt apperception of effort.

The reflective dive into the depths of self-intimacy – an eidetic devoid of image or associations of ideas – provides no access to the power of representation. This dive, though triggered by an initial act, knows no end. It passes through multiple degrees of intimacy that reflection seizes to grasp the distinct phenomena of consciousness. Indeed, in the chapter on hearing disorders, Biran emphasizes the central thesis of his book, namely that a genuine science of man must become indifferent to causal explanations (RPM 122–123). Better than any other sensory event, sound phenomena highlight the theoretically inexplicable yet observed relationship between raw nature and intelligent nature, the feeling world and the thinking world. In his analysis of hearing disorders, Biran seeks to clarify and deepen the meaning of the data that the inner self collects when there is a break in the usually regulated order between these two worlds. Sound experience in its natural state is a reminder that causal explanations are futile in accounting for the disorders and alterations of perception that physiology attempts to explain.

The most intimate experience in which the ego perceives itself as distinct is indeed sound experience.[7] The sense of hearing exemplifies reflection without representation (MDP 171). There is something that the inner self sees and hears before the faculty of understanding gives it 'voice'. Instead of departing from its native state – of which we have no idea – let us consider this experience in the state in which it lends itself to a possible representation: the clear perception of successive and coordinated sounds, that is, the music that man creates with noises extracted from raw nature. Usually this extraction goes unnoticed; we spontaneously consider sounds transposed into a musical structure as nature's way of expressing itself and communicating with us. Biran describes the role of habitus in the intelligent activity that orders and plays with sounds as 'certain very specific modes of passive hearing'. How do we prevent this purely affective

---

[7] For a detailed analysis of the role of sound experience in Maine de Biran, see A. Devarieux, *Maine de Biran. L'individualité persévérante*, Grenoble: J. Millon, 2004, pp. 17–20, 291–304.

component of hearing from being eclipsed by the intelligent activity that produces music?

Biran notes that even a completely deaf individual is stirred at the centre of his inner sensory receptors when exposed to the full force of sound impressions. Sound is invasive to the point that we probably never succeed in eliminating it completely by plugging our ears, unlike the eye, for example, which can easily be shut off from sight. Sound impressions that have such an effect as to deprive the hearing subject of its autonomy are characterized by a specific timbre. The same also occurs with individuals gifted with perfect hearing: some vocal or instrumental timbres have an affective impact that does not involve auditory perception. The timbre that generates emotional impressions is even more significant in that it is secondary and insignificant in the musical structure of sounds. Indeed, timbre, or more generally the tonal colour, is not a principle of musical organization on par with rhythm, melody or harmony. The latter weave as it were the musical thread, creating a tonal space in which its movement is heard; timbre, by contrast, remains a secondary aspect. The physical cause of the phenomenon of tonality is well known: the tonality of a sound is the product of its overtones. But in attempting to describe the timbre itself, i.e. the thing we actually hear when we hear the timbre, we quickly become perplexed. Either we identify timbre by means of its physical cause (say, the sound of an oboe), or we revert to metaphor because words fail us in the attempt to capture a truly unique sound. At any rate, in describing a sound's timbre, we are not in a musical discourse, nor do we describe anything essential to timbre as musical. For example, the orchestration or reduction of a piece is generally perceived as a version of the same piece, not as a new musical entity. The timbre has something unique and inimitable that puts it on a different plane from all the other components of sound experience. A primitive duality emerges within the musical space in which a meaning resistant to the network of meanings arises, revealing an outside within its own interior.

The primitive duality of timbre and rhythm/melody/harmony with respect to organized and representable sounds points up another primitive duality, one that is deeper and more universal because constitutive of consciousness. Hearing is twofold: it establishes a close relationship between the voice and hearing, the sensory expression of the relationship between activity and passivity that is characteristic of consciousness, companionship with oneself in a shared dialogue between one's soul and that of others. With respect to myself, I am at once active and passive: the voice that projects and the ear that hears. On the one hand, I have the power to create impressions in myself, since I have the power to give myself auditory sensations, to hear the sounds that my voice produces. On the other hand, however, this activity is saturated with passivity. Although unlimited in principle, my activity is limited in fact because it is linked to nature. While I have within me the theoretical power to produce all the sounds that I can hear, there are certain sounds that I cannot produce as a physical matter. Moreover, since there is always a gulf between the act that I perform and the result produced by this act, my act is always surpassed by the result in the sounds that I produce. Yet sound, like consciousness, is an act. Although we may be passive with respect to the sounds we hear, we only hear the sounds that we can somehow produce by reproducing them, at least theoretically.

Sound is subjective reality, too close to thought for thought to make it an object and know it other than by an act. But the two registers of this subjective reality, hearing and voice, mirror one another. Voice is a gesture of the body, which in its materiality is inadequate to the sound form, but which nonetheless tends towards this form. It does so in a way that goes beyond the sound form: it creates a dynamic sound space, similar to the visual space. As Maurice Blanchot clearly stated: 'Voice is thus not only the organ of subjective interiority, but rather the resounding of a *space* open to the *outside*.'[8] Between sound and vocal gesture, there is a kind of reciprocity, one contours to the other such that vocal gesture outlines sound without pronouncing it. Biran wrote: 'Auditory perceptibility is much more related to the active organ that repeats internally and imitates first, as by a kind of instinct of sympathy, the sounds that strike the ear, than to the passive sense that receives immediate impressions' (MDP 172). The active organ, the voice, appears initially in a kind of passive activity, imitation. The vocal instrument 'repeats the outside sound and echoes it', so that the impression is internally reflected and intensifies in one's interior. Thus, the attention that we direct towards an external sound that reaches our ear is meaningless without the inner reflection that reproduces it. When the sound is reproduced internally, it is already almost immediately a memory. The active echo-like repetition expands the present, which now includes an infinitesimal difference from itself – an almost immediate memory of the present. What becomes of this immediate memory, which is as it were glued to the extended present, when it detaches from the present and invites us to pay attention to and reflect upon an organized series of sounds (melody or speech) that we have heard? The audible and the vocal then compete with

---

[8] M. Blanchot, *Infinite Conversation (Theory and History of Literature)*, Minneapolis, MN: University of Minnesota Press, 1992, p. 386.

each other, engaging in a game of eclipses whereby attention and thinking dominate each other in turn. If thinking dominates attention, the *timbre* reverberates and persists, as it were, on its own, without any recall effort, in the passive imagination. If instead we pay attention to what has taken place, voice predominates, i.e. '*tone*, accent, measure, all things we can imitate and reproduce' (MDP 178), in short, rhythm. The imitable (vocalizable) part of sound is the framework of this sound, and this framework is 'an identity of *power*, which is that of *our own being*'. In short, the voice consists of an active part and a passive part: the active part mimics the sounds that come from the outside, whereby our own being is manifested in the slight delay with respect to the passive part. The passive part, by contrast, does not imitate anything and corresponds to a sensation that determines our being in an immediate and uncontrollable way. What is heard (physical sound) is not heard (as a function of the understanding) unless it is repeated in purely potential kinaesthesia, i.e. 'oral keys' (MDP 181) or moving parts of the mouth, tongue, teeth, lips, etc. in which our entire being is engaged. Potential kinaesthesia are reminiscent of childhood and the moment when we start talking and hear ourselves for the first time. Finally, when thought achieves understanding in 'the regular action of thought', it does so against the backdrop of a 'kind of speech that we speak softly to ourselves'. When this happens, the voice function is not exercised, yet 'oral keys are pressed and put into play'.

As a purely potential kinaesthetic habitus, the framework of understanding (interior sound imitating exterior sound) is thus not a product of passive imagination; not only does it not physically repeat what is heard, but it does not 'pronounce' anything in imagination. Organic corporeality and imagination are taken out of play, leaving only kinaesthesia that are purely potential, but that take action as potential. If they did not, the interplay of the vocal and the audible would never free itself from its interiority to become constituted and recognizable meaning. The voice, which at first is enclosed in the strangely hollow cavity that is the head, initially occupies no space precisely because it resonates in a head that gives the impression of being empty. But once it is propagated outside, the voice becomes audible like any other sound that strikes the ear without declaring its origin. The voice situates the head in space; as a result, the head is filled, organic physicality reclaims its rights, and meaning is able to constitute itself by the interplay of imagination that situates my head vis-à-vis other heads.

However, as a series of organized sounds that never reaches the level of a representational discourse, music essentially involves feelings and the nuances (accents) of feeling, without any involvement of ideas (MDP 183).

In this sense, it's the flip side of conceptual thinking, which also navigates between two registers: concepts and sense data.

Cognition – the ability to construct – precedes recognition.[9] Forming a concept is tending to recreate a sense datum as if it had never existed. But if consciousness indulges the pretention of believing itself at the origin of sensory consciousness, it is only by default. Indeed, concepts could never completely capture sense data; the latter are concrete and rich, while the former are empty and abstract. The concept is always filled by the sensible before the sensible is exhausted; indeed, the sensible is inexhaustible. Thought attempts to *reduce* sense data to its operation with a view to constituting the objective world. But if in constituting the object, thought captures it incompletely, it is because thought is unable to capture itself completely; all it can do is see itself at work in a work that surpasses it. Concepts derive from the union between thought and an exterior given – a union that lacks the legitimacy of a duly recognized and registered paternity; concepts are the illegitimate children of this union. However, constructive thought is not the only form of thought. There is another form of thought whose paternity is confirmed by the very experience of thought in its own acts: creative thought. Musical thought is the prototype of this kind of thought. Indeed, when applied to sound, thought encounters a material that is its closest relative. Thought can perform its pure acts upon sound with an immediate spontaneity. Hearing creates the given, generating it instead of reconstructing it. Sight and intelligence presuppose this given as a spectacle that they do not produce. Musical thought, although not conceptual thought, returns to the source of all thought. In doing so, it captures sensation in its most concrete quality. Thus, sound and the sound form symbolize the act by which consciousness constructs the world by creating it.

Before focusing on voice, body gesture is musically present in response to sound in the generality of its vital space. The sound form retains from this body gesture only a rhythm, i.e. the alternation of its tensions and releases, its restraints and impulses, which traces an imaginary and symbolic curve in the sound space. But among all musical gestures, vocal gesture is the one that is embodied immediately in this curve; it thus conveys vital activity before becoming the realizing agent of the will. The voice is a subtle gesture that is an agent of expression because the will controls it. Biran explains how reflective consciousness gradually takes control over the spontaneous cry and subjects it to its own laws. The voice becomes the

---

[9] See G. Brelet, *Le Temps Musical*, Paris, PUF: 1949, pp. 480–481.

embodiment of the will; the will recognizes itself in vocal gesture, which mirrors the will itself. Better still, the voice becomes a spiritual gesture that regulates other bodily gestures, as well as an instrument of self-control. Yielding to the vocal gesture, the body remains motionless and empties its passions. This immobility is the moment when the purely potential habitus appears, when it acts while remaining potential; it is also the moment when the body stands at attention, ready to listen.

In the modern sense, '*entendre*' means perceiving by hearing. This meaning has supplanted the old verb '*ouïr*' while maintaining its connotations from the Old French 'pay attention to (what someone says)' and the seventeenth-century 'perceive by the intellect'. '*Prêter son attention*' (which means 'paying attention', or literally 'lending one's attention') is making attention available for some task for a specified time. '*Entendre*' is 'to hear', 'accept with favour', while '*écouter*' ('to listen to') derives from '*auscultare*' ('listen carefully to', 'intently attempting to hear'). Juxtaposed against this etymology, listening to music is a remarkable phenomenon because the listener (as well as the composer or performer, for that matter) cannot suspend the passage of time, which defies its resolute attempts to hear. The passage of time is a constantly ongoing process of ever-new productions of consciousness. Every act of listening entails grappling with the constant evanescence of the present, with time as continuous uninterrupted flow, as a constant and regular series of 'nows' fastened to one another. Riveted to the flow of the sound phenomenon, the auditor has no time to modify the present imposed from outside. She is not at liberty to organize the timing of her reception, unlike a reader or a museum art goer that can return, resume, linger or otherwise skim, skip over, shorten. In music, it is impossible to return to the moment in which one lost concentration, to dwell on a passage that seemed beautiful; it is already gone, continuously pushed into an increasingly distant past, at an ever greater distance from the present that continues producing novelty. It is impossible to remember a passage of music when the music, obstinately, continues to play.

Yet memory is also implicated in the process of listening. Without memory, hearing would be a succession of moments disjoint from one other (RPM 55–57). Biran criticizes all conceptions of sensory memory as a weak perception of the original sensation. These conceptions are based on a causal explanation. Under these conceptions, once the object that first caused the sensation disappears, the reproduction of the sensation produces the same sensorial impact that originally created the sensation, only in an attenuated form. To such conceptions of memory Biran opposes a conception of the soul as active force: 'The same repetition that imperceptibly wears out, alters and erases passive sensation and all the subordinate faculties which originate in it, serves on the contrary to perfect, illuminate, and develop the mind's *perception*, as well as all the intellectual operations whose veritable principle or source is the soul's motor activity' (RPM 55–57). 'Perception' is a word that covers a very broad spectrum of meanings, from sensation to cognition and concept. However, perception is and can only be present. In the philosophical tradition, time is kept at a distance as if it did not exist, or as if perception did not take time into account. The alliance between perception and the present within this philosophical tradition is forged by the primacy that it accords to sight over hearing. Indeed, the relationship between 'seeing' and 'perceiving' is straightforward. The relationship between 'hearing' and 'perceiving', however, is more complex. If perceiving means having direct and present contact with an object, it obviously does not encompass hearing. Does the perception of a melody consist in the perception of one note followed by another? A high-pitch note, a low-pitch note, a shrill note, a weak note, a short note, a long note, etc.? At no point do I *perceive* a symphony, and yet I *hear* it. When Biran identifies perception in a series of sensations modified by the mere passage of time, he invites us to think about the deeper meaning of this enlargement of the present that music creates: how, by the act of listening, does hearing also become perceiving?

The answer is that the past cannot grow weaker because the remembrance of a melody and the sounds that make it up is the remembrance of an act. The remembrance of an act contrasts with the fleeting remembrance of an impression. The remembrance of an impression fades with the impression itself, but the remembrance of an act is still the very same act. If the sensorial impressions that compose a melody disappear one after the other, we nonetheless retain the power to recreate its form – a power that we can always exercise again. Through its remembrance, the act is thus split into two acts. We can describe these two acts as a succession that takes place within us, relying on the conceptual tools that Husserl utilized in his considerations on the intimate consciousness of time. Act I: everything begins with sound vibrations that come from the outside (MDP 182); the impressions thus created have the unique feature of being preserved by the auditory organ through its natural vibrational tendencies that keep the movement going. Act II: the preserved movement would dissipate in a diminishing wave motion if it were not supported by the voice that accompanies hearing. At the conclusion of these two acts, sounds are strictly speaking perceived. Two sound series unfold in parallel: on the one hand, the sound series recorded in the exact present by the inner movement of the auditory sense; on the other hand, the sound series that is preserved in the primary memory that is 'tacked on to' this exact present. Obviously, the primary memory can only precisely reproduce the order of the sounds perceived in the present if we posit a form of listening that records absolutely everything in an uninterrupted series of exact presents. For this reason, primary memory is supplemented by 'judgement, which operates by comparing or assessing the relationship that successive sounds have with each other'. Judgement perceives the relationship between sounds the way that successive sounds are first perceived in listening. The power to reactivate a musical structure implies a significant shift from attention to reflection, without which the two series of sounds would always remain foreign to one other: put another way, a 'first idea' must precede and inform future cognitive relations; or put still another way, appreciation is informed by and foreshadowed in an association that preceded it. How does this shift from attention to reflection work? Reflection is the subjective act that distinguishes the result of the act from the act itself, so that the subject can take credit for the result by connecting it with her own power. It is a double apperception insofar as the actual perception is foreign to the result of the act. For its part, attention obscures the sensation of performing the act in favour of its sensory outcome, which then prevails over that sensation. Attention focuses first on successive sounds – the sensory outcome, which is also 'the motive of the first association'. Thought then takes over for this first association and allows it to develop into appreciation via 'the inner active modes'.

When I listen to music, I sometimes find myself concentrating on the perception of a particular sequence of notes or chords. This is especially true at the beginning of a piece. But the effort required to sustain this concentration can be overwhelming and ultimately inhibiting. I then immerse myself in the memory of what I have heard by trying not to hear the fleeting sounds that I am given to hear now (if they were just given to me in mass, this diversion would not be possible). Decisive here is what we might call the attentional drift. It happens occasionally in everyday life that musical phrases or melodies arise suddenly in a flux of thoughts that do not have any a priori relationship with them. The inverse situation is seemingly more common: that imaged thoughts arise suddenly while one listens to music – figurations that are unrelated to what is heard. In both cases, we observe a game of eclipses whereby perception and emotion overshadow each another in turn. I listen to this song, and I can look out the window and watch the passage of clouds, think of a poem, and look forward to seeing a friend tomorrow – I daydream without letting myself simply be lulled by the music: the driving force of the soul is still there, in the form of a basso continuo. From time to time, I turn my attention back to the music and then let it go adrift again. Psychology may well discern paradigmatic musical structures that awaken characteristic images, and that are themselves determined by the past experiences of the listener. In the attentional drift, by contrast, everything occurs in the present in intervals of thought superposed on the musical flux itself. Each phase of the drift coincides with the need for a cognitive appraisal of the relationship between the sounds. Either the listener zones out despite his efforts to remain attentive to the expressive content, or zones out without even realizing it. Whatever the modality of the zoning out, conscience tackles the central cognitive problem of a temporal flux by living it. How does the perception of a succession become a succession of perceptions? How is a past present in the present, such that the listener is not inexorably lost in a tonal chaos? Phenomenologically, the interval of the drift is when I quasi-hear the sound. In the quasi-hearing – as in the visual perception of a thing that is not there in the flesh[10] – the thing that I hear is given neither as existing nor as not existing; that is, it is not given in any positional modality but with a modification of positionality. As for the music itself, as a temporal object, it drifts in its own way thanks to its organized system of modulations. The fundamental fact is that these two drifts could never coincide or overlap perfectly. If they coincide, the music would not be 'alive'; it would not capture my attention before lending itself to my reflection.

Attention and reflection impose themselves intermittently in turn. This does not mean, as Biran noted, that attention and reflection cannot be exercised simultaneously. The two parallel series of sounds can actually coincide at a particular time, but this coincidence never excludes a past or future contrast. This is why the double series of sounds, based on the double exercise of attention and reflection, which in turn is reflected in the double exercise of hearing and voice, may be generalized for the most complex as well as the most basic musical structures. The melody can thus provide the backdrop for the harmony and vice versa.

The simultaneous occurrence of attention and reflection is, however, subject to a condition: that the ear be already accustomed to hearing a series of sounds. Without this prior habituation, memory would not place its own series in parallel with the original series. For a subject that is beginning to realize the potential of the self in the initial emblematic action of reflection, everything begins with a sort of basso continuo over which neither consciousness nor even the will have control (CDM 90–92). No one has

---

[10] Husserl describes this perception in §111 of the first book of *Ideen*, 'Quasi' translates 'gleichsam': no actual object is seized upon, but instead precisely a picture, a fictum.

ever escaped this bass, which is also a *base* in the deepest sense, such that the first hint of the self that is exposed in this nascent reflective experience does not differentiate one self from another. Thus, music has, *in and of itself*, a universal scope that addresses all of humanity, even if *in fact* it only invites and mobilizes reflection if it draws upon an already acquired and culturally determined habituation.

The more the senses feel, the less intelligence thinks and discerns. How do we think about this lived fact that everyone immediately experiences, without relying on a theoretical basis which would be illusory? Maine de Biran's analysis reveals that sound experience offers the most appropriate way to think about this question. A given sound is the cause of a given experience within me, but the meaning of what I hear lies in the erasure of the cause: the impact retained in the inner experience of hearing. The erasure of the cause is coupled with a failure to escape the grip of sound completely. Losing its role as external cause, sound becomes the condition of a wholly inner shock. Biran invites us to imagine the beginning of life as a purely emotional state that only becomes more magnified with the habits of maturity: a state that is unknowing and unenlightened, that is, a kind of grand habitus (an absolutely primitive cause) without an identifiable beginning. To borrow a term from Heidegger, let us call this state the *Stimmung*, which precedes absolutely, is impossible to grasp through intuition and has no identifiable beginning in consciousness. Heidegger immediately characterizes the *Stimmung* as the tonality of existence without distinguishing the tonality from the timbre. In fact, the Biranian distinction allows us to compare it more fundamentally to the timbre of a sound wave that never ceases to ring, in the *final* forgetting of the substantial component that it transmits. For this reason, the timbre cannot by nature become the object of attention. We are transfixed by these affective dispositions imposed by the timbre, which a retroactive grasp (a representation) from the subject cannot move past. We are not only affected by these affective dispositions; we become them without noticing it. When we exercise thought and the sense, these unnoticed products of life remain united. But the impossibility of a retroactive grasp does not prevent us from making an effort to comprehend them. This effort comes closest to succeeding when these products become recognizable by certain 'sympathetic' signs that completely invade the intimacy of our lives. It is possible that the unnoticed products may pass themselves off as something that has been noticed in order to appear as 'objects' within a particular tonality; hence the objective illusion of owning them and acting upon them to condition them to a particular mood. In reality, they only give the timbre of our existence, and although absolutely intimate, they *seem* to come from the outside due to a kind of *fatum*. Because they are indifferent to things and images, these habits are characterized by instability, charm turning on a whim into disgust or vice versa, love into hate, etc. They therefore do not fix any destiny, even if it seems that one cannot escape them. Their semblance of objectivity is the only way in which a purely potential kinaesthetic habitus comes to manifest itself as a possibility. More specifically regarding music, there is not and there never will be a dictionary capable of translating unequivocally each musical form into a corresponding affect, but the always failed *attempt* at translation is the life of thought inasmuch as it is consubstantial with music.

This *Stimmung* coloured by timbre at first seems purely private and incommunicable in its changing immediacy through the intermediary of language. However, as evidenced by affective experiences such as night-time dreams, the *Stimmung* can still seem like a product of the passive imagination (RPM 149). It is then akin to a *belief* tethered to immediate affect. This *Stimmung* – which is original belief, or a sort of mechanical faith – differs from the intelligence that rationalizes its grounds for belief and that is preceded by which faith. The *Stimmung* communicates with our purely sensory nature (RPM 143). Biran nonetheless discovers that, although recalcitrant to language, this continuous bass, which never ceases to intensify throughout life, ultimately exceeds the limits of a private sensation. While it is never expressed, it nevertheless seeks expression through the voice. It is intersubjective because in each of its moments (or each of the passions it induces) it seems to correspond to a particular manner of speech (RPM 123). My manner of speech can be imitated to a certain extent, thereby inviting others to sympathize with it (me) even if they do not understand it (me). The sympathetic signs that I experience within me seek expression; they seek to empathize with other souls in order to be heard. The original belief that occurs in my conscience is an appeal for communication with all those who can hear the signs in my sympathetic signs. If the *Stimmung* exists for each of us individually, with its changing phases that are always unique to it, its accent is disseminated and heard as 'this profound cry of the soul, which all souls hear and to which they all reply in unison'.

INDEX